THE CRITICAL EDGE

THE CRITICAL EDGE
Controversy in Recent American Architecture

Edited by
Tod A. Marder

The Jane Voorhees Zimmerli Art Museum
Rutgers, The State University of New Jersey

THE STATE UNIVERSITY OF NEW JERSEY
RUTGERS

The MIT Press
Cambridge, Massachusetts
London, England

**THE CRITICAL EDGE: CONTROVERSY IN RECENT
AMERICAN ARCHITECTURE**

© 1985 by the Jane Voorhees Zimmerli Art Museum
and The Massachusetts Institute of Technology.

Printed and bound in the United States of America

Library of Congress catalogue card number: 84-063027
ISBN 0-262-13207-9

Designed by Jeffrey Wechsler
Cover design by Design & Illustration and Jeffrey Wechsler

THE CRITICAL EDGE
Controversy in Recent American Architecture

This book is based on an exhibition of the same title
organized by the Jane Voorhees Zimmerli Art Museum,
Rutgers, The State University of New Jersey,
New Brunswick, New Jersey

Research for the book and exhibition
was carried out in a seminar in the Department of
Art History, Rutgers University

The exhibition and book were supported by grants from
AT&T FOUNDATION
and
THE NATIONAL ENDOWMENT FOR THE ARTS
a federal agency in Washington, D.C.

The exhibition was curated by:

Tod A. Marder
Associate Professor of Art History
Rutgers, The State University of New Jersey

Jeffrey Wechsler
Assistant Director
Jane Voorhees Zimmerli Art Museum

The exhibition was presented at the following institutions:

Jane Voorhees Zimmerli Art Museum,
Rutgers, The State University of New Jersey
New Brunswick, New Jersey .... March 24—June 9, 1985

Newport Harbor Art Museum
Newport Beach, California .... July 25—September 25, 1985

Ackland Art Museum,
University of North Carolina,
Chapel Hill, North Carolina .... October 11—December 1, 1985

University Art Museum,
Berkeley, California .... January 8—March 9, 1986

The Nelson-Atkins Museum of Art,
Kansas City, Missouri .... May 8—June 8, 1986

ACKNOWLEDGMENTS

During the course of our work on "The Critical Edge," we have had the advice and assistance of many generous and interested people without whom this book and the accompanying exhibition could not have been realized. We want to acknowledge these individuals, listed below according to the building with which they were involved. AT&T Corporate Headquarters: Philip Johnson, James Peck, and Alan Ritchie of John Burgee Architects with Philip Johnson, New York; Joseph D'Urso, Manager of Building Operations, AT&T Corporate Headquarters, New York. Bronx Developmental Center: Richard Meier and Ron Monroe of Richard Meier and Associates, New York. East Building, National Gallery of Art: David W. Scott and Richard Saito of the National Gallery of Art Planning Office; Leonard Jacobsen and Peter X. Ksiezopolski of I.M. Pei and Partners, New York. Governor Nelson A. Rockefeller Empire State Plaza: at the Empire State Plaza, Dale Loucks of the Office of Design and Construction, Charles Wheeler of the Office of Tourism and Conventions, Walter Cummings and Joan Whitbeck of the Office of General Services, Thomas Cooper of the Office of Public Information; James Hoben of the Albany Public Library. Gehry House: Frank and Berta Gehry, Santa Monica; Eamonn O'Mahony of Frank O. Gehry and Associates, Venice, California. The J. Paul Getty Museum: Mitchell Hearns Bishop and John Walsh, Jr. of the J. Paul Getty Museum, Malibu; Pebble Wilkins of Langdon Wilson Mumper Architects, Los Angeles. House VI: Peter Eisenman and Susan Knauer, Eisenman/Robertson Architects, New York; Richard and Suzanne Frank, New York. Indeterminate Facade, Best Company Showroom: Joan Durand, Alison Sky, Quentin Thomas, and James Wines of SITE, Inc., New York. Piazza d'Italia: R. Allen Eskew of Perez Associates Architects, New Orleans; Joseph Maselli of Venice, Inc.; Ron Filson of Tulane University, New Orleans. The Portland Building: Alan Prusis and Karen Wheeler of Michael Graves Architect, Princeton. Renaissance Center: Stanley Steinberg, Danielle Martin, John Hayes III, and Nancy Williams of John Portman and Associates, Atlanta; Robert B. Devine, General Manager, Renaissance Center Venture, Detroit. Vietnam Veterans Memorial: Jan Scruggs and Robert Carter of the Vietnam Veterans Memorial Fund, Washington, D.C.; Kent Cooper, William Lecky, and Carla Corbin of the Cooper-Lecky Partnership, Georgetown; Judith Tannenbaum, Director of the Freedman Gallery, Albright College, Reading.

On the art historical side, we would like to thank Robert Bruegmann, Alan Colquhoun, Martin Filler, William Foulks, and Kenneth Frampton for various kinds of advice; Riva Feshbach, Esther Sandrof, and Lisa Gittleman for their dedicated services as research assistants; and Dean Tilden Edelstein and Associate Dean Iris Müller of the Faculty of Arts and Sciences at Rutgers University for their steadfast support of the project. For bibliographic assistance we are grateful to Ferris Olin of the Art Library at Rutgers and to our friends at the Architecture Library, Princeton University. At the Zimmerli Art Museum, we want to thank Phillip Dennis Cate, Director; Anne Schneider, Editor; Marilyn Tatrai, Registrar; Stephanie Grunberg, Curator of Education; and Ferenc Varga and E.A. Racette, Installers and Preparators, for their usual care and attention on this project.

Finally, a word about the essays on the individual buildings. The material for this book was presented in a graduate seminar in the Rutgers University Department of Art History, and the participants were fully responsible for the research related to each building. In order to compile a consistent discussion, however, it was necessary to apply a heavy editorial hand to the written work produced in the seminar. The operative fact is that the book has been an entirely cooperative scholarly venture, for which the editor happily assumes joint responsibility with his younger collaborators.

Tod A. Marder
Jeffrey Wechsler

CONTENTS

Introduction:
A Plea for History

Tod A. Marder

"The Critical Edge" is concerned with a group of controversial buildings constructed in the United States during the last fifteen years and with their critical reputations. What we have in mind is a contribution to the history of a period in American architecture that has been heralded as one of the most exciting of this century. In the last decade-and-a-half the profession has demonstrated more energy and more creative diversity than it has at any other time since the Victorian era, and the public has become widely involved in this phenomenon. Architects have become public personalities, and their work is regularly featured in daily newspapers, weekly news magazines, and on television. The architecture book publishing industry is thriving, and opinions in the media, on campus, and among lay citizens have become more frequent, often more polemical, and generally more sophisticated. Our goal is to bring together a representative selection of opinions about a group of controversial buildings in order to gain some understanding of the architectural concerns of the period.

When we began this enterprise three years ago, we consulted with various architects, critics, and historians and quickly realized that no group of buildings would begin to satisfy every observer's view of what was "most important" or even "most controversial." We also realized that much of the advice we were getting directly reflected the differences in taste, in perceptions of quality, and in judgements of moral and ethical values that we had hoped to present in a more equitable and dispassionate manner. But the history of architecture, like the practice of architecture, has yet to embrace the quantitative methods used by social scientists to assess broadly based public opinion. Our methods for choosing the buildings to study therefore had to depend on other criteria, and none was more appropriate to our interests than the amount of printed commentary inspired by the various buildings. As a result, the shape of our work reflects the significance of the press as an arbiter of taste. To have realized a "democratic" choice of buildings representing all parts of the country and all persuasions of design would have required us to sacrifice the opportunity of taking stock of the most prominent currents in architecture and criticism.

These currents of theory and practice and the widespread interest in them cannot be communicated through the buildings alone, however eloquent they may be, for the buildings are but one component, albeit the most important, in a wide field of activity.[1] Thus, rather than orchestrating an anthology of buildings defined by type (civic, corporate, domestic, institutional) or by region or on the basis of subjective judgements based on quality, we have chosen the buildings that have generated the most frequent discussion in the professional architectural press and in local and national news media. While we did not intend to include all types of buildings, some diversity was desired, and we do have a substantial variety of domestic, civic, speculative, memorial, urban, and suburban structures, large and small. And although it was not our intention to balance the choice of buildings geographically, our twelve examples do represent the vitality of the architectural profession in various parts of the country.

It is appropriate that the essays on each of our buildings are not identical in length or approach, but each of them has as its goal a synthesis of viewpoints drawn from the critical literature. As editor, I have tried to insure that the notes on each building contain a representative, if not exhaustive, collection of the literature from a variety of sources. In general, we have concentrated on publications from the United States because we have been interested in architecture and criticism in this country. We have not excluded European sources, but our coverage of them has not been extensive. As a result, we look forward to the contribution of others who would investigate the European response to American architecture more thoroughly.

The purpose of our work has been to present the raw materials for further discussion. To this end, the introduction and two papers of a more subjective character are followed by twelve essays dealing with the critical literature on each of the buildings in our group. These twelve discussions involve issues that range from the initial conception of the building to advanced phases of its use. We have tried to include as many controversial questions as possible, from planning, theory, and financing through construction, use, misuse, and disuse, wherever these

1. House VI and immediate environs

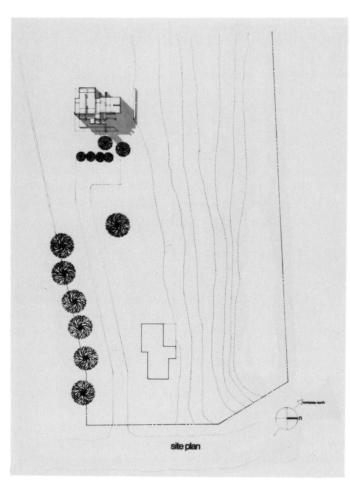

site plan

2. Site plan of House VI

matters have been raised in the literature. In short, the twelve essays may be considered case-histories. They may indicate the degree to which criticism anticipates, accompanies, or follows the realization of a building, and how the complexion of criticism can change during the construction process and later use. Some distinctions among the kinds of commentaries available in publications (ranging from professional journals to airline magazines) may also be gleaned from the information presented in these essays. They may suggest that the manner in which an architectural commission is awarded sometimes relates to or affects the subsequent reputation of the building. As much as possible, however, we have tried to leave such broader conclusions to our readers, for we have learned that identical evidence — visual or written — can be interpreted in any number of ways. Our purpose is to present the buildings and a short compendium of the interest and anxieties expressed in print about them.

While the twelve essays are not intended to call attention to improprieties or excesses in architectural practice or critical writing, we have all become aware of issues that deserve further consideration. In the remaining pages of this introduction, I would like to suggest some of the issues that might be worth further investigation. For example, I have been frequently struck by the repetitive use of a canonical group of photographs for each building. These photographs, which are often works of art themselves, have the potential to influence the writer's commentary and the reader's understanding of a

3. Model of the Piazza d'Italia, as illustrated in *Progressive Architecture*, January 1976, page 83

building. A canonical set of photographs also serves to limit discussion to features that are easily captured on film. Among the less consequential examples of such features, there is the little sloping front lawn of the Gehry House, which gives added dimensions, real and implied, to an element that is consistently flat and featureless on neighbors' properties. The fact that the lawn is hard to photograph may account for the lack of comment about it in the literature on the house. And who would know from published photographs that House VI, a diffident statement of self-referential sculpture, is perched on the edge of a wooded ravine with a meandering stream at its foot? The piquant effect of that design on the site is unmistakable (even if influenced by pre-existing foundations), and it deserves more comment than it has received.

Out of practical necessity, of course, one is regularly forced to conjure up the presence of a building on the basis of photographs that are inevitably insufficient to the task, but it is dangerous to take the visual evidence for granted in any situation. There have been occasions, furthermore, when critical judgements have been made and discussed on the basis of changing sets of evidence. In 1976, the jury for *Progressive Architecture* gave an award to the design of the Piazza d'Italia on the basis of a model. That model differed significantly from what was later constructed, which amounted to the first phase of a much altered multi-phase scheme. The executed portions — a fountain, the piazza, and street entrances — were

highly praised in a *Progressive Architecture* review in 1978. During the extensive and highly charged debates about the Piazza in subsequent issues of the journal, however, no one cared to observe that the scheme being alternately attacked and defended was only the first installment of a multi-phase commercial and cultural complex.[2] It is impossible to know if opinions would have been so intense had the fountain-and-piazza component been presented with the shops, restaurants, and amenities planned for it, but the fact remains that a historical reality had been swept under the thick rug of differing opinion.

The unrecognized changing of evidence for the assessments of Piazza d'Italia in its various incarnations is not unique. When the winning design for the Vietnam Memorial was announced, it was not made public using the original and poetic drawings submitted on the competition boards, but rather with a rudimentary model that had been worked up virtually overnight by the architectural office of a member of the jury committee. About a week later, as I understand it, perspective renderings were commissioned and when completed, in turn, they became the source by which the winning scheme (which had still not been displayed in the original drawings) was judged in the press.[3] These are nothing more than facts of life in professional architectural circles, but they ought to be documented when definitive histories of the period and of the monuments are written. It is, after all, just possible that the emotive qualities of the Memorial cap-

3

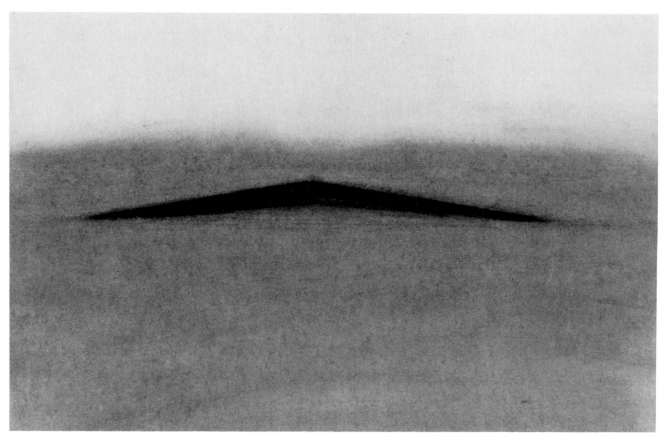

4. Pastel drawing by Maya Ying Lin of her proposed design for the Vietnam Veterans Memorial

tured in the pastels on the competition drawings would not have made as many enemies as did the stiffly formal and severe model or black and white renderings, whose abstract qualities were more readily communicated than the meditative aura of the original scheme.

The AT&T Corporate Headquarters remains the outstanding example of a building on which critical judgement had been rendered by all of the major critics well before ground was broken; here, too, perspective renderings in black and white were the objects of the criticism. Such a practice is common and perfectly legitimate, but only a few critics bothered to caution restraint in judging the building before its completion. When the question of zoning was raised, none of those with adamant opinions on the matter seem to have consulted the shadow studies produced in the architectural office to show where the sun would strike neighboring buildings at a given time of the day in a given month of the year. Press deadlines work against the possibility that a journalist will have the time to rummage through hundreds of drawings in the office archive for such materials, but the opportunity remains where the investigator is intrepid and architects accommodating. In this regard, one can only applaud the author of an article in the *Architectural Record* who, swimming against most fashionable currents, wrote extensively not about the shape of the facade or the stone cladding of the AT&T Headquarters, but about its structure and engineering.[4]

While the AT&T Headquarters was largely judged on the merits of renderings, the Portland Building has been judged too much as a product of drawing, a criticism firmly but unfairly based on the designer's reputation as a draftsman. (After a hostile critic characterized Michael Graves's Portland Building as "wallpaper," Philip Johnson made a visual pun of the remark: he papered the walls of a room at the Museum of Modern Art with the same repetitive window scheme used on the walls of the building Johnson had on display there.[5]) Whatever one thinks about the Portland Building, there is no denying that it has become a scapegoat for all that is deemed willful, subversive, and nefarious or, contrarily, the rallying point for all that is judged spirited, contextually appropriate, and uplifting in post-modernism. The opponents muster the testimony of the building's users, who complain that the small windows make it "the world's tallest basement."[6] The adherents interview the proverbial man-on-the-street, who has been likely to say that the building is exciting, colorful, and "different." But the real issue for present and future historians is why we are all so committed to discussing it. Why is it so inescapably visible on the horizon of its time, and what is the source of its ability to make us so adamant about it?

The same questions might be asked about the Governor Nelson A. Rockefeller Empire State Plaza in Albany, New York. In the early planning phases through the 1960s, hardly any attention was paid to its aesthetic mer-

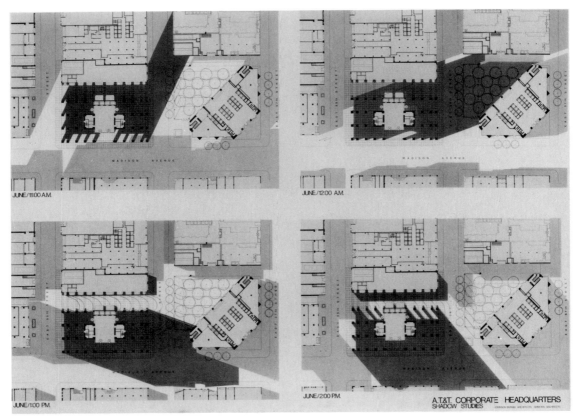

5. Shadow studies prepared for AT&T Corporate Headquarters

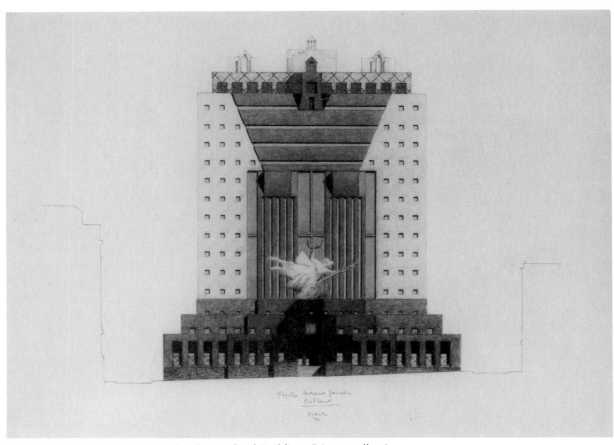

6. Drawing by Michael Graves for the Portland Building. Private collection

7. Cultural Education Center, Empire State Plaza

its and demerits, apart from some brief and dismissive notices. Yet upon its completion in the 1970s, the Albany Mall was greeted with a small flood of hostile responses that are an indication of the recent interest in architecture. To be sure, it was an outdated design by the time it was completed in 1979, and most commentators had unpleasant associations with its imagery. But the Mall serves the useful purpose of reminding us that associative imagery has not in itself been a consistently positive element, and that there is evidently "good" imagery and "bad" imagery, in addition to imagery that is merely successful or unsuccessful.

The critical fortunes of the Empire State Plaza have been largely, though not exclusively, dictated by a flow of events far beyond the control of architects. If the work had been completed more promptly, and if it had been invested with less personal significance for the governor who promoted it, it might have been as easy for us to

8. Bronx Developmental Center

accept today as any number of other large urban enterprises of that time. Such hypotheses are not worth pursuing; the important point is that the lives of buildings can follow courses that are largely out of the hands of the designer. Thus, to some extent, the reputation of the Bronx Developmental Center for the mentally retarded has been compromised by circumstances beyond the command of the architect, such as changing concepts of social policy, developing notions of therapeutic techniques, stringent budgets, and poor administrative decision-making.[7] And who is to say, ultimately, whether the carefully wrought formal vocabulary of the Bronx Developmental Center is either cold, spare, impersonal, and forbidding or polished, personalized, and lovingly crafted down to the smallest detail?

In matters of aesthetics, there will always be differences of opinion and diversity in points of view. As the essay on the Piazza d'Italia points out, the very essence of architectural categories seems to be at stake: where Charles Jencks saw the unlimited, ambiguous character of the space as a characteristic of post-modernism, Christian Norberg-Schulz saw the same quality as characteristic of modernism. All the same, the responses to the East Building of the National Gallery in Washington, D.C. have been so diverse as to make us wonder whether we are reading commentary about the same building. Different points of view are useful, but there are sensible limits to opinion that can be defined by available information. For instance, one critic has lately suggested that the East Building "probably looked so good in the drawings that those had to be reproduced," whereas the realities of the design process were quite different.[8] It was the dissatisfaction with the early drawings that led the architects to commission a succession of perspective renderings in order to study the much discussed lobby area. The renderings were used to project the experience of the space in

9. Early design for atrium, East Building, National Gallery of Art. Rendering by Steven Oles

10. East Building atrium, view toward main entrance

three dimensions, not "the linearity of an isometric projection" as posited by the critic. In fact, the extensive use of renderings in the design process of the East Building is rather exceptional and remarkable for that reason.

The two most persistent issues in the critical literature on the East Building involve its style in relation to its context on the Mall in Washington and the complexity of the design in relation to its function as a museum. The accusation that triangular shapes do not function well as exhibition spaces is to some extent both self-evident and

11. The J. Paul Getty Museum, peristyle garden

12. The Getty Museum, the Basilica

irrelevant, for there are almost no triangular rooms in the new galleries, each of which is "nested" within wall configurations designed to match the needs of changing exhibitions; the structural walls of the building, which appear prominently in published plans, are not visible to the visitor in the galleries.[9] These issues offer a telling contrast to the reception of John Russell Pope's neo-classical National Gallery in 1941, when its grand size and expense seemed more debatable than anything else. Even in Pope's time, however, the notion of consistency of style on the Mall had been an issue. In 1939, Eliel and Eero Saarinen's modernist scheme for the Smithsonian Gallery of Art won a nationwide competition but was subsequently left unexecuted by the agencies that thought it too progressive for the location.[10] It is ironic that the same progressive wing of the architectural profession that supported the Saarinens in 1939 might well have sympathized with the recent call for more classical allusions in the East Building: progressive modernists in one era have become progressive classicists in another. Speculation aside, there is surely an interesting contribution to be made to the history of taste in comparing the Pei extension to the schemes for additions on the same site projected earlier by Warner, Morris and Wilson (1953?), Eggers and Higgins (1953), and Pietro Belluschi (1967).

To a considerable degree the times, not the buildings, make the controversies. On a display board in one of the first galleries at the J. Paul Getty Museum in Malibu, a statement by the founder says, "The museum is aware that it is somewhat controversial to display authentic classical artifacts in a far-from-neutral setting." Nevertheless, it is hard to imagine that Mr. Getty could have anticipated the range of responses to his recreation of an ancient Roman villa, for much of the reaction was based on the revival of interest in classical motifs and imagery among architects in the early 1970s. Suddenly, commentators had to become archaeologists capable of evaluating whether the colors used in the decorative mural paintings were too bright or not bright enough, the composition of the building too loosely derived from its sources or too slavishly archaeological. Suddenly, too, the old art-versus-the-gallery issue was put on new footing when critics complained that the recreation of the villa was not authentic, hence uncomplementary to the art, or, alternatively, that the recreation was too accurate and thus distracting or forbidding. For some it was too decorative, for others it was too clean, too orderly, and too sterile for the art it was meant to display. In the midst of these debates, the taxonomists found it hard to decide whether the museum fit the definition of early post-modern classicism or modern fantasy architecture, or both, as well as other categories.

The Getty Museum has been likened by some observers to Disneyland, Knott's Berry Farm, the Assyrian style rubber factory, and other architectural extravaganzas typical, so it is said, of Los Angeles and Southern California. But the Gehry House in Santa Monica has also been

13. Gehry House, detail of kitchen window/skylight

touted as an example of regional style, although it has nothing in common with the museum a few miles away. As our essays make clear, the earliest and strongest adverse criticism of the Gehry House came from its neighbors, just as the Getty was most unmercifully censured by local journalists. It would be easy to write off this phenomenon as self-consciousness or mere coincidence, but clearly there is something that is not so comfortably "regional" about these buildings. In general, the critics

had little doubt that the rugged vocabulary of exposed studs, chain link, raw plywood, and corrugated metal at the Gehry House derived from the Southern California environment, and the architect agreed. But there is no more or less of these materials in and around Los Angeles than in the environs of many other American cities. If such a vocabulary were to have appeared in one of these cities, would the result have been considered regional? If the composition of the Gehry House is reminiscent of

9

14. Indeterminate Facade, Best Products Showroom, and neighboring stores

California after the earthquake, as several critics suggested in jest, could the same be said of the dislocated forms of the Best Showroom in Houston, Texas? It is possible to rationalize the use of the term regional in almost any context, but that fact only compromises the term's usefulness.

Many of the most prominent critical opinions published on architecture are packed with partially hidden agendas, poorly disguised sub-plots, and what have been called "in-innuendos." Beyond those thinly veiled thrusts and parries, however, there are genuinely influential notions that have affected thinking and writing in significant ways. For example, the influence of Peter Eisenman, Kenneth Frampton, and others associated with the Institute for Architecture and Urban Studies in New York is evident in the critique of the Gehry exhibition that was published in *Skyline* in 1978, where terms like "rotation" and phrases like "specific internal references" appear. But I also detect the same influence, at many removes, in the critique of the Gehry House in *Progressive Architecture* in 1980, where Suzanne Stephens insisted that "By appropriating modern art's abstracted relationships and non-objective qualities for a habitable dwelling, Gehry violates the basic premise of modern art, that it be about art and its own process."[11] Stephens provided broader implications for this observation, which I take out of context only to illustrate a possible echo of Eisenman's insistence on the purely formal demands of architectural composition. Eisenman's dialectics, like those expressed in House VI, gained conviction with every executed building and, regardless of their critical success, inflected our thinking about houses in particular and architecture in general.

Reflections of architectural theory in critical writing are but one index of the success of a monument or its imagery in communicating its meaning and encouraging its acceptance. Another gauge of success is the degree to which buildings are used and their imagery incorporated in the popular culture. Features of the Piazza d'Italia are incorporated in the yearly posters for the Festa d'Italia in New Orleans, but also in the advertising campaigns of local banks, car dealers, and other merchandisers. The Portland Building has spawned a raft of imagery in that city, ranging from earrings and cookie jars to T-shirts, which consolidates the image of the city in its most conspicuous symbol. Nor are such manifestations of popular acceptance limited to the architecture of post-modern persuasion.

Is the role of architecture to satisfy or to uplift the taste of the public? If the role of the architect is to broaden and deepen our understanding of the art, under what circumstances is it defensible to aim for profit? As a long-time associate and partner in the office of John Portman and Associates made clear, the goal of that firm is to please people, both clients and users, because what satisfies also sells.[12] Thus, despite the focus on the inner city and its prospects for revitalization, Portman's is not an altruistic, socially-committed architectural office, but rather a profit-making company that seeks to incorporate as much salable design in architecture as is financially feasible. That the designs do satisfy the needs of the convention hotels for which Portman has become famous is amply proved by the fact that his dramatically soaring atrium lobbies with glass-enclosed elevators have become a cliché. That the Renaissance Center in Detroit has become a symbol of urban revitalization in the 1970s is indicated by its prominence on the catalog cover and the poster for the exhibition *Transformations in Modern Architecture* (Museum of Modern Art, 1979). Those who have learned to love the American vernacular have not always recognized it in the making, but the fact that Portman's work has concerned the literati is evidenced by the interview published by the Institute for Architecture and Urban Studies.[13]

15. Renaissance Center atrium

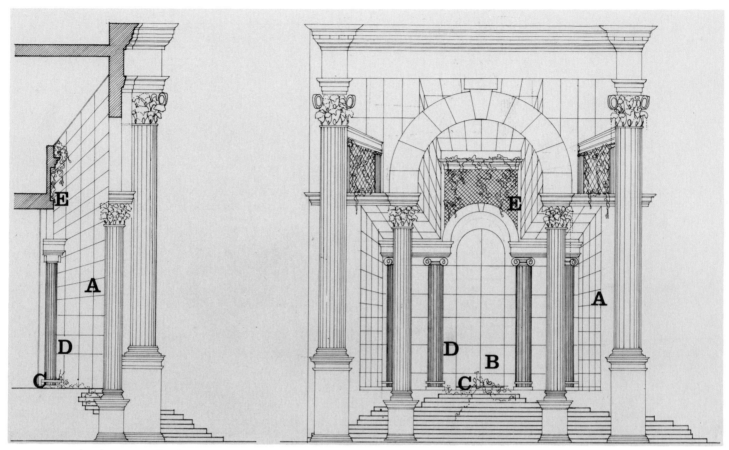

16. Drawing for the Piazza d'Italia

That the field of architecture needs stars is not unusual. It is rather the number of stars in current practice and the way stardom is attained and maintained that deserves more attention. Charles W. Moore is widely credited with the design of the Piazza d'Italia, yet the competition for the commission was won by project designers R. Allen Eskew and Malcolm Heard from Perez Associates. According to Eskew, it was a matter of chance that the Moore design team was brought in. Moore had been the first runner-up in the competition, and it was apparently on his way to Europe that Moore stopped in New Orleans for the public announcement of the results.[14]

Over celebratory cocktails, someone from the mayor's office suggested a collaboration, and all concerned welcomed the idea with enthusiasm. In retrospect, Moore's presence can hardly have been a matter of chance, and the circumstances of the whole story require more thorough investigation. Certainly, there is only steadfast loyalty among the protagonists. But the facts as known still suggest that a useful study could be made of the differences and especially the striking similarities of the Eskew/Heard and the Moore competition designs, as well as the exchange of ideas that resulted in the final form of the Piazza. In New Orleans, it is rumored that the invention of the famous Delicatessen Order, which was to complement the five classical Orders of architec-

ture, was the invention of Marty Schwartz, although Charles Moore is invariably given credit for it, as he often is for the whole Piazza in the literature. Such matters as these are full of the pitfalls of pedantry, but they may also begin to reveal the dynamics of a collaborative creative process that may be more characteristic of practice today than the emphasis on stars would suggest.

The prospect of a history of architecture and criticism that is so recent may itself be controversial, but that argument is hardly a persuasive reason to avoid trying to keep some systematic account of events over the last fifteen years. On the contrary, there are indications that the time is right to begin these kinds of endeavors as a period of critical reassessment emerges. Through the 1970s *Progressive Architecture* was one of the few professional journals of established authority that consistently fostered debate; now other journals, old and new, have begun to follow suit. In August 1984, for example, the *Architectural Review* ran extensive articles on viewpoints regarding the AT&T Headquarters and other recent and nominally classical buildings; and in the winter of 1984, an issue of *Places,* a new journal published at the Massachusetts Institute of Technology, was devoted to various critical opinions and recollections about the Piazza d'Italia.[15] These are typical rather than isolated examples of current publishing trends. In 1977, the distinguished author and architect Peter Blake wrote a book entitled

Form Follows Fiasco, Why Modern Architecture Hasn't Worked; lately, he has been writing about the reasons why he believes post-modernism isn't working.[16] The correlative statement to Blake's critique of architectural practice is Ada Louise Huxtable's commentary on the literature. In an essay for the *New York Review of Books* in December 1983, she complained that although "Polemical works are to be expected in a transitional period with aesthetic axes to grind," much of the writing on recent architecture has begun to cross "the line between persuasive and critical commentary."[17] "How much of this writing is manipulatory rather than expository?" she asks.

Huxtable's skepticism about the character of critical writing on recent architecture has kept pace with her skepticism about many developments in recent architecture, so that where the latter opinions may be in question, the former may seem easy to dismiss. But the issues are real, and the questions do not disappear. A significant portion of writing on recent architecture is frankly partisan without any pretensions of objectivity. Part of the reason for this situation is that the majority of those who have assumed the title of historian are architects who prefer the role of critic to that of practitioner without having developed the tools that are the stock-in-trade of historians of science, culture, and philosophy. Thus, despite the abundance of "historians" of contemporary architecture, there are but few who have not aligned themselves to a current architectural camp, school, or manner that precludes a dispassionate evaluation of the burgeoning developments in style, technology, design process, and construction practices. To put it bluntly, most "historians" of contemporary architecture are critics, who regularly assess the relative merits of professional performances and only secondarily attempt to understand them in the fullest possible context. For such contributions we must be grateful, and truly so, but surely there is more to do.

As strange as it sounds, we need more scholars of recent American architecture. We need more dispassionate voices to deepen our understanding of recent practice and to guide our cultural institutions in identifying, acquiring, and exhibiting the materials that will further this effort. A dedicated group of research-oriented scholars with training and experience in the earlier eras of architectural history and catholic interests in current architectural events can help us to see those events in new light. Absolute objectivity is unattainable, but the fear of being captive to a given place and time has never been a sensible reason to ignore them. The drawings of Palladio and those from the Ecole des Beaux-Arts have had enormous impact on all aspects of the profession through exhibitions; who will be guiding the formation of similar materials for the architecture of our time? It appears that the Architekturmuseum in Frankfurt, West Germany, is leading the way in this direction; but surely there is room for similarly aggressive collecting, guided by trained historians, in our country.

The enormity of the challenges of scholarship can, of course, be deflated by accusations of pedantry or chauvinism, just as an organized effort to acquire study materials may be dismissed for lack of funds when lack of resolve is the real problem. Today, there is a lively commercial trade in architectural drawings, but my experience in the offices of our architects would indicate that the larger portion of potential materials for future study lays untapped and, in many cases, literally wasted. The apparent lack of resources, of primary materials or the funds to gather them, the apparent confusion of critical opinions, and the complacence induced by the presence of the buildings and the architects in our country should not preclude our most ambitious efforts to transmit as much as we can of the present to the future. We are living in exciting times, architecturally speaking, and we will be judged by our response to them.

Notes

1. A pictorial survey consisting of more than four hundred photographs of buildings from the last twenty years was mounted at the Museum of Modern Art in the exhibition *Transformations in Modern Architecture* in 1979. For an overview of the themes presented, see the catalog by Arthur Drexler, *Transformations in Modern Architecture,* New York, 1979. Drexler clarified the goals of the show in "Response: Arthur Drexler on Transformations," *Skyline,* Summer 1979, 6.

2. The limits of the first and subsequent phases of construction are clearly outlined in a document entitled *Piazza d'Italia* (n.d.) at the office of Perez Associates Architects. The references to the publications in *Progressive Architecture* are contained in the essay on Piazza d'Italia in this book.

3. Personal interview with Jan Scruggs, the president of the Vietnam Veterans Memorial Fund, Washington, D.C., April 2, 1984.

4. Robert Fischer, "Behind a 'Renaissance' Tower: a Contemporary Structure That Lets It Work," *Architectural Record,* 168, October 1980, 106-111.

5. Johnson's was the only room in the exhibition to be decorated with such "wallpaper," derived from Johnson/Burgee's International Place at Fort Hill Square, Boston (design 1982-83). It is illustrated in the catalog by Arthur Drexler, *Three New Skyscrapers,* New York, 1983.

6. Quoted in Donald Judd, "A Long Discussion Not about Masterpieces But Why There Are So Few of Them, " *Art in America,* 72, September 1984, 15.

7. For a tough-minded assessment of the problems at the Bronx Developmental Center, see Carter Wiseman, "When a Pretty Face Is Not Enough," *New York,* January 18, 1982, 66–67.

8. Judd, "A Long Discussion," 17. The drawings for the East Building were published in a catalog to the exhibition *I.M. Pei and Partners: Drawings for the East Building, National Gallery of Art—Its Evolution in Sketches, Renderings, and Models 1968-1978,* Adams Davidson Galleries, Washington, D.C., 1979.

9. The one exception is the Matisse room in the southwest tower, if one grants that the entrance area is not, properly speaking, a gallery. I want to thank Dr. David Scott for pointing out these facts to me.

10. See the fine essay by David De Long, "Eliel Saarinen and the Cranbrook Tradition in Architecture and Urban Design" in *Design in America, the Cranbrook Vision 1925–1950,* New York, 1983, 68–69, with documentation and further references.

11. For references to the Stephens quotation and the *Skyline* review, see my essay on the Gehry House in this book.

12. Personal interview with Stanley Steinberg, a partner at John Portman and Associates, Atlanta, June 1, 1984.

13. See *Skyline,* January 1983, 12–15. See also the interview, "Architect/Developer John Portman," *R.I.B.A. Journal,* 84, December 1977, 504–513.

14. Personal interview with Allen Eskew of Perez Associates Architects, New Orleans, May 29, 1984. I would also like to thank Joseph Maselli of New Orleans for sharing with me his insights and recollections of the planning stages of the Piazza d'Italia. On the personalities involved in the planning from the Italian community, see Evans Casso, *Staying in Step: A Continuing Italian Renaissance,* New Orleans, 1984, 56 ff.

15. See William Curtis, "On Appearing Too Classical," and Reyner Banham, "A.T.&T.: The Post-Post Déco Skyscraper," *Architectural Review,* 176, August 1984, 11–21 and 25–27, respectively; and "Place Debate: Piazza d'Italia," *Places,* 1, Winter 1984, 7–31 (various authors).

16. Peter Blake, "What on Earth Is Happening to Our Buildings?," *Pennsylvania Gazette* (University of Pennsylvania), February 1984, 32–38. This was kindly brought to my attention by Kent Cooper.

17. Ada Louise Huxtable, "After Modern Architecture," *New York Review of Books,* December 8, 1983, 29–35.

Utilitas, Firmitas, Venustas and the Vox Populi: A Context for Controversy

Robert Bruegmann

If there is a single conclusion to be drawn from this book, it is that architectural criticism, or at least architectural controversy, is surely in a golden age. This will probably come as something of a revelation to many people who will disagree violently with much of the criticism of the buildings in the book and disagree routinely with all of the major critics. But in terms of quantity, the degree of passion aroused, and the range of people who wish to be heard, it is hard to deny that we are witnessing a significant phenomenon.

In fact, architecture seems to be generating the kind of widespread discussion that only painting or sculpture among the visual arts used to stimulate. The East Building of the National Gallery or the Getty Museum are routinely accused of upstaging the art within them. Michael Graves and Philip Johnson have become as well known as any living American painter or sculptor. It is particularly telling that the Vietnam Veterans Memorial, perhaps the most hotly contested monument of recent memory, is usually considered a work of architecture rather than sculpture, and that so many sculptors seem to be doing work that is clearly architectonic.

One has only to read critics attacking certain infamous nineteenth-century paintings as "dangerous" to glimpse the seriousness of the subject of painting in that century. Public commissions for murals or sculptural monuments were seen as a direct reflection on civic virtues and aspirations. The criticism of buildings, on the other hand, was more the province of specialists and it tended to be carried out at much lower temperatures. It is hard to think of a single building in the nineteenth or early twentieth century capable of creating such a juicy scandal as Manet's Olympia, for example.

Today, by contrast, it seems to be architecture that upholds or challenges the morality of the public. It is hard to remember a painting in recent years that has been called "dangerous." Violence, pornography, even self-mutilation seem to be acceptable subjects of artistic expression, leaving very little left up the artist's sleeve that can still shock. On the other hand, when modernist critic Wolf von Eckardt characterized the Portland Building of Michael Graves with the word "dangerous," it

seems he was perfectly serious. Von Eckardt no doubt saw the building as a real challenge to truth and integrity in architecture and, by extension, as a direct threat to the moral fabric of the citizenry.

Clearly, not everyone is thrilled with the new boom industry of architectural criticism. Writes Ada Louise Huxtable:

> Criticism is not doing the job. That is not surprising at a time when being part of the action is more important than asking questions about meaning and value. The media has created a false culture of celebrityhood and cult, fed only by the more sensational, entertaining, superficial aspects of the arts. Publicity is its own reward.[1]

On the other hand, it has been seriously suggested that criticism may be the great art form of today. Emancipated from its role as subservient to what it describes, criticism has taken on a whole new identity. Much recent architectural criticism takes buildings as its point of departure but then develops in a way independent of the buildings. For example, the essay by William Gass on House VI that appeared in Progressive Architecture is as much a conscious aesthetic effort as the house itself.

There can be little question that this book and exhibition betray certain biases about architecture and about criticism that would have been unacceptable to most modernists of an earlier era. The building itself, like a painting, was the work of art and the only thing that really mattered, the modernists would have argued. Documentation of the architect's intentions and the response of the viewer might be interesting in a sociological way, but these had no essential bearing on the work, which should be complete and self-sufficient without any explanation. Certainly, the modernists would add, this kind of documentation would not belong in the museum. For this book, however, it has been assumed that the artist's intentions, the creation of the work, and its reception by the public are all integral parts of the architectural experience. None can really be understood without taking the others into account.

The buildings represented in this book seem quite diverse. Geographically they are scattered around the country. They range from those highly constrained by programmatic and budget limitations (Renaissance Center) to those as free from specific physical restraints as works of architecture can normally be (Vietnam Veterans Memorial), from quite private (Gehry House) to very public (Portland Building), in budget from very cheap (Indeterminate Facade) to those that represent sizeable chunks of the gross national product (Albany Mall).

The range of viewpoint expressed here is prodigious. The students who gathered the research materials for the essays managed to collect something like twenty-four pounds of photocopies. Surely the number of works written about the AT&T or Portland Buildings must already rival the total for any previous structure in the history of architecture. Among the commentaries are irate letters to the editors of local newspapers, the glib pronouncements of the national newsweeklies, and the fluffy prose of the popular magazines, in addition to the articles in the standard architectural journals.

A little scrutiny shows that the apparent diversity is deceptive. It is significant that all of the twelve buildings tend to cluster along the coasts. Almost every structure here is in a large city or its suburbs. More significant is the distribution of architects. There are no architects represented from the mid-west, the plains states, the mountain states, the southwest, the Pacific northwest. The architects of virtually every building, moreover, work either in the New York or Los Angeles area. In fact at least eight of the twelve designers represented here work in New York or at a distance of a short train ride.

In the case of the criticism, likewise, for all its apparent diversity when the discussion leaves political, economic, and social matters and enters the realm of matters more purely architectural, the remarkable thing is how similar these professional architectural writers sound even when their conclusions are dramatically different. Whether the writer is a dyed-in-the-wool modernist, a fellow traveler of the post-modernists or a spokesman for old-fashioned common sense as it might be understood by a mid-western businessman, the differences are minimal. The same criteria are evoked, the same architects discussed. Even the writing style is often similar. This is actually not at all surprising. The debate, despite all of the obvious widening of interest in matters architectural, is still spearheaded by a small elite in a few cities. Almost all of the writers grew up reading the same architectural journals and going to the same schools.

What conclusions can we draw from this evidence? One conclusion might be that the most controversial architects and critics live in a few cities on the coasts. Presumably the vast majority of American architects and critics from anywhere else are viewed as inherently less controversial. There may be some truth to this. For instance, most buildings that are well publicized and considered controversial are also, despite their apparent

diversity, examples of High Art. Such a group of buildings by definition excludes not only over ninety-percent of the built environment which is innocent of architects, but also most of what is done by architects outside the very small circle certified as important by the national architectural press, professors in the major schools, and a few prominent practitioners.

The apparent exception is most instructive. The Indeterminate Facade is the one building which many critics have refused to accept as significant. Indeed, the structure seems to have been in part a deliberate slap at the established order of the profession. But SITE's astonishingly successful use of the media for self-publicity seems to have worked. Enough ink has been spilled on behalf of SITE to overcome any amount of critical disdain. The appointment of its co-founder James Wines, as chairman of the Environmental Design Department at Parsons is an excellent example of the interloper forcing his way into the inner circle.

What this example suggests is that in the rarified councils of High Art, being "good" or "bad" is less important than being discussed. The Albany Mall, for example, seems to have been thoroughly disliked by almost everyone writing in the architectural press, but at least it was discussed. The very vehemence of denunciations leads one to suspect something more than meets the eye. Consider the relish with which an anonymous writer in *Progressive Architecture* attacked it:

> Half a cantaloupe sliced on the bias, a croquet wicket with avoirdupois, an upside-down orange half from a Kraft salad, and four little towers and a high tower resembling forms of cubistic coition are the major elements in the South Mall Plan proposed—seriously, we presume—for the Capital of New York State.[2]

How far can this be from a camp classic, a building so bad it is good? How soon will loving to hate it turn to just plain loving it as all of its presumed vices are turned into virtue by the young Turks of the next generation? Much worse than being declared terrible is the fate that befalls most buildings, including countless others better known to the public at large: they are simply ignored.

To many people who are not protagonists in the admittedly small and elite circle of architects and critics writing in the architectural press, the debate over post-modernism and perhaps much of the controversy represented here will seem like so much academic hair splitting. But underneath the flood of words issued in reaction to these buildings are some indications that the way architecture is perceived is changing in fundamental ways. This book, because it looks in depth at a few buildings over a fairly narrow time frame, affords an excellent sample from which to draw some conclusions on how criticism changed at a critical moment. By the early 1970s something clearly had happened to the "Modern

17. Empire State Plaza

Movement." While well-known architectural firms like
I.M. Pei, Roche and Dinkeloo, and Skidmore, Owings
and Merrill continued to produce buildings that met with
acclaim and stood firmly in line with the great modernist
tradition of pioneers like Mies Van der Rohe, Walter
Gropius, and Le Corbusier, an increasing number of architects seemed ready to move on to something new. In
buildings by Robert Venturi, Charles Moore, and others,
gables and dormers, columns and capitals, references to
surrounding buildings and to historic structures started to
appear. They were published in the architecture press
where they were greeted with storms of criticism and
called irresponsible, arbitrary, and silly. Another much
smaller group including men like John Barrington Bayley,
who had been producing buildings in the classical tradition all along, acquired new respectability. At the same
time, buildings by a group of Europeans calling themselves the "Tendenza" and led by Aldo Rossi of Italy

started to appear in American journals. Their work was
characterized by an attempt to create new buildings
based on the kind of structure that they saw around them
in the historic city centers of Europe, but their relation to
the older buildings was much more abstract and ideal-
ized than the literal historic references of the Americans.

Publications accompanied practice. Venturi's *Complexity and Contradiction in Architecture,* published in
1966, argued for a messy vitality as opposed to the clear,
straightforward solutions of modernism. There also appeared a stream of articles and books with titles like *The
Failure of Modern Architecture* (by Brent Brolin, 1976) or
Form Follows Fiasco (by Peter Blake, 1977). Finally,
Charles Jencks's polemical book, *The Language of Post-
Modern Architecture* of 1977, provided the catch-word
necessary for the debate to break out in earnest. "Post-
modernism" has most often been used as a stylistic label
for any structure that does not look like a minimal con-

crete, steel, and glass box, especially if it has keystones, arches, or other specific historical elements; it has also been used more recently in a more basic way to indicate a fundamental shift of world view away from all of the certainties of the last fifty years, and, some theorists have argued, from the entire tradition of western humanism altogether. Needless to say, the whole idea has been extremely controversial.

This compilation represents, then, a very complex group of interactions. Critics ranging from very conservative to quite avant-garde are looking at buildings that range in style from modern (Bronx Developmental Center) to post-modern (Portland Building) to pre-modern (Getty Museum), and which are the creations of architects with very different philosophies of design. Perhaps the best way to analyze the criticism here is to study in turn each of the time-honored categories, first proposed by the ancient Roman architect Vitruvius, of "Commodity, Firmness, and Delight," *(Utilitas, Firmitas, et Venustas)*—or loosely translated, programmatic fitness, structural soundness, and aesthetic pleasure. These elements have been recognized from ancient times to ours as a reasonable starting point for criticism, a fact which is even more remarkable than the diversity of conclusions which has been drawn from them. Perhaps the best short exposition of this "Vitruvian Triad" was given by Geoffrey Scott in his classic work, *The Architecture of Humanism,* published in 1914. Let us look briefly at each.

A. FIRMNESS

Perhaps the most straightforward of the three categories is "Firmness." Writes Geoffrey Scott:

> On every hand the study of architecture encounters physics, statics, and dynamics, suggesting, controlling, justifying its design. It is open to us, therefore, to look in buildings for the logical expression of material properties and material laws. Without these, architecture is impossible, its history unintelligible. And if, finding these everywhere paramount, we seek, in terms of material properties and material laws, not merely to account for the history of architecture but to assess its value, then architecture will be judged by the exactness and sincerity with which it expresses constructive facts, and conforms to constructive laws.[3]

Firmness, then, is about structure and construction. A building should not only be sound and logical in its construction, but it should appear this way as well. For Scott and for classical architects this demand had implications that extended remarkably far, leading to the creation of a whole catalogue of "rules." Every column or piece of wall should stand clearly on a support below and so on down to the ground. Lighter, more "feminine" Corinthian columns should surmount heavier Doric ones in multi-

storied buildings employing the orders. But these strictures were always considered rules that, under certain circumstances and to create certain effects, could be broken. With the advent of new steel and concrete technology many of the practical limitations that lay behind the old rules were eliminated. Structurally, the rules could be broken with impunity. At first it seems ironic that at just this moment theoreticians such as Viollet-le-Duc fortified the old arguments with new strictures that were even more firmly based on moral principles, but this was clearly a necessary reaction to avoid the chaos of form the new materials made possible. "Truth to materials" and "structural rationalism" became catch-words for over a century. They represented an attempt to remove irrational, conventional standards and to replace them by more rational ones. This process reached its apogee in the theories advanced by the extreme leftist wing of modernism. For certain German architects especially, structure and program became the only criteria. If beauty was mentioned at all, it would be explained as the result of a perfectly rational, appropriate structure. Something similar happened in painting, reaching its most developed point in writings by critics like Clement Greenberg. The materials of painting, the canvas and pigments, became the basis for extraordinarily restrictive moral imperatives. Paintings had to be flat, reinforcing the picture plane, and non-illusionistic, never pretending to be anything other than paint on canvas.

Few of the critics in this book speak much about structure, but where it is an issue, they document a break with the modernist rules. In the criticism of the work of Peter Eisenman, for example, there has been almost no talk about the actual structure since it is nearly impossible to perceive behind the smooth surfaces and the camouflage of redundant structural elements intended not to hold up the building but to mark the process of its creation. As a number of critics pointed out, Eisenman's designs seemed to ignore gravity to the extent that models could be and were inadvertently displayed upside-down.

In the case of SITE's Indeterminate Facade, despite constant reminders from Wines that the building was about "incompleteness," that is about not being finished, critics invariably spoke about it as finished but already in a state of ruin. Perhaps the best description comes from Gerald Allen in *Architectural Record:*

> The image of a big chunk falling out of the corner of a building or the building jacked up on one side, or collapsing, or being altogether roofed over by an asphalt parking lot in some final apocalyptic triumph of the automobile, all of this can be seen as pessimistic. But it is also funny and fun, and profitable and very powerful. SITE's juxtaposition of the modestly familiar with the stunningly unfamiliar is like a bomb that arrives in a shoebox.[4]

18. Indeterminate Facade, cascade of bricks

The Indeterminate Facade, whatever the intention of the architect, has been read as a direct negation of conventional standards of "firmness." Hardly a voice was raised to claim that the building was wrong, only that it was nonsensical. Obviously, firmness has lost some of its power as a critical standard.

B. COMMODITY

If "Firmness" seems at present somewhat less important a critical criteria than heretofore, the same is true, although to a lesser degree, with "Commodity." Geoffrey Scott wrote:

> Buildings may be judged by the success with which they supply practical ends they are designed to meet. Or, by a natural extension, we may judge them by the value of these ends themselves; that is to say, by the external purposes which they reflect. These, indeed are two very different questions. The last makes a moral reference which the first avoids, but both spring, and spring inevitably from the link which architecture has with life.[5]

Commodity thus refers both to the actual physical functioning of the building and to the expression of its function. By the mid-nineteenth century this criterion had become quite rigid and, as in the case of firmness, based on moral imperatives. The great English critic John Ruskin believed, for example, that a building devoted to work should have little or no ornament, whereas a building devoted to higher purposes, a church, for example, required ornament. The kind of ornament was also important. In the nineteenth century the choice of a style for the Houses of Parliament or the Foreign Office in London could become a national issue because this kind

19

19. The Portland Building

20. Bronx Developmental Center

of choice reflected the aspirations of the government and the people. Should the universality and continuity of the classic tradition, for example, be more appropriate for such buildings than the particularly British sensibility revealed in certain British medieval buildings?

Twentieth-century modernists, while accepting the moral basis for functional expression, rejected the use of historical ornamental styles. By concentrating on the universal needs of mankind, they hoped to arrive at universally valid forms that would have no need of merely conventional elements. The stone columns on the front of a steel frame bank, after all, did not really assure the strength of the bank. One of European modernism's fondest hopes was that conventional elements like the columns could be eliminated. The building would become simply itself, physically and visually.

In recent years this modernist notion has been under heavy attack, especially by writers interested in semiotics, the study of signs. These writers argued that the modernists, in a naive attempt to avoid conventional symbolic meaning, deprived their architecture of elements that were readily understood by the public. The new forms they created, moreover, far from simply signifying themselves, actually carried with them a whole series of associations, many of them undesirable. Semiotics became a major movement in the 1970s, as architects and critics tried to decide how to recover for architecture some of the legibility it once had. The results were largely unsatisfactory since the transfer of ideas from language to architecture proved highly problematic. In the end the search to regain appropriate expression for all kinds of building types has been carried out on a more

intuitive level. Curiously, this search has led right back to the Battle of the Styles of the nineteenth century.

The most publicized of all attempts to return to traditional architectural elements in an effort to recapture a building's ability to communicate its function in the city has been the Portland Building. This building seems to have become the focus of debate on the entire enterprise. The result has been a savage cross-fire of opinions. On the one hand there was an initial burst of reactions from many modernists, who believed that the idea of returning to a classical style was futile or simply foolish. The classical styles are no longer a continuous tradition, they argued, and classical detailing is by this time as dead a language as Latin. On the other hand, there were the writers who presumably accepted the idea that a classical vocabulary could still speak but thought the Portland Building was not classical. As a number of the writers argued, the Portland Building was profoundly modernist in its two-dimensionality, its use of a kind of collage of classical elements presented in layers in a screen-like manner. But because the building was neither classical nor modern, the critics were at a loss to know what standard to apply to it.

The expression of function turns out to be a quite complex matter. The Bronx Developmental Center provides an excellent example. Repeatedly, medical authorities were cited as saying that the building should have a "home-like" character. Although this might at first seem self-evident, the discussion that followed—turning on the question of whether "home-like" meant the arrangement of rooms, the exterior appearance, whether the latter should make references to little bungalows with pitched

21. East Building atrium

roofs, or the apartment buildings like the ones most of the children came from—made it clear that the phrase itself was an abstraction.

A further extension of the arguments about Commodity is apparent in the discussions of the East Building of the National Gallery. The advice of the director of the National Gallery that the new, museum-going public tended to spend less than forty-five minutes at a time looking at the art, for example, was accepted by many writers as a reasonable basis for programmatic decisions, such as the small galleries and the enormous atrium. When Richard Hennessy lashed out in *Artforum* at the "shocking fun-house atmosphere," the "deeply philistine unseriousness," of "airport 78" and the "ringing affirmation of the morbid restlessness of crowds," he was not reviewing the forms so much as making a judgement on the museum's administration, the architect, and the general public for accepting a vision of the museum quite different from his own.[6]

We have moved from a critique of the building to a critique of society as exemplified in the building. Much recent criticism is of this kind. Since there seems to be less and less agreement on the most basic assumptions about the needs of "mankind," it is not surprising that discussion turns increasingly from the means to the ends. With both Firmness and Commodity, however, most people believe there are still some apparently objective criteria left. I have not read a single critic who suggests that buildings that actually fall down (as opposed to looking like they have) or endanger the life of their occupants are acceptable designs.

C. DELIGHT

In moving from Firmness and Commodity to Delight, we enter a different world.

> We may trace in architecture a third and different factor—the disinterested desire for beauty. This desire does not, it is true, culminate here in a purely aesthetic result, for it has to deal with a concrete basis which is utilitarian. It is, nonetheless, a purely aesthetic impulse, an impulse distinct from all the others which architecture may simultaneously satisfy, an impulse by virtue of which architecture becomes art. It is a separate instinct. It will borrow a suggestion from the laws of firmness or commodity; sometimes it will run counter to them, or be offended by the forms they would dictate. It has its own standard, and claims its own authority.[7]

For Scott, beauty was not a problem. He spoke of the desire for beauty as an "impulse" or an "instinct." This implies something inborn, a reality that is independent of man, something that cannot be learned, only discovered. This was not just Scott's belief. It was shared by almost everyone up until the mid-twentieth century. Even the vast majority of European modernists, often accused of being utilitarian functionalists, still believed that there were immutable natural laws and that some forms were inherently better than others. Smooth, simple geometric shapes, for example, were thought to inspire positive psychological responses in man. Modernists believed that the job of the architect, at least the genuine avant-garde architect, was to discover what these laws were and to insist on them even if they ran counter to society's expectations. In fact, as the nineteenth century progressed, the avant-garde moved further and further from the tastes of the population at large.

By the mid-1970s, there was ample evidence that the whole idea of the modernist avant-garde was under siege. The single most important attack came from Robert Venturi. The first words of Venturi's landmark *Complexity and Contradiction in Architecture* were not "Architecture should be," as a modernist might have written, but "I like." This tended to remove beauty wholly into the realm of taste. Venturi and his wife Denise Scott Brown further, but probably unwittingly, opened the door to a position of extreme relativism in their *Learning from Las Vegas* of 1972, by introducing from sociology the idea of taste cultures, the idea that the tastes of different groups in a society differed markedly and that they were all valid.

The seemingly inevitable conclusion of Venturi's line of thought, but one with which Venturi himself would almost certainly not agree, seems to be that all aesthetic questions are relative, that "beauty is in the eye of the beholder." By discounting the modernists' claims for the architect as economic and social engineer, then proposing that architects have no monopoly in the field of taste,

Venturi knocked out the last prop of authority the profession could claim. No longer the repository of an authority based on God or moral humanistic principles, the architect was reduced to the status of any other professional competing in the market place.

To the faithful the sharp decline of the idea of the avant-garde is particularly painful. Here, for example, is a passage from an article by Bruce Goodwin, writing in *Architecture and Urbanism:*

> For the past decade, a cultural temperament of insidious pleasantness has debilitated the appreciation of architectural intelligence. The strident social idealism of the sixties in America reminiscent of the post–World War I era in Europe and post–World War II in Japan, was unable to thwart the triumph of adhesive daisies and Barry Manilow. Now the architectural consumer wallows in batter-whipped mediocrity. The vitality of art is possible only in confrontation and opposition to middle class values.[8]

It appears that the only architect represented in this book who still maintains a belief in the avant-garde and in absolute standards of beauty is Peter Eisenman. Denying firmness and commodity as determinants of form, he is left with the idea that certain relationships of line and plane are more significant or resonant, if not more beautiful, than others. He calls them archetypal and attempts to preserve them as much as possible autonomously, as little subject to the materials out of which they are made or the uses to which they will be put as is compatible with the necessity of finding a client. William Gass indicated the way in which Eisenman's House VI attempts to transcend man and his needs altogether to rise to the level of pure form:

> These walls did not guard or shelter or enclose, the windows did not cowtow to me, or frame scenes, or provide an excuse for drapery. The world of this house was Copernican. Its spaces did not flow from me as though I were their source and center. Its surfaces were not the limits of my spirit and movement, places for paintings, shepherds of privacy, backgrounds for my furniture. Nor did the floor exist to support rugs or serve to assure me, always, that I was safe on the hard and even earth.... Thank God, I thought. This house has no concern for me and mine, over which it has no rights, but displays in every aspect and angle and fall of light the concern for the nature and beauty of building, that is the architect's trust and obligation.[9]

For almost every other architect and critic in this book, however, the eclipse of many of modernism's certainties necessitated the adoption of much more subjective critical standards. For example, with a few

22. House VI

exceptions, most of the critics represented here are careful to avoid calling a building "good" or "bad" but have said rather it is "interesting," or "powerful," or "important." Architectural criticism, like architecture itself, seems to be heading inexorably toward the conclusion reached by Philip Johnson who has stated that the only absolute today is that there are no rules. The statement by Pierre Rastnay quoted by James Wines is relevant here:

> Art will no longer aspire to account for everything; it will have left forever the ambiguous sphere of transcending for the scattered humble everyday universe of the relative.[10]

If this line of reasoning is taken to its logical conclusion, on what basis can the architect of the post-modern age make any choices at all? Like society, architecture needs some rules to function. One possibility is that even without the existence of inevitable "natural" laws, architecture can make its own rules. Rules governing various games, for example, are arbitrary but as long as everyone accepts them, they work. This is the thesis of a provocative recent book, *Complicity and Conviction: Steps Toward an Architecture of Convention,* whose very title seems to indicate a reaction to the Pandora's box opened by the Venturis in the 1970s.[11]

If the critical writing discussed in this compilation is any evidence, a real consensus is still far off. Indeed the increasingly rapid swings of opinion within the profession would argue this point. Witness the case of the East

23. Piazza d'Italia

Building of the National Gallery where the initial responses were largely favorable, followed by a flood of adverse criticism that appeared in the next couple of years. Juan Pablo Bonta, in an interesting book called *Architecture and Its Interpretation,* has documented this phenomenon in a striking fashion. He shows, for example, that the Folger Library by Paul Cret, considered among the finest American buildings in a poll of architects in 1948, became within a generation a matter of scorn when it was remembered at all.[12]

If a broadly based consensus on architectural design is a desirable goal, it would be important to know not only what the professionals but non-professionals think. It is obvious in the writings gathered in this book, especially those on the most public buildings like Pei's East Building and Graves's Portland Building, that the architectural press has recognized this need. A great deal of attention was paid, for example, to the reactions of employees in the Portland Building to the relatively small windows or to the response of the Italian-American community to the Piazza d'Italia. In fact, during the *Progressive Architecture* awards selection, Cesar Pelli decisively linked the Piazza's value to its popular acceptance: "A project like this can't be judged until after it's built; if people use it, it's good, if they don't, forget it."[13] It is telling, however, that even long after the opening of the Piazza, comments by critics ranged from Martin Filler's assertion that the fountain is a resounding success in the Italian community (except for the neon) to Tom Aidala's statement that the design deeply offends the Italian community because it exploits ethnic stereotypes.

Almost every other business that provides a product or service in any way dependent on the public's image of it spends enormous amounts of time and money trying to determine the tastes of each sector of the market and to influence them. The evidence of this book indicates that the architectural profession is interested primarily in the latter. Nowhere in any of the writings about these buildings is there any hint that any systematic opinion sampling was done except for one reference to a poll taken of architecture students.[14] In that case the fact that the students named Michael Graves the most important architect today makes one wonder if any schools west of Philadelphia were included.

Does the population at large admire the Bronx Developmental Center and dislike the Albany Mall as much as the critics? In the case of the Renaissance Center and the Best Showroom, a number of writers implied that the design's effectiveness could be gauged in financial terms. If people like a building, the argument goes, they would come there more often to shop. Evidence consisted of a few sales figures at the Best Showroom and the Renaissance Center. But lacking any kind of analysis of how a standard showroom would have done in that area of Houston or how well or badly the Renaissance Center did in comparison with other buildings in Detroit, whose economy in the late 1970s and early 1980s had all but collapsed, the conclusions are hardly convincing. It is also quite possible that design was not an important factor in these cases. In fact, it appears that the old notion that the job of architects is to educate the public into liking what it ought to like is still very much with us, even

24. Vietnam Veterans Memorial

in an era when the profession is wrestling with the suspicion that all of the principles they are seeking to instill may be just a matter of taste. Curiously, it is in the very largest, most public issues that the tendency to resort to categorical statements or moral certainties is strongest. Writing about the AT&T building, for example, Paul Goldberger says:

> If there is anything that the city's current boom, one of the largest in history, has proved, it is that there are limits to density and that midtown Manhattan has now almost certainly reached them.[15]

But nagging doubts remain. Goldberger has the honesty to admit that just this lament has been issued many, many times before and yet the density has just continued to increase. In this case, moreover, if enough New Yorkers agreed with Goldberger, they could impose their views by electing officials who would considerably tighten zoning restrictions. In fact, zoning is a perennially thorny political issue with partisans arguing for a wide variety of different solutions. This is also true in the case of all the other, and fast multiplying, restrictions on land use and design: landmark designations, energy conservation measures, sign ordinances, design review, scenic conservation restrictions.

Perhaps the most revealing glimpse of public opinion provided in this book is the history of the Vietnam Veterans Memorial. It seems to indicate that "public opinion" is much more diverse and less predetermined by political, social, or class distinctions than anyone might have thought. A modernist might well argue that the Vietnam Veterans Memorial is a perfect argument for the chaos that ensues when design decisions are removed from the hands of the "experts" and become political decisions. But the tide seems to be running the other way. The surge of excitement about architecture seems to be related to the perception that a new consensus about architecture is being formed and a lot of people seem to be interested in the result. The controversy documented in this book may be just a foretaste of the struggle ahead in reaching some kind of agreement on how architecture should function in an era searching for rules. It may be a difficult time to make convincing architecture, but it is also a time that promises to provide more architectural controversy.

Notes

1. Ada Louise Huxtable, "State of the Arts: Architecture, Classicism in a Contemporary Context," *New York Times,* September 6, 1981, 21.
2. "Cacophony of Forms in New York Capital," *Progressive Architecture,* 44, September 1963, 70.
3. Geoffrey Scott, *The Architecture of Humanism,* London, 1914, 2.
4. Gerald Allen, "Bringing In the Business," *Architectural Record,* 161, March 1977, 115.
5. Scott, *Architecture of Humanism,* 3–4.
6. Richard Hennessy, "Type and Progeny: Recent Monumental Architecture," *Artforum,* 17, November 1978, 70.
7. Scott, *Architecture of Humanism,* 4.
8. Bruce Goodwin, "Architecture of the Id," *Architecture and Urbanism* (A+U), 117, 1980, 113.
9. William Gass, "House VI," *Progressive Architecture,* 58, June 1977, 64.
10. *Best Products Co. Houston Showroom by SITE, Inc.* (published by SITE), New York, 1975.
11. William Hubbard, *Complicity and Conviction: Steps Toward an Architecture of Convention,* Princeton, 1980.
12. Juan Pablo Bonta, *Architecture and Its Interpretation: A Study of Expressive Systems in Architecture,* New York, 1979, 176.
13. "The Twenty-third Awards Program: August Perez and Associates," *Progressive Architecture,* 57, January 1976, 83.
14. See Filler in "The Gallant Gamble of Michael Graves," *House and Garden,* January 1983, 168.
15. Paul Goldberger, "The Limits of Urban Growth," *New York Times Magazine,* November 14, 1982, 46–68.

Selected Bibliography

"Beyond the Modern Movement," *Harvard Architectural Review,* Spring 1980.The introduction and the article by Robert Stern, "The Doubles of Post-Modernism," are perhaps the best statements on the subject of post-modernism in architecture in the broadest sense of the term.

Bonta, Juan Pablo. *Architecture and Its Interpretation: A Study of Expressive Systems in Architecture.* New York, 1979. A short study on how architecture is perceived with an admirable short explanation of how semiotics was important in the overthrow of modernist doctrine.

Collins, Peter. *Changing Ideals in Modern Architecture.* London, 1965. Probably the best single book on modern architectural theory, especially as it was formulated in the nineteenth century.

Hubbard, William. *Complicity and Conviction: Steps Toward an Architecture of Convention.* Cambridge, Massachusetts, 1980. This author proposes that architecture could develop its own set of rules by analogy with other human activities such as games, typography, and the law.

Portoghesi, Paolo. *After Modern Architecture.* New York, 1980. A brief popular book on some of the causes for the decline of modernism and the rise of post-modernism.

Scott, Geoffrey. *The Architecture of Humanism.* London, 1914. A classic text on judging architecture, with an eloquent defense of the importance of purely aesthetic criteria.

Scruton, Roger. *The Aesthetics of Architecture.* Princeton, 1979. This is the best introduction to the subject of "Delight" in architecture.

Venturi, Robert. *Complexity and Contradiction in Architecture.* New York, 1966. This classic text was the opening salvo in the attack on modernist certainties.

Venturi, Robert, Steven Izenour, and Denise Scott Brown. *Learning from Las Vegas.* Cambridge, Massachusetts, 1972. This book attempted to study American strip architecture to find lessons that could apply to High Architecture. It was also the place where Venturi and Scott Brown introduced from sociology the notion of taste cultures.

Watkins, David. *Morality and Architecture.* Oxford, 1977. An interesting attempt to trace the rise of morality as a criterion for judgments in modern architecture.

American Architecture and Its Criticism: Reflections of the State of the Arts

Martin Filler

If American architecture is, as many people believe it to be, in a crucial phase of transition — as well as a high level of creativity and world influence — why is this moment not also accompanied by a comparably high level of architectural criticism? There can be little question that architecture has a far more pervasive influence on the daily lives of people than any of the other arts, and yet the level of critical discourse on the subject lags far behind — in quality as well as quantity — that pertaining to painting, sculpture, music, theater, dance, and film. Why is this so, how has it been able to happen, and what is the likelihood that the conditions permitting this anomalous situation will change?

To provide an answer, we must examine the attitudes that currently inform the practice of architectural criticism in this country. First, there is the issue of expectations. With the exception of a handful of individual critics who have achieved strong voices of their own, there has been an absence of a strongly-developed (or at least strongly-sustained) critical tradition in the evaluation of our architecture. There are several contributing factors. The relative newness of the United States and the resultant late start it got in matters artistic had the effect of making criticism a generally suspect enterprise. The very fact that a community was able to raise a courthouse or town hall or orphanage was deemed such a justifiable source of civic pride that evaluation of its aesthetic merits was usually considered by most citizens to be a secondary, if not wholly irrelevant, question. Thus, with the exception of such isolated worthies as Horatio Greenough — whose investigation of the philosophical and social principles of architecture as practiced in this country still has a clear contemporary relevance more than a century and a quarter after his death — there was precious little written before the Civil War deserving of the designation of architectural criticism.

It was not until the United States achieved the high measure of economic prosperity based on industrial innovation following the Civil War that a climate of sufficient self-confidence allowed evaluation of the arts to be regarded as something more than civic boosterism. The writings of Montgomery Schuyler — "the first full-fledged critic of architecture in America" in Lewis Mumford's estimation — continue to be relevant not only for their acute perceptiveness (his critique of the Brooklyn Bridge on its opening in 1883 remains unsurpassed), but also for the manner in which he was able to identify social issues that must pertain in the evaluation of architecture, above and beyond the aesthetic concerns that might alone suffice in the discussion of the visual arts. This is at the heart of the matter: whereas the layman might willingly defer to "expert" opinion in the definition of standards of beauty (which in any event tend to vary greatly from one epoch to another), it is quite another thing to accept dictums on what is morally correct as it applies to society as a whole, especially in a country where the virtues of individualism and self-determination have been raised to almost mythic status.

Another important factor has been the degree to which the criticism of architecture has been considered (in a manner not paralleled by the other media) as inimical to the very practice of the art form and, as it is more often seen by those who pursue it, the profession. Though painting, sculpture, and music since the end of the Age of Absolutism have become increasingly independent of patronage, architecture remains tied to commissions, even if the patron is today more likely to be a board of directors or a building committee than a monarch or a mogul. Virtually alone among the arts today, architecture can be carried out only if the support of a client is engaged. Faced with critical indifference or rejection, the painter can still buy canvas and pigment, the sculptor a block of stone, or the composer have ready access to a piano. The architect, however, must enjoy the endorsement of a sponsor if his work is ever to proceed beyond paper.

The stakes in architectural criticism are therefore deemed to be much higher than elsewhere on the contemporary creative scene, though in fact it would seem that the commercial impact of criticism in other fields is far more immediate and quantifiable. For example, an unfavorable review of a Broadway play — especially if written by a critic of the omnipotent *New York Times* — is sufficient cause for a show to close, while enthusiastic critiques of books in widely read journals likewise help to propel titles toward the best-seller lists. Who has ever heard of a corporate client deciding not to use Philip Johnson because of the controversy one of his latest buildings has prompted, or a search committee deciding to call in an unknown young firm because of a rave received in one of the professional architecture magazines? The absurdity of real estate developer Donald Trump's recent lawsuit against Paul Gapp, the architecture critic of the *Chicago Tribune,* after his piece decrying Trump's plan to erect a 150-story skyscraper in Lower Manhattan, was rightly ridiculed by Paul Goldberger, the architecture critic of the *New York Times* (who nonetheless enjoys greater journalistic power than his colleague, but who left it to Gapp to take on this development in Goldberger's own backyard).

More to the point is the fact that because of the self-imposed prohibitions of The American Institute of Architects, which remained in effect until only recently, architects in this country were traditionally barred from advertising their services, and therefore had come to view criticism — that is to say positive reviews of their work — as the only ethically permissible form of publicity open to them. Encouraged over the years by the support of the professional architecture journals (whose controlled readership remains almost exclusively architects and allied professionals, and whose source of income remains almost exclusively advertising revenues from building product manufacturers), American architects have become accustomed to conditions unthinkable if compared to those which pertain in the other art forms. True, an art dealer or a theatrical producer — if willing to spend enough on advertising — could at least partially counteract the impression the public might receive from a negative notice. But on the other hand, there is little or nothing that they could do to deny public access to a work presented for public consumption.

Quite different circumstances prevail in architecture, however, and these conditions have had a very direct bearing on the free exercise of the critical evaluation process. If a critic has incurred the wrath of this gallery owner or that impresario, it might indeed be possible to have that writer barred from seeing a work in advance (as indeed happened not long ago when theater producer David Merrick cancelled a preview performance of a musical rather than allow a particularly detested critic the privilege of seeing the show prior to its official opening). Even given such tactics, there is really no way that access to the artifact can be permanently withheld. But the reverse is often the case in architecture. The cooperation of the architect — for permission to visit privately-owned structures, for copies of building plans and lists of specifications, and for the revealing anecdotal information which sometimes provides the real keys to understanding a building's social significance — is required for all but the most public projects. Without that help, there is often no story.

No one is more aware of that fact than the architect, who is frequently willing to use the threat — direct or implied — of noncooperation to exact from publications the conditions he deems likely to achieve the goal he wants, which more often than not amounts to a completely positive (or at least uncritical) treatment that can ultimately be used as a public relations handout for potential clients. As unequivocal as this assertion might appear, it is based on this writer's personal experience as a staff member at two of this country's three major professional architectural journals, as well as one of its leading popular decorating magazines, in addition to writing on a regular basis for publications ranging from the most scholarly to the most popular.

Though the specifics vary from case to case, the basic scenario is usually the same. The public for design criticism in this country remains both relatively small — virtually all of the 55,000 registered architects in the United States subscribe to all three professional magazines, *Architecture, Architectural Record,* and *Progressive Architecture*—and fairly constant. The two most prestigious decorating magazines, *Architectural Digest* and *House & Garden* each have circulations of about 600,000 and monthly newsstand sales of about 100,000; despite individual fluctuations, the total market tends to remain the same. Competition among design publications for the small amount of desirable work available for publication is intense. The long-standing practice of exclusivity — including prohibitions against publishing a project elsewhere within a specified period, the "brand loyalty" of an architect offering first refusal of his work to a magazine that has treated his work favorably in the past, and the reluctance of magazines to run buildings that have been published by their competitors (with the exception of highly important public works that demand to be written about widely) — feeds into a climate in which it is the creator, rather than the critic, who calls the tune.

The need for a publication to seem up-to-date and journalistically aware of the latest developments in an art form that is notoriously slow-moving likewise prompts responses not always, to put it tactfully, in the best interests of a detached and dispassionate assessment of architecture. The desire to be first (difficult enough in a profession wherein very few buildings are completed on schedule) often leads publications and their writers into making hasty evaluations before the most crucial phase of a building's life: its occupancy by its users. Thus critiques rushed into print as soon as possible after a structure's opening cannot hope to evaluate how successfully a design fulfills the client's programmatic and functional requirements. What ought to be a central component of the critical analysis of a building — how well it does its job and how it enhances the lives of the people who use it — is thereby either ignored or left to the twilight zone of innuendo and hearsay. For years, the only systematic attempt to rectify this astonishing omission has been the "post-occupancy studies" that have appeared in the *AIA*

Journal (recently renamed *Architecture*). Not surprisingly, those reports occasionally came up with judgments rather different from those which greeted those buildings' initial appearance.

Of course, the prevailing practice of instant coverage rather neatly exempts publications from having to delve into potentially uncomfortable areas of investigation, thereby perpetuating the celebratory tone in what generally passes for architectural "criticism." It is easy to understand the tendency. Architecture is an endeavor so fraught with obstacles of so many kinds that if the lay person were aware of all the problems the architect in America today commonly confronts in the pursuit of his career, the response would be one of amazement that anything ever gets built at all, regardless of its quality. So daunting a struggle is it for most practitioners that the attitude adopted by the professional architecture publications (which have as their sole constituency those very fighters against seemingly impossible odds) is habitually one of unqualified support.

For years, the avowed editorial principle of *Architectural Record* had been "If it gets built, it's good for the profession." In recent years, however, *Record* has adopted a more critical tone (though, it must be added, only within the context of overall approval — buildings that would have to be panned are simply not published), bringing it somewhat closer to the less timid approach of its closest rival, *Progressive Architecture,* which in contrast has not been afraid of running negative critiques. Even at *P/A,* though, there have been sporadic failures of nerve, as in its occasional resort to the so-called "round table" format for important buildings that for one reason or another are unlikely to receive a favorable evaluation from most of the staff writers. In those instances the "forum" approach — short comments arranged thematically, with a "pro" and "con" representation on each issue — has allowed the critical voices of certain editors to be, if not muffled, then at least diluted by others to give a more "balanced" view.

Not surprisingly, the prevailing situation at popular publications is even less committed to the development of a serious critical standard for judging architecture and evaluating its impact on society. Paradoxically, given the extent to which these mass market magazines deal with design at the very point it becomes accessible to the public at large, there is even less interest with the actual effect that design has on people's lives, or even an awareness of what popular adaptations of high-style design says about society.

Increasingly, it is to popular publications of the past that historians are now turning for the kind of revealing contemporary insights sought by proponents of the Braudelian *annales* approach to history. Those magazines provide an incomparable commentary on the times that produced them, and that remains true of design periodicals today, whether or not that is their conscious intention. Why then do publications that cover architecture today not apply the same standards that pertain in the press toward much less significant efforts in the production of food, rock music, or clothing? Is it because architecture is deemed to be such a central aspect of our common experience that it must be held to a higher standard of accountability? One would think not. The real reason is twofold: the lack of widespread precedent, and, more tellingly, the lack of sufficient desire.

It is remarkable to consider that the critical criteria applied by art publications in America are not shared by their sister publications in architecture. When informed by this writer of the usual attempts by architects to control visual materials, have manuscript review, and receive assurances of a favorable attitude, Elizabeth C. Baker, the editor-in-chief of *Art in America,* offered that if architects in this country wanted to be considered as artists — one of the major objectives among the contemporary architectural avant-garde — then they would have to expect the same critical standards to which artists are standardly subject. If there is to be any significant change in the way in which architects and their work are treated in our press, it will be because of such insistence.

Historically, the establishment of a critical voice in architecture in this country has usually depended more on the support given a writer by a publication rather than his or her own evolution of a set of principles and values. Perhaps the most extraordinary run of architecture criticism in an American periodical was that of Lewis Mumford for *The New Yorker* from 1931 to 1963. Those 187 articles, which appeared under the heading "The Sky Line," compose one of the most cogent bodies of occasional and topical architecture criticism ever published, and *The New Yorker* during those three decades was the primary platform for America's most distinguished architecture critic. Yet in the twenty-two years since "The Sky Line" ceased to appear, that magazine has neither seen fit to replace Mumford, nor to continue to cover architecture in any systematic fashion, save for an occasional "Profile" or a "Talk of the Town" squib. The only inference one can draw from this is that while *The New Yorker* was willing for over half its life to make room for the work of one of the most important literary figures of his time, the fact that his major field of interest was architecture was rather incidental; it would seem as though *The New Yorker* was interested in publishing Mumford on architecture, but was not sufficiently interested in publishing architecture criticism by anyone else.

Although several daily newspapers in the United States have established regular architecture criticism as an integral part of their coverage of the arts, it has been only a fairly recent development, generally dated to the appointment of Ada Louise Huxtable as architecture critic of the *New York Times* in 1963. Two decades later, it would have been unthinkable for the *Times* to have simply done away with architecture criticism after Huxtable's retirement, as *The New Yorker* did after Mumford. But despite that continuity of commitment, there have been special problems in the exercise of critics' opinions in newspaper journalism that parallel the rather different set of constraints placed on the magazine writer. It does not take a very highly developed sense of literary judgment to notice the striking disparity of tone in architecture criticism as it appears in most newspapers and the criticism of drama, music, movies, and restaurants in those same pages. When it comes to architecture, there is a cautiousness, a tendency to circumlocution, and an evaluative evasiveness that one rarely finds in the withering notices that often accompany the appearance of a new play, opera, film, or bistro. It has been suggested by some observers that large metropolitan dailies — a major part of whose revenue comes from real estate advertising — have been particularly hesitant about offending the established interests which sponsor major architectural projects. That accusation is impossible to verify as an expression of official publication policy, but there are clear indications that in several specific instances negative evaluations of major architectural schemes have resulted in the censure and even dismissal of newspaper writers.

One such incident occurred in the months prior to September 1975, when John Pastier, architecture critic of the *Los Angeles Times* was fired at least in part for his coverage of a downtown Los Angeles redevelopment scheme in which the paper's parent corporation, the Times-Mirror Co., had a major interest. Pastier set into motion this chain of events innocently enough in an article by questioning not only the specific plans for the renovation and expansion of the landmark Los Angeles Central Library (designed by Bertram Goodhue in 1931) but also by asking whether or not a main library was even desirable, given the decentralized nature of that city. This was by no means the first time that Pastier had run afoul of powers at the *Times*. (He reports that copies of his clippings with the word "NEGATIVE" boldly scrawled across them were routinely sent to his editor by the publisher-owner's mother, Dorothy Buffum Chandler.) Eventually, a somewhat fictionalized account of Pastier's dismissal became the subject of an episode of the television series "Lou Grant," although the television version concluded with the publisher's ultimate siding with the reporter against the real estate developers, an ending happier than that in real life.

In New York, Carter B. Horsley, whose incisive reportage on the real estate market had long been among the best writing on architecture in the *New York Times*, was demoted in 1982 to checking facts for wedding notices on the society page after his investigative coverage of the redevelopment of the old Army Terminal complex on the Brooklyn waterfront — leased under a sweetheart deal by the city government to a local real estate tycoon — drew the wrath of the *Times* management. Shortly

thereafter, the real estate section itself began to take on a much less substantial tone.

Needless to say, the specifics of such case histories are difficult to substantiate, since no newspaper is eager to admit muzzling staff members in the pursuit of truth and justice. Yet enough such tales have circulated in recent years to indicate that there is a real reluctance on the part of some newspapers to antagonize vested financial interests where issues of architecture and urban planning are concerned.

Of course, that reticent attitude often proceeds from well-intentioned (if not exactly laudable) boosterism. Since the construction of new buildings (whatever their design merit) has long been deemed one of the most visible manifestations of "progress," in many instances it is therefore considered inimical to the good of the community to criticize a project which will create jobs, afford a municipality a sense of modernity, and enhance the economic well-being of the town. It is thus understandable why the *New York Times*, for instance, has put virtually every redevelopment scheme for the Times Square area on its front page, regardless of its merits; its editorial offices are smack in the middle of that ultimate urban squalor, and one can sympathize with the belief that almost anything else would be an improvement. But standards of serious evaluation are often thereby dispensed with, or at least not given sufficient emphasis, and it is the public that is often the loser.

This then brings us to the crux of the issue: why is the quality of our architecture criticism no better than it is? The answer is simply that more is not wanted, or at least not wanted badly enough for the public to demand it, the profession to require it, and publications to provide it. Architecture is the only one of the major arts which is not systematically taught in some manner to schoolchildren in America. They are instructed in music, art, and drama, but are not encouraged to think about architecture even though in their adult lives they will not only have greater daily contact with it than any other art form, but also are likely — as members of any number of business or civic organizations — to be involved in the commissioning, alteration, or preservation of a work of architecture. Furthermore, the lack of awareness that the average educated layman has about architecture — its history, its process, and its possibilities for enhancing human experience — adds greatly to the widely-held perception that it is a subject beyond the easy comprehension of all but the professional.

This is no doubt a major contributing factor toward the lack of informed public discourse on the direction of architecture in our country today. But the ultimate responsibility for this unfortunate state of affairs must rest with the press, both popular and professional. It is, after all, the primary means by which both the practicing architect and the layman receive information about new directions and important issues in architecture; while not totally at fault for the lack of engagement on the part of the public in architectural evaluation and decision making, the press is at least partially culpable.

Certainly, a convincing case for a greater role for the press in the exposition of architectural issues and ideas has been made much more convincingly of late in England, a country in which lively and incisive criticism has flourished to a degree largely unknown in America, despite the existence of libel laws a great deal more stringent than, but seemingly not as restrictive as, those in effect in the United States. The most recent example of this has been the heated (not to say vitriolic) debate that has surrounded two projects proposed for construction in London: Peter Ahrends's addition to the National Gallery and the long-postponed Mansion House Square tower by Ludwig Mies van der Rohe for the real estate developer Peter Palumbo.

The press commentary inspired by both schemes has far exceeded that engendered by even the most controversial American designs both in quantity and conviction, and that coverage is further noteworthy for its appearance even before construction plans for those designs have been finalized. The upshot is that one of them (the National Gallery addition) has been set aside, while the final approval of the second (a 19-story office tower in the City) seems at this writing virtually certain of being overruled. The equivalent happening in this country is, by recent evidence, virtually inconceivable. Although there were those who were displeased with the scheme prepared by I. M. Pei for the East Building of the National Gallery of Art in Washington, it is unimaginable that a high-ranking member of the establishment in this country would have denounced it — as Prince Charles did the Ahrends design in a widely-publicized speech before the members of the Royal Institute of British Architects, in which he castigated (with ample justification) the National Gallery addition as "a carbuncle on the face of an old and elegant friend." Though his attack on the Mansion House Square tower ("a glass stump more appropriate to Chicago than to London") is rather less well taken, at least his opinion was heard, and played its part in bringing the debate to a wider audience than otherwise might have been aware of it.

Yet the erection of an altogether inappropriate building on perhaps the most prestigious piece of land in the United States — the triangle on the Mall in Washington directly facing the Capitol Building — was met with virtually no opposition (let alone from a child of the chief of state), even though in the opinion of at least one critic it is no less a carbuncle than the proposed addition to its sister institution in the British capital. Although our national capital is by no means the venerable relic that

London is, it is nonetheless the most carefully preserved of our major cities in terms of local laws governing its architectural character, the conception of which has remained remarkably intact since the first days of the republic. Whatever the merits of the buildings under discussion in London and their recent counterparts in the United States, it cannot be doubted that a much more vigorous forum for the intelligent appraisal of architectural issues now exists in England than it does in the United States. Therefore, although the situations in America and England are by no means directly comparable, they nonetheless provide an instructive demonstration of the degree of influence the press can exercise where a critical voice has been established, maintained, and frequently exercised.

How, then, is it possible to raise the general standard of criticism in American architecture? One essential approach is to attempt to break down the wall of professional hocus-pocus that surrounds both the profession of architecture and much of the writing about it. To a greater extent than pertains in media that produce works that can be kept behind closed doors but still be enjoyed by people, architecture virtually demands the kind of consensus that can emerge only if the public is constantly instructed in the concepts and concerns that ought to inform architectural initiative and decision making.

Thus far in the United States, that awareness on the part of the public has been most successfully captured in three areas: historic preservation, ecology, and zoning. One of the most pernicious critiques of contemporary architecture is the apprehension of at least part of the public that anything which replaces existing construction is likely to be of inferior design quality. While that, alas, is often the case, it is not inevitably so. Nonetheless, this notion has stimulated active preservation groups in many communities where architectural advocacy bodies had not existed before. The increasing concern in this country about the impact our built environment has on our natural environment is another burgeoning focus of interest about what gets built, where, and why. And the quality of life as it is led within already-developed districts — most notably our big cities — is the most important potential catalyst toward a more widespread understanding of our zoning and regional planning laws. If a broader sense of involvement is to come from the population at large, it is likely that it will proceed from those three issues, either singly or in combination — most beneficially the latter if the complexity of the architectural process is understood.

There is a great deal of work to be done by the press in the United States before it can be said to be fulfilling its role as educator, evaluator, expositor, and advocate in regard to other essentially social forms of endeavor.

For too long the treatment of architecture in the popular and professional press has been more one of coverage than criticism, of acceptance rather than questioning, and typified by a passivity that seems seriously negligent in light of the permanence that most architecture enjoys. (Even in our disposable culture, almost any building is likely to remain standing for at least twenty years.) The question is not why there has been so much controversy in American architecture since 1970 — as readers of this book and viewers of its related exhibition might be led to believe — but rather why there has not been more of it. The highly visible and well known buildings discussed in these pages are less the tip of an iceberg than a goodly part of its mass.

The architecture that a society, culture, or civilization leaves behind inevitably bears the stamp of the values most important to those who built it, whether or not such a revealing record was their intention. Without question this is a time of great social change and equally great uncertainty; but so also were the Renaissance, the Counter-Reformation, and the Age of Romanticism. Yet through all those previous periods there prevailed a coherent social order that has largely been eroded in the modern world. In place of that order, it has been left to us as individuals (rather than to our institutions) to re-evaluate, redefine, and reintegrate the arts and the role they play in our culture. That is happening among many practitioners of architecture no less than it is among the exponents of its sister arts, but the carry-over to the public consciousness that we have witnessed since the beginning of the culture boom in this country twenty years ago has not included architecture. It must. If it can be said that people receive the government they deserve, then it is equally true that they receive the architecture they deserve. There are those of us who believe that we deserve better; but that will come about only if more of our fellow citizens can be made aware of why that is so and how it can be achieved.

If we are to get better architecture in our country, then more of us are going to have to become active in determining what it is we want from our buildings and how we can best go about achieving those goals. Leaving it to entrenched real estate interests, speculators, and bureaucrats is not going to result in the architecture which concerned people talk about but very rarely see built: that is, architecture that gives to the public more than it takes, that provides pleasure for the eye, stimulation for the mind, and comfort for the body — which, in sum, makes us feel more intensely alive. Determining how those qualities translate into built form is not easy, but it is impossible to begin without a dialogue that can proceed only on the premise of an educated public. Mere information is not the answer: rather, we need analysis, judgement, and above all moral teaching in its least restrictive and most liberating sense.

AT&T Corporate Headquarters, New York, New York. Photo: Esto © Wolfgang Hoyt

Bronx Developmental Center, Bronx, New York. Photo: Esto © Ezra Stoller

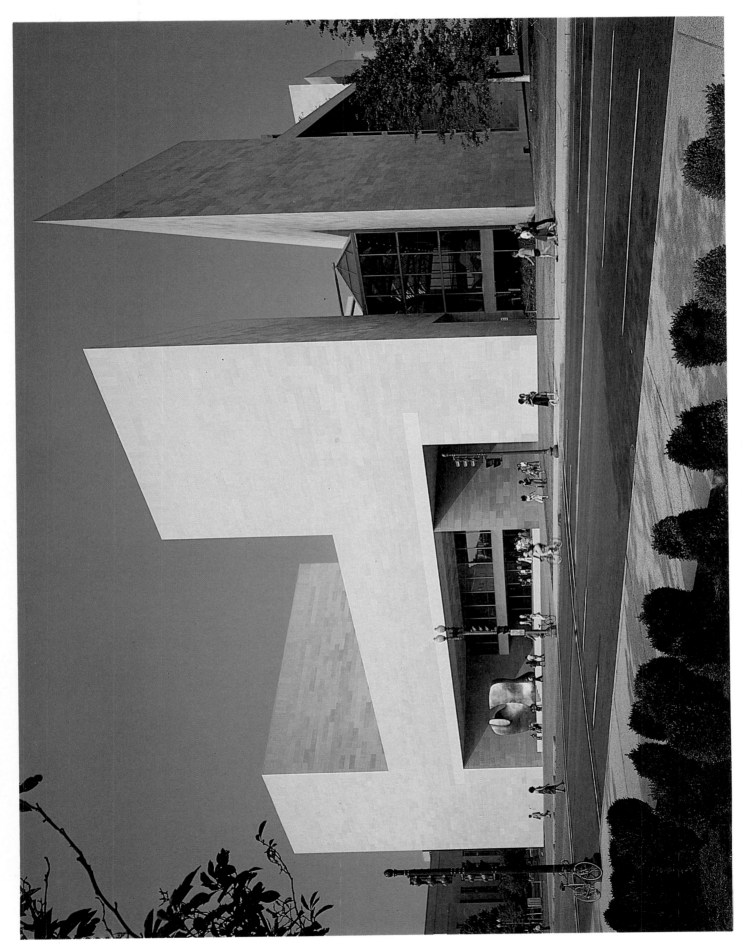

East Building, National Gallery of Art, Washington, D.C. Photo: Esto © Ezra Stoller

35

Gov. Nelson A. Rockefeller **Empire State Plaza**, Albany, New York. Photo: Esto © Ezra Stoller

36

Gehry House, Santa Monica, California. Photo: Tod A. Marder

The J. Paul Getty Museum, Malibu, California. Photo: courtesy Langdon • Wilson • Mumper, Architects

House VI, Cornwall, Connecticut. Photo: courtesy Eisenman/Robertson

39

Indeterminate Facade, Best Products Showroom, Houston, Texas. Photo: courtesy SITE, Inc.

Piazza d'Italia, New Orleans, Louisiana. Photo: © Alan Karchmer

41

The Portland Building, Portland, Oregon. Photo: Esto © Peter Aaron

42

Renaissance Center, Detroit, Michigan. Photo: Alexandre Georges, courtesy John Portman and Associates

43

Vietnam Veterans Memorial, Washington, D.C. Photo: Christopher Lark, © Lark Ltd.

25. AT&T Corporate Headquarters (color plate on page 33)

AT&T CORPORATE HEADQUARTERS

New York, New York

Architects: Johnson/Burgee

In 1978, the office of Johnson/Burgee designed the American Telegraph and Telephone Company's new corporate headquarters in New York City, and construction was completed in 1984.[1] On March 31, 1978, the *New York Times* made public Philip Johnson's proposed design for the AT&T building. The newspaper featured a rendering of the high-rise tower on its front page, and the accompanying article promoted the building as a symbol of New York's fiscal strength and its status as a leading communications center.[2] As an anonymous writer for *Architectural Record* observed, the nominal reason for coverage of the building was the good news that AT&T intended to build a new headquarters in Manhattan, but "no *Times* reader had to be an architect to understand that in this case the news was the architecture."[3] This skyscraper was conceived in a classicizing style by one of the leading American proponents of modernist architecture, prompting Paul Goldberger to remark that rarely in the history of the field has so prominent a figure made so dramatic a shift in sensibility.[4] Shortly after the plan was published, it met with widespread skepticism among members of the architectural community and the general public: many were either confused or outraged by Johnson's adoption of a classical vocabulary.[5] In fact, much of the initial controversy surrounding the AT&T tower did not deal directly with its design, but focused on the building as a disturbing anomaly in Johnson's career. In addition, many of the critics rushed to judgment and formed opinions long before designs were finalized, and longer still before the building was completed. As such, the short history of the AT&T Corporate Headquarters serves as the outstanding example of critical opinion based on preliminary schemes rather than the actual structure.

The AT&T Corporate Headquarters is situated on the front half of a square-shaped lot that occupies the entire block between 55th and 56th Streets at 550 Madison Avenue.[6] Measuring 100 feet by 200 feet at the base, Johnson's structure is a slender, rectangular slab that soars upward from the street in a sheer vertical rise without setbacks. The structural frame of the building is a heavily reinforced steel skeleton, which is entirely sheathed in thick panels of Stony Creek granite, a pinkish marble-like variety speckled with gray and white veining.[7] This granite veneer dominates the exterior, with only thirty percent of its surface devoted to glazing.

The tower is divided into a clearly articulated tripartite scheme of base, shaft, and crown, and ascends 660 feet from grade level to peak. The shaft rises to a monumental pediment thirty feet high that is broken in the center by a circular opening called an orbiculum. This imposing ornamental crown conceals the tower's mechanical service equipment and gives the building its distinctive, albeit controversial, silhouette.

The tower's base encloses a public plaza at grade level, and in the center of the Madison Avenue side is a towering arched portal 110 feet high that is flanked on either side by three sixty-foot-high rectangular entranceways separated by massive piers. At the rear of the site, connecting 55th and 56th Streets, is a covered galleria that links the office complex to a box-like four-story structure that was originally built as a communications museum.[8] In his plans for the galleria, Johnson also proposed the inclusion of ground level shops and an area reserved for a sidewalk cafe.

When Johnson's plan was first published, writers attempted to identify the formal precedents for the building's major elements: one critic found the base to be reminiscent of Alberti's facade for the church of Sant' Andrea in Mantua, while the shaft was generally linked to the historicizing skyscrapers of the 1920s; the tower's pediment was alternately believed to have been inspired by the visionary classical designs of Boullée, or dismissed by writers as a humorous enlargement of a Chippendale furniture ornament.[9]

In the first full-length review of the building published in the *New York Times* in March of 1978, Paul Goldberger wrote that it was ". . . the most provocative and daring—if disconcerting—skyscraper to be proposed for New York since the Chrysler building. . . ," noting that Johnson intended it to be a reproval of the repetitive modernist structures that dominate midtown Manhattan, which the critic referred to as an "esthetic disaster."[10] Goldberger was more concerned with analyzing how

26. Drawing depicting planned usage of galleria

successfully the architect employed the mode: "There is no problem with the basic philosophy behind the building—the question is simply whether the physical form that philosophy has yielded is going to work as well as it might in the cityscape."[11] Although Goldberger questioned the suitability of utilizing a Chippendale motif for the tower's crown (the form would perhaps not function effectively at such a massive scale), his assessment of the plan was positive, especially with regard to the monumental colonnades and covered plaza at grade level.

In 1978, Ada Louise Huxtable, then senior architectural critic for the *New York Times,* wrote a less favorable review of the AT&T proposal in an article entitled "Johnson's Latest—Clever Tricks or Art." Unlike Goldberger, Huxtable was not sympathetic to the architect's interest in experimenting with what she described as "the rubric of the new eclecticism." For Huxtable,

> What Mr. Johnson has produced, from that Pop pediment on down, is a pastiche of historical references . . . blown up gigantically in unconventional and unsettling relationships. . . . The more arcane the borrowings of design elements, and the more perverse their combination, the more provocative and progressive the result. . . . The outcry may well be because both the knowing and naive suspect an architectural rabbit punch.[12]

Huxtable, like Goldberger, questioned how successfully the tower would relate to its Madison Avenue setting. In her opinion, the building was a statement about corporate architecture in search of a Park Avenue location. Huxtable also emphasized that the 660-foot structure was far too massive for its narrow lot, and criticized zoning ordinances that permitted such a plan in exchange for a pedestrian plaza and proposed retail space.

In his review Goldberger had remarked that the building's distinctive quality would stem from the grandeur of its monumental scale. For Huxtable, the tower's heroic dimensions would perhaps be its only redeeming feature, serving to obscure weaknesses in Johnson's overall design: ". . . the building's impact will not come from [its] creative power or stylistic integration."[13]

The articles by Goldberger and Huxtable in the *New York Times* were followed by reviews by Wolf von Eckardt in the *Washington Post* and Paul Gapp in the *Chicago Tribune.* In his article for the *Post* in April 1978, "The Defiant Architect: Philip Johnson Upsets the Modernists," von Eckardt likened Johnson's abrupt shift in style to Le Corbusier's adoption of an expressionist architectural idiom with his design for Notre Dame du Haut at Ronchamp. The critic asserted that "Johnson's act of defiance is just as drastic and, in the short run, possibly just as divisive."[14] In his analysis of the building, von Eckardt noted that Johnson relied on the tripartite scheme of early twentieth-century skyscrapers. While for others the pediment was an outlandish borrowing from Chippendale furniture, von Eckardt found it to be an attractive and appropriate solution to the tower's historicizing program; and given the peak's grandiose size, he believed it was most likely inspired by ancient Roman or baroque architectural motifs.[15] Von Eckardt also suggested that although the AT&T building had been considered "a major monument to post-modernism," Johnson was not closely aligned with this development, but was actually forging a unique, alternative course in contemporary American architecture:

> . . . If Johnson's new historicism proves as popular as I think it will, the Modernists, post-modernists, ex-modernists . . . who giggle derisively about the 'Chippendale skyscraper' will in the long run come around. . . . In short I believe Johnson may well unite contemporary architecture again and lead it out of both the glass box and the concrete sculpture to a new economic gentility.[16]

On April 23, 1978, Paul Gapp's " 'Chippendale' Architecture—Near-Kitsch or Top Drawer?" in the *Chicago Tribune*, maintained that it was Johnson's conversion to post-modernism that had stimulated much of the controversy over the AT&T plan and he pointed out that, at a national design seminar in 1977, Johnson had already declared architects to be free from the modern movement.[17] In Gapp's view, however, Johnson was clearly adapting classical forms to the structural rigor of modernist architecture, and he saw the Chippendale pediment as a creative indulgence. In questioning the architect's motives for adopting a radically classical mode, Gapp maintained that Johnson wanted to incite debate and to promote an image of himself as a perennial innovator:

> Johnson . . . wanted to leave behind at least one great monument to himself that would prove he was out in front of the action right to the very end. . . . Johnson wanted to raise hell in his cool, urbane way.[18]

In May of 1978, Michael Leapman wrote an article on the AT&T building for the *Times* of London, the first time that newspaper had previewed an architectural project.[19] Entitled "Skyscraper That Upset New York," Leapman's piece stressed that while Johnson's proposal had met with criticism, the architect's plan was a unique design that represented a sharp move away from the modernist style of the past twenty years. Johnson, who was interviewed for the article, commented that his historicizing scheme for the AT&T tower was an attempt to honor an architectural idiom that was indigenous to New York City, and when asked about the controversy surrounding his project, Johnson said in mock dismay "Here I am, a modern architect, and look what I've done."[20] Leapman closed his article by asserting, "It is an astonishing building by an astonishing architect, and this city is the richer for both of them."

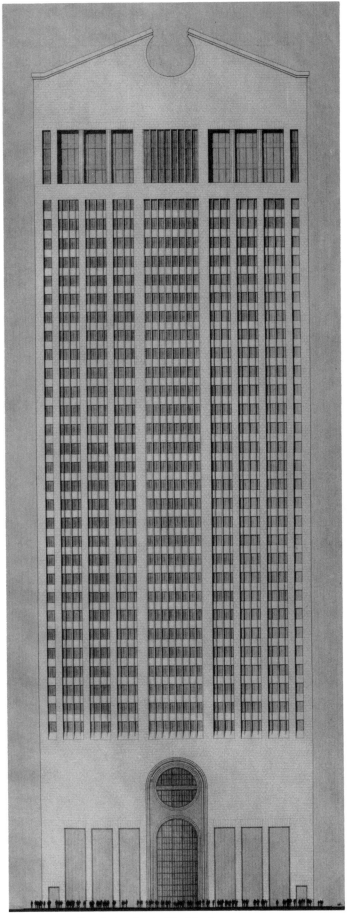

27. Facade. Rendering by Judith Ginsberg

28. Detail of figure 27

When the AT&T plan was first published, the building's distinctive pedimental crown became an instant target for derision, stimulating the largest amount of controversy. In fact, the outcry was so great that AT&T began to reconsider Johnson's original design for the pediment. As public relations vice president Edward M. Block commented, "Initially [the design] didn't strike us as being odd, and it wasn't a big issue until others made it one," and after the architects presented alternative designs for the crown to AT&T executives, the corporation decided that the first choice had been the most appropriate.[21] At first, many critics and the general public felt that the Chippendale peak was intended to be a satirical device, as it appeared to be somewhat arbitrarily attached to the structure; however, a writer for *New York* magazine reported that Johnson had first thought of utilizing the pediment as a way of unifying the verticality and symmetry of the facade by raising the middle section

higher.[22] Moreover, Johnson said the idea for the ornamental crown was in keeping with the classical scheme established for the building and that it was derived from his interest in the masonry skyscrapers of the 1890s, which often had classical cornices. Carleton Knight III wrote that Johnson's interest in creating a distinctive top for the AT&T tower may have been inspired in part by the view from his thirty-seventh floor office in the Seagram Building. According to Knight, Johnson was critical of the Citicorp Building, whose crown is dramatically pitched, and once remarked, "I'm going to do something better than that."[23]

A good deal of the criticism engendered by the pediment was linked to the problem of scale, for while such a broken pediment is suitable as an ornament for furniture, the classical grace of the form is subverted by transforming it into a thirty-foot peak. Amplified to this massive scale, it becomes an eccentric shape on the skyline. In March 1978, Goldberger remarked that if lit dramatically, Johnson's broken pediment would create a stunning visual effect, interjecting an element of fantasy and romanticism back into the cityscape.[24] In June 1978, however, J.M. Dixon commented, "Blown up 50 times domestic scale, this pediment is perversely simplified to the rudimentary detail of a doll house doorway."[25] Dixon also found the pediment to be a superficial element that recalled the inauthentic detailing of mock Georgian structures, and thus for Dixon this so-called radical feature was simply a dull, commonplace solution that could be found on thousands of small-town churches and city halls across the nation. In a later article that appeared in an issue of *Progressive Architecture* in 1984, which was devoted to the work of Johnson, Susan Doubilet noted that Johnson's gracefully arching pediment served to disrupt the bland uniformity of the New York skyline.[26]

Robert Hughes likened Johnson's ornamental device to Claes Oldenburg's large-scale sculptures of banal objects, which function as absurdist monuments to popular culture.[27] In keeping with Oldenburg's approach, Hughes claimed, Johnson had wrenched a classical motif from its normal context and recast it in the form of an outsized, contemporary icon. Although Johnson relied on a classical vocabulary, it was filtered through a modern, populist sensibility and presented as ironic quotation.[28] Like Oldenburg's monuments, Johnson's pediment may allude to our society's penchant for transforming aspects of American culture into readily identifiable symbols. Johnson's Chippendale crown does act as an effective corporate emblem for AT&T, and no doubt its prominence on the skyline was intended to reflect the importance of the telephone in a city that depends heavily on communications technology. Yet, other writers have also interpreted the crown as a satirical thrust at the pretensions of architecture, and many post-modernist designers might have felt that Johnson was lampooning their movement.[29]

In addition to the controversy dealing with the pediment, many writers have criticized the building's overall design scheme. In a review of 1978, Huxtable commented that while the structural elements of the building were juxtaposed in a provocative manner, there was little stylistic integration to the design.[30] Suzanne Stephens and, later, Paul Goldberger analyzed this problem more fully. In *Progressive Architecture* in 1979, Stephens remarked that the divisions in the tripartite plan were too emphatic, adding that the building lacked the cohesiveness of the office towers of the 1920s that Johnson had supposedly emulated.[31] In his 1982 survey history of the skyscraper, Goldberger stated that the parts of the building ". . . require a certain coherence, a certain sense of

29. View of midtown Manhattan, with AT&T Headquarters

appropriateness together, as well as good proportions, and here is where AT&T seems to fall short. There is a feeling that the parts of it have little in common."[32]

Several writers, such as Suzanne Stephens and William J. Curtis, have also written that Johnson's design is a seemingly arbitrary arrangement of classicizing motifs that mask a standard steel frame.[33] This observation was made by Charles Jencks in 1977 in *The Language of Post-Modern Architecture*, in which he declared that the building was nothing more than a modernist steel skeleton with historical quotations applied to it in a cosmetic fashion.[34] However, in a later article entitled "Late Modernism and Post Modernism" that was published in *Architectural Design* in 1978, Jencks remarked that Johnson's mixing of modernist and historicist elements could result in a witty and appropriate synthesis.[35] In combining the two modes, Johnson was honoring the two major architectural styles associated with New York City—the historicizing trend of the 1920s and the modernist tradition. As Jencks remarked, "a degree of credit should go to Johnson . . . for the sensitivity with which he has combined local New York codes."

30. View from Madison Avenue of AT&T Headquarters

Johnson's treatment of the tower's shaft has also been criticized and many writers find it to be the least successful feature of the building. The shaft has nine strips of vertical fenestration that rise for twenty-eight floors and are arranged in a tightly structured grid that is deeply set into the fabric of the building. Paul Goldberger asserted that despite the use of recessed fenestration and various textural effects on the shaft, they were not varied enough to relieve its unrelenting flatness.[36] And Susan Doubilet noted that while Johnson tried to animate the shaft with an alternative pattern of window strips, this grid-like arrangement of glazing remains a dull, repetitive design.[37]

A number of writers have regarded the building's monumental entranceway and flanking loggias to be its most outstanding feature, yet these elements have also met with a wide range of observations. In appraising the plaza, J. M. Dixon has written that while it is a welcome addition to New York's scarce supply of aesthetically pleasing public space, its open construction will provide little protection during cold or rainy weather.[38] Dixon also remarked that although glazing on the building was limited to only thirty percent for energy conservation purposes, views from the upper lobby and dining areas were limited to a few large portholes and these do not even face the major thoroughfare of Madison Avenue.[39] On the other hand, Paul Goldberger had hailed the building's towering entrance and plaza as being the most valuable aspects of the design; he maintained that their grandiose scale has an almost uplifting effect, adding that their classical character provides a humanistic presence to a city that has become dominated by sterile modernist structures.[40] Doubilet, however, has written that while the flanking loggias and the galleria at the rear of the building are dramatic and expansive spaces, the relationships between these areas are not clearly defined within the structure.[41]

31. View of entranceway

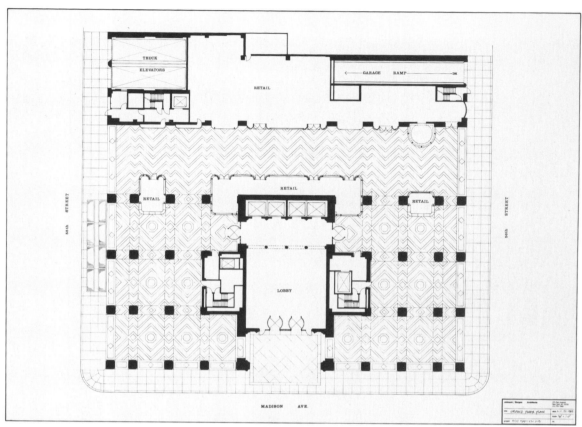

32. Ground floor plan, showing geometric pavement design

33. Lobby elevator

The massive scale and grandeur of the exterior is carried over to the lobby, which is seventy feet high, lined in granite, and paved with black and white tiles in a geometric design. The walls of the lobby facing north and south are lined with blind arcades, and at the end of the lobby an arcade with four arched openings screens a bank of four paneled elevators. Passages between the arcaded screen and the elevators lead, left and right, into the covered plaza areas, or loggias. The lobby space is dominated by Evelyn Beatrice Longman's gilded statue, *The Genius of Electricity,* and is covered by a cross-vaulted, gilded ceiling. The *Genius of Electricity* (popularly known as the Golden Boy) originally stood atop the old AT&T headquarters at 195 Broadway. During the planning stages, even the use of the statue for the lobby became a focus for controversy when in 1980 the New York Landmarks Conservancy attempted to persuade Charles L. Brown, AT&T's chairman, that the statue should be left where it was. The Conservancy argued that the statue was one of the best-known symbols on the lower Manhattan skyline and that it had been designed to be viewed from a great distance. Ellen Posner wrote that "In the new lobby, close up, Golden Boy can be seen for what he always was: a naked man wrapped grotesquely in telephone wire."[42] Both Goldberger and Doubilet also found fault with the lobby's design, which they regarded as too narrow, particularly for Longman's towering statue. As indicated, this massive gilded figure dominates the constricted space of the lobby, and Gold-

54

34. View into lobby, showing the statue *The Genius of Electricity*

berger remarked that one can only get a full view of this work by standing on the east side of Madison Avenue and looking westward towards the building's lower facade.[43] By contrast, in 1983, Colin Amery praised the scheme for the lobby, remarking on Johnson's pride in the space and maintaining that "It is too soon to judge the building as a whole, but this great room already has the impact of one of the great indoor spaces of New York."[44] Other writers have found the lobby to be overly ostentatious,[45] and Doubilet has suggested that the various design components of the lobby are not successfully integrated, as the rounded Byzantine arcades and the rosy, richly grained granite walls clash with the geometric pattern of the floor tiles.[46]

As construction progressed in the early 1980s, critics realized that earlier evaluations of the plan would have to be reassessed in light of issues dealing with contextual considerations. As early as 1978, Huxtable had argued that the towering, unrelieved bulk of the AT&T plan was ill-suited to the narrow measurements of its lot on Madison Avenue.[47] It is important to stress that this problem of context has been one of the more carefully considered and widely debated issues involving the AT&T project, and many writers have found the inappropriateness of the building to its site to be one of the plan's overiding failures. In *Progressive Architecture*, J. M. Dixon noted that "the imperial scale and symmetry" would only face the modest expanse of Madison Avenue, relating to nothing in the surrounding cityscape.[48] Yet for Goldberger,

> . . . part of the pleasure of this building comes from the drama of the huge expansion of wide scale on narrow Madison Avenue. To come upon AT&T from a side street and have the immense entrance arch burst upon you is to experience a kind of drama that is common to baroque Rome, but rare indeed in twentieth-century Manhattan.[49]

In an article entitled "Corporate Form Givers," Suzanne Stephens argued that the classical character and lightly colored stone of the AT&T building would clash sharply with the dark, modernist slab of Edward Barnes's IBM Corporation Building, which stands to the north on the corner of 56th Street and Madison Avenue. For Stephens, this juxtaposition of styles would only add to the city's visual chaos.[50] For Paul Goldberger, however, successful urban vistas are created by such a mixing of architectural modes and materials. Goldberger argued that New York's environment has suffered from its overly homogeneous modernist skyline and that such structures as the AT&T building will give midtown Manhattan a more diversified appearance.[51]

It must be noted that many of the early reviews of the AT&T building that discussed contextual problems or design issues were based on drawings and models. Goldberger has pointed out that there are various problems in analyzing architectural designs by relying on such preparatory aids. He wrote that a building judged in plans and models is invariably viewed as sculptural form, rather than as a structure with contextual relationships, and that the awkward proportions and eccentric shape of the AT&T tower were less noticeable in the densely built area of midtown Manhattan.[52] The idea that the AT&T tower would become integrated into this congested visual field served to point up the problem of escalating urban growth that Huxtable had voiced. As a thirty-seven-story structure that was placed only a short distance from the street, and was to span an entire city block, the AT&T building was clearly adding to this urban congestion. Goldberger was not unmindful of this issue, remarking that "No one can question that it is too big a building for an already crowded part of New York. But it intrudes on one's sense of scale less . . . than the neighboring I.B.M. building."[53]

In addition to the contextual and formal issues relating to the AT&T tower, it is important to note that a number of the articles written on the building reflect a tendency among critics to assess the design in light of their attitudes toward Johnson. For example, in an article that appeared in the *AIA Journal* in June 1979, Andrea O. Dean noted that the response of critics to Johnson's rejection of modernism "has been predictably extreme. Most have tended to either elevate Johnson to position of seer or reduce him to self-seeking publicist."[54] Such a remark could be applied to the opposing views taken by von Eckardt and Gapp in their reviews of the AT&T building: von Eckardt saw the AT&T tower as a seminal work that would launch a new unified movement in contemporary architecture; for Gapp the building was a monument to Johnson's egocentricism and his desire to remain an arbiter of taste. In discussing Johnson's experimentation with new design trends in the AT&T building, Goldberger pointed out how "Johnson's critics have already called his shift further proof of his alleged inconsistency and glibness; on the other hand his supporters have seen it as evidence that his agile mind is still questioning, still searching."[55]

Philip Johnson has been regarded as one of the leading American proponents of the International Style since the early 1950s. In 1932, the architect and Henry-Russell Hitchcock codified the formal tenets of the movement in *The International Style*, and during the following decades Johnson designed such influential modernist structures as his Glass House in 1949 and, under Mies van der Rohe, the Seagram Building in New York City in 1956. However, beginning in the middle 1960s, a generation of younger architects began to challenge the premises of modernism, reintroducing vocabularies that were culled from a wide range of sources. In the 1970s, critics began to refer to this loosely defined development under the umbrella term "post-modernism," and with his design for the AT&T building, Johnson appeared to be aligning himself with this current. Thus, it may be that Johnson's rather dramatic shift to a post-modern sensibility prompted the strong and sometimes negative reactions to the AT&T scheme; in effect, some critics may have been attacking a dominant figure in architecture in their commentary on the AT&T building, instead of focusing on the building itself.

The widespread interest in the AT&T tower involved more than just a change in Johnson's development, however, for the design was also an important indication that a profound shift was taking place in contemporary architecture. In an article that was published in the *AIA Journal* in May of 1978, Paul Goldberger discussed Philip Johnson's recent involvement with "post-modernism." Goldberger wrote:

> [the AT&T building] . . . is a serious and earnest attempt to reinterpret historical form in a way that will never be directly imitative of historical styles nor conventionally modern. . . . The move away from the International Style . . . is now something more than an academic crusade . . . [and] in one gesture, Philip Johnson has stretched out an arm of the architectural establishment to embrace it.[56]

In 1978 and 1979, a number of articles appeared in the popular press promoting Johnson as the conspicuous leader of the post-modernist movement in architecture.[57] Johnson also cast himself in the role as a chief polemicist of the new tendency, writing a series of articles in which he espoused such non-modernist concerns as the revival of historical forms and regional architectural idioms.[58] Leland Roth, in his 1979 textbook, *A Concise History of American Architecture,* even closed his survey of American architecture with a discussion of Johnson's AT&T tower, indicating that it represented a radical and challenging direction for American architecture beyond the exhausted formulas of modernism.[59]

Indeed, a good deal of the controversy that was generated by Johnson's plan stemmed from its potential importance as a trendsetting design, and it was this very realization that triggered such decisive critical attacks from modernists. In his *Washington Post* review, Wolf von Eckardt wrote, "Not since Le Corbusier surprised them with his Chapel at Ronchamp have modern architects been so upset."[60] Paul Gapp exclaimed in the *Chicago Tribune,* "If Mies van der Rohe were alive today, he would regard this design with loathing, because it is the antithesis of everything he believed in."[61] Many modern architects actually felt that Johnson was abandoning the modernist cause, and a letter written by Moshe Safdie perhaps best represented this reaction. Published in *Skyline* magazine, the letter read:

> I cannot agree more with the statements attributed to you that the so-called International Style and much in the name of Modern Architecture has lacked richness. . . . It is in an understanding of the shortcomings of the architecture of the last 30 or 40 years that, I believe, lie the

35. Model of AT&T Corporate Headquarters

> seeds for growth and positive evolution of architecture. It is by broadening the base of the considerations of the form-making process, not by ignoring them or substituting whim and whimsy, that we shall move forward.[62]

As early as 1978, Charles Jencks speculated that both modernist and post-modernist factions would find Johnson's design disturbing.[63] This proved to be the case, since many architects who had based their careers on challenging modernist concepts did not accept Paul Goldberger's assessment that the AT&T building was a major monument to post-modernism. For example, Charles Moore commented, "Philip's a genius and a gadfly. . . . But people's expectations that he would sum up all the currents in architecture today with the AT&T building are simply wishful thinking."[64] Still others were concerned, as Paul Gapp explained, that the modernist's sudden foray into post-modernism would impede the orderly development of the movement.[65] Perhaps it was felt that as an adherent of modernism, Johnson would not be entirely fluent in current avant-garde design principles, nor would he properly endorse their ideological premises.

Johnson's reliance on an historicizing vocabulary in the AT&T building was also perceived as an opportunistic attempt to align himself with a mode that was rapidly growing in popularity. In an article on Johnson for *Saturday Review* in 1979, Denise Scott Brown, who is a partner in the firm of Venturi, Rauch, and Scott Brown, wrote that in 1968, she and her husband Robert Venturi invented a mythical Motel Monticello, whose sign was "a silhouette of an enormous Chippendale highboy."[66] This mention of the Motel Monticello had appeared in the Venturis' *Learning from Las Vegas* of 1972, and Brown wryly commented that "fantasy is sometimes prophecy," noting that she was dumbfounded to find their motel sign proposed for the facade of a Manhattan corporate structure. Further, Brown viewed with irony the phenomenon of an orthodox modernist being hailed as a leading figure in post-modernism: "He has bypassed the mess of populism, rhetoric, and kitsch that bubbled up with the social swirls of the 1960s. . . . Johnson's luck is that the word 'controversial' cannot kill his firm's career. . . ."[67] Brown's article seemed to suggest that Johnson had assumed the leadership of a movement he had not actively helped to forge; however, as Robert Hughes has stressed, "Johnson did not create the way of thinking that this building reflects. But he helped bring it about, and now he has given it a degree of . . . validity that cannot help affecting other corporate clients."[68]

During the last stages of construction on the AT&T tower in 1983 and 1984, several writers challenged earlier assessments of the building, noting particular aspects of the plan that had been difficult to discern in the early models and architectural renderings. For example, the use of granite and the crisply articulated details on the tower give it a striking sculptural quality that was not conveyed in drawings. As Goldberger exclaimed, ". . . it is impossible to stand in front of it and not think about the nature of space, the nature of light and the nature of stone."[69] Goldberger also indicated that the architect's interest in exploiting the sensuous qualities of the stone and the emphasis on expertly crafted details make this monumental structure a less intrusive presence.[70]

In the same article, which was published in September of 1983, Goldberger noted that once the building was complete, it seemed somewhat overblown and grandiose.[71] Moreover, Goldberger conceded, "Mr. Johnson and Mr. Burgee's commitment to classical architecture, which seemed so daring in 1978, now seems, oddly, not to go far enough." However, Goldberger praised the rich effects of the building's granite sheathing and carefully executed decorative program, maintaining that the building would herald a new era in architectural design:

> It reminds us, more firmly than anything in New York yet has, that the stark glass and steel boxes of the International Style are something of

an era already gone. For if the triumph of modern architecture was largely due to its acceptance as the American corporate style . . . the decision by AT&T . . . to try something else . . . must rank as the beginning of the withdrawal of that acceptance.[72]

As the AT&T building reached completion in 1984, other writers offered reassessments of the tower. For instance, Sam Kaplan of the *Los Angeles Times* wrote that the building had helped to lend credence to the postmodernist movement and commented that it also demonstrated Johnson's notorious ability to gain recognition by appropriating architectural styles that were pioneered by others.[73] Kaplan also remarked that once the building had been erected, the controversial pediment did not seem as prominent an element of the design, since it was difficult to view in the densely developed midtown area. Further, he advanced a critique of the towering entranceway that was markedly different from Goldberger's appraisal, as he felt its monumental scale makes "a visitor feel very small. There is something cold and calculating about the building. . . . [It is] out of scale and of touch with the flow of humanity around it."[74] Susan Doubilet was more sympathetic, even as she admitted that it is "not quite the scintillating Post-Modern morsel that would delight fans and infuriate Modernists."[75] Doubilet, unlike Kaplan, commented that the majestic scale of the tower's loggias and the superb handling of the construction materials offered to the pedestrian an extraordinary architectural experience that was unrivaled in midtown Manhattan; she maintained that the building's status as a "landmark of the Post-Modern movement" could not be discounted. In a *Washington Post* article from April 1984 entitled "Towers of Excellence," Benjamin Forgey also took issue with the negative reactions to the tower's crown and shaft and claimed that the pediment, once realized in stone, proved to be a striking feature of the design and that the varied window treatment on the shaft was a welcome departure from the repetitive, ribbon-like scheme found on most modern high-rise buildings.[76] In addition, Forgey echoed the sentiments of many critics by maintaining that Johnson's AT&T Corporate Headquarters had become a symbol of the ascendancy of the post-modernist trend in architecture.

Since Johnson's plan was first published in 1978, such controversial designs as Michael Graves's Portland Building and many other similarly adventuresome office towers have been built all over the country. Ironically, many critics now regard the AT&T building as being a somewhat restrained and conventional example of current design tendencies, but no one can deny its historical importance. Definitive histories of the period may well conclude, as some critics and scholars have, that the AT&T Corporate Headquarters is a pivotal work that served to usher in a new era of large-scale post-modernist office buildings.[77]

Gregory Gilbert

36. View at night

Notes

1. See "AT&T Sets Architects Survey," *Wall Street Journal,* June 21, 1977, 3, which reported that AT&T had hired Johnson to do a feasibility study for a new corporate headquarters building at 55th Street and Madison Avenue. A short piece in the "Notes on People" section of the *New York Times,* June 17, 1977, A, 23, had already announced that the firm of Johnson/Burgee had been selected by AT&T to design the company's new skyscraper headquarters in New York City at Madison Avenue and 55th Street. Johnson was quoted as saying that the building would be a "landmark headquarters, hopefully for this generation what the Seagram building was for a generation ago."

2. For additional articles dealing with announcements of the plan, see "AT&T Set to Build New Headquarters in Mid-Manhattan," *Wall Street Journal,* March 29, 1978, 44; "Midtown Is Where It's AT&T," *Daily News,* March 30, 1978, 5; "Thanks, Ma!," *Herald Tribune,* March 31, 1978, 4 and 26; "American Telephone Officially Airs Plans for Its New Building: Facility to Cost $110 Million; Plan Is Called a Vote of Confidence in New York," *Wall Street Journal,* March 31, 1978, 32; "Shattering Glass," *Daily News,* April 2, 1978, 55.

3. "Philip Johnson Designs a Post-Modernist Tower for AT&T," *Architectural Record,* 163, May 1978, 34.

4. Paul Goldberger, "The New Age of Philip Johnson," *New York Times Magazine,* May 14, 1978, 73.

5. Throughout 1978, the *New York Times* received letters from readers commenting on their reaction to Johnson's design. See the letter to the editor from Francis Brennan, April 10, 1978, 22, which commented that Johnson's design indicated a possible return to architectural romanticism; Eugene J. Johnson wrote a letter to the editor, June 25, 1978, 78, comparing Johnson's plan to a large pay telephone and James Stevenson proposed a series of comical designs for the AT&T headquarters based on phone books and a stack of dimes; Stephen H. Stempler wrote a letter to the editor, July 1, 1979, 46, in which he criticized Johnson's design, commenting that it was "a massive, costly joke on the telephone users who will bear the cost of this monstrosity."

6. For a detailed technical description of Johnson's AT&T design and related plans, see Giorgio Ciucci, Kenneth Frampton, and Craig Owens, *Processes: The Glass House, 1949 and the AT&T Corporate Headquarters,* Cambridge, Massachusetts, 1978, 61-71.

7. For an article dealing with the use of granite in the construction of AT&T tower, see Robert E. Tomasson, "Quarries Cutting More Granite for Skyline," *New York Times,* September 15, 1979, 22. Also, for additional articles that discuss the construction and engineering of the AT&T building, see Robert Fischer, "Renaissance Tower: A Contemporary Structure That Lets It Work," *Architectural Record,* 168, October, 1980, 106-111; Carter Wiseman, "So You Want to Build a Skyscraper," *New York,* February 2, 1981, 40-42; Robert Teitelman,

"The Soul of a New Machine," *Forbes,* February 13, 1984, 140–141ff.

8. Because of the corporation's divestiture plan, less space at 550 Madison Avenue was needed by the company. For information on this matter, see Martin Gottlieb, "AT&T Planning Change in Pact with City for Museum at Tower," *New York Times,* May 25, 1984, A, 1; and Martin Gottlieb, "AT&T, in a Reversal, to Open Exhibition Space," *New York Times,* July 11, 1984, B, 2.

9. See Paul Goldberger, "A Major Monument of Post-Modernism," *New York Times,* March 31, 1978, B, 4; and Paul Gapp, " 'Chippendale' Architecture—Near Kitsch or Top-Drawer?," *Chicago Tribune,* April 23, 1978, VI, 13. Arthur Drexler of the Museum of Modern Art has been credited as the first to compare the AT&T building to a Chippendale highboy. See Carleton Knight III, "Significant Clients: Ma Bell Builds Big," *AIA Journal,* 72, July 1983, 64.

10. Goldberger, "A Major Monument," B, 4.

11. *Ibid.*

12. Ada Louise Huxtable, "Johnson's Latest—Clever Tricks or True Art," *New York Times,* April 16, 1978, D, 26,31.

13. Huxtable, "Johnson's Latest," D, 31. Also, for an excellent summary of Huxtable's and Goldberger's critical views of the AT&T building, see Eric Marcus, "For Whom the Bell Tolls," *Metropolis,* November 1984, 16-17 and 28.

14. Wolf von Eckardt, "The Defiant Architect: Philip Johnson Upsets the Modernists," *Washington Post,* April 22, 1978, C, 1.

15. Von Eckardt, "The Defiant Architect," C, 2.

16. *Ibid.*

17. Gapp, "Chippendale Architecture," VI, 13.

18. *Ibid.*

19. Michael Leapman, "Skyscraper That Upset New York," *Times* (London), May 13, 1978, 1 and 4; in his *Architecture Today,* New York, 1982, 125, Charles Jencks remarked that before AT&T no architectural project had ever been previewed in the *Times.* For additional foreign articles relating to Johnson's AT&T building, see Philip Jodidio, "Architecture: l'après modernisme?," *Connaissance des Arts,* 334, December 1979, 80-85; Alessandro Mendini, "Dear Philip Johnson," *Domus,* 608, July-August 1980, 1; "Il post-modernismo," *Casabella,* 44, November-December 1980, 110; Marco Mattei, "Philip Johnson: modernismo o post?," *Casabella,* 45, April 1981, 48-51; "Sky-high Success!," *Southend Standard Recorder* (England), August 20, 1982, 1.

20. Leapman, "Skyscraper That Upset New York," 4.

21. Craig Unger, "Tower of Power," *New York,* November 22, 1982, 48; and Knight, "Significant Clients," 64. In addition, see "Architecture as a Corporate Asset," *Business Week,* October 4, 1982, 124-126, for a discussion of how distinctive architectural design for corporate buildings can enhance a company's image (for specific reference to AT&T building see page 126); also, for information dealing with financial and real estate matters connected to the AT&T building, see the following articles: "Three Proposed Midtown Towers to Get Nearly $30 million in Abatements," *New York Times,* Decem-

ber 20, 1978, B, 2; Randall Smith, "AT&T Is Searching to Lease About Half of New Headquarters," *Wall Street Journal,* September 16, 1983, 6; Diane Henry, "AT&T in Role of Landlord," *New York Times,* September 29, 1982, D, 24.

22. Unger, "Tower of Power," 52.

23. Knight, "Significant Clients," 64.

24. Goldberger, "A Major Monument," B, 4.

25. J. M. Dixon, "Take It from the Top," *Progressive Architecture,* 59, June 1978, 8.

26. Susan Doubilet, "Not Enough Said," *Progressive Architecture,* 65, February 1984, 70.

27. Robert Hughes, "Doing Their Own Thing," *Time,* January 8, 1978, 59.

28. *Ibid.*

29. Gapp, "Chippendale Architecture," VI, 12.

30. Huxtable, "Johnson's Latest," D, 31.

31. Suzanne Stephens, "Corporate Form Givers," *Progressive Architecture,* 60, June 1979, 59.

32. Paul Goldberger, *The Skyscraper,* New York, 1981, 153.

33. Stephens, "Corporate Form Givers," 59, and William J. Curtis, *Modern Architecture Since 1900,* Englewood Cliffs, 1982, 373-374.

34. Charles A. Jencks, *The Language of Post-Modern Architecture,* New York, 1977, 131; also, see Douglas Davis and Maggie Malone, "The Sky's the Limit," *Newsweek,* November 8, 1982, 50, where Johnson himself admitted, "Outside, AT&T is a reawakening of the early skyscraper. Inside, the plan is pure Mies van der Rohe—a modern grid." Richard Pommer, "Philip Johnson and History," *Artforum,* 17, October, 1978, 26-29, advanced a more polemical view of the modernist aspects of Johnson's AT&T design. Pommer wrote that the postmodernist architects who had come of age in the 1960s and 1970s (Venturi, Moore) had mastered the modernist heritage and were able to reconcile it with past traditions; however, such modernist architects as Philip Johnson (trained "under the most ahistorical of the modernists, Gropius, or his imitators") saw developments in architecture as stemming from a rejection of prior conventions. Pommer continued, "Not having known much about the origins of modernism, they accepted its own self-image as a complete break with the past. . . . It followed that the next change would have to be just as drastic—that history proceeded by revolutions. . . ." Therefore, as Pommer argued, although Johnson utilized a historicizing approach in the AT&T building, his renunciation of modernism in favor of other styles still reflected a modernist sensibility.

35. Charles Jencks, "Late Modernism and Post Modernism," *Architectural Design,* 48, November-December 1978, 600. In her book *Johnson/Burgee: Architecture,* New York, 1979, 113, Nory Miller also commented that in designing the AT&T tower Johnson was responsive to its urban context, namely, the existence of both neoclassical and modernist structures in the city. Further, Miller wrote that Johnson's design was also influenced by the neoclassical style of AT&T's former headquarters at 195 Broadway.

36. Paul Goldberger, "AT&T Building: A Harbinger of a New Era," *New York Times,* September 28, 1983, B, 9.

37. Doubilet, "Not Enough Said," 70. Also, in Colin Amery, "Johnson's Cookie Cutter Modern," *Architect's Journal,* 177, February 16, 1983, 53, Henry-Russell Hitchcock is reported as saying that the shaft of the AT&T building is "like a good speech, fine in the beginning and the end—but you can't remember what happened in the middle."

38. Dixon, "Take It from the Top," 8.

39. *Ibid.*

40. Goldberger, *On the Rise: Architecture and Design in a Postmodern Age,* New York, 1983, 110.

41. Doubilet, "Not Enough Said," 75.

42. For a discussion of this issue and a general reassessment of Johnson's AT&T plan, see Ellen Posner, "Learning to Love Ma Bell's New Building," *Wall Street Journal,* October 12, 1983, 26.

43. Goldberger, "Harbinger," B, 9.

44. Amery, "Johnson's Cookie Cutter Modern," 53.

45. Mention of this criticism appeared in Posner, "Learning to Love Ma Bell's New Building," 26.

46. Doubilet, "Not Enough Said," 75.

47. Huxtable, "Johnson's Latest," D, 31. Even before Huxtable's first review of the AT&T design had appeared in April of 1978, she had written on contextual problems related to the building in "Today the Cards Are All in the Builders' Hands," *New York Times,* March 26, 1978, 29. For additional articles by Huxtable that contain references to the AT&T tower, see "Radical Change on the City's Skyline," *New York Times,* July 22, 1979, 27; "The Boom in Bigness Goes On," *New York Times,* December 28, 1980, 25; "State of the Arts: Architecture, Classicism in a Contemporary Context," *New York Times,* September 6, 1981, 21.

48. Dixon, "Take It from the Top," 8.

49. Goldberger, *On the Rise,* 110. For additional references to the building's relation to its setting, see P. Viladas, "Philip Johnson: Predictably Unpredictable," *House and Garden,* February 1981, 131; and Janet Abrams, "Manhattan Masterpiece," *Building Design,* August 6, 1982, in which the author comments that the narrow space of Madison Avenue makes it impossible to get a full view of the AT&T tower.

50. Stephens, "Corporate Form Givers," 59.

51. Goldberger, *On the Rise,* 110.

52. Paul Goldberger, "Those New Buildings: Promise Versus the Reality," *New York Times,* June 9, 1983, C, 18. For an article discussing the donation of a model of the AT&T tower to the Queens Museum, see David Dunlap, "Building Boom Outpaces a Scale Model of the City," *New York Times,* December 20, 1981, 52.

53. Goldberger, *On the Rise,* 109. Although Huxtable has consistently focused on the contextual issues relating to the AT&T building, Goldberger has also discussed the matter in several articles, most notably in "The Limits of Urban Growth," *New York Times Magazine,* November 14, 1982, 46-68. Even earlier, Goldberger had commented on the impact that the AT&T building

would have on its urban environment in "Design Notebook," *New York Times,* May 18, 1978, C, 10; and "New Madison Avenue Buildings, a New New York?," *New York Times,* December 18, 1980, 21. With reference to Johnson's comments on the contextual and zoning issues surrounding the AT&T building, see David W. Dunlap's "A Graceful Move 'Upstairs'," *New York Times,* May 23, 1982, 6. Further, it is important to note that the controversy centering on the zoning problems relating to the AT&T building resulted in new zoning ordinances limiting the size of midtown skyscrapers (see Smith, "Searching to Lease," 6). In a short piece in *Alive and Well and Living in New York City,* published by the Saint Patrick's Cathedral, October, 1982, there is also mention of the problems of congestion in the midtown area and Johnson's attempts to alleviate them by raising the plaza for the AT&T building.

54. Andrea O. Dean, "Conversations: Philip Johnson," *AIA Journal,* 68, June 1979, 45,

55. Goldberger, "The New Age of Philip Johnson," 73. Although such projects as the AT&T building were generating a great deal of controversy, Johnson continued to be a respected figure in the field and received a number of prestigious awards after the AT&T plan had been made public. For a listing of articles on these honors, see Nory Miller, "Convention '78: Remarks by Gold Medalist Johnson," *AIA Journal,* 67, July 1978, 16-22; Paul Goldberger, "Philip Johnson Awarded $100,000 Pritzker Prize," *New York Times,* May 23, 1979, C, 26; Charlotte Curtis, "An Honor for Philip Johnson," *New York Times,* December 6, 1983, C, 16.

56. Paul Goldberger, "Design Direction: Other Voices," *AIA Journal,* 67, Mid-May 1978, 162.

57. Wolf von Eckardt, "Philip Johnson, Shining Bright," *Horizon,* May 1978, 50-56; Peter Blake, "Philip Johnson Knows Too Much," *New York,* May 15, 1978, 58-61; Hughes, "Doing Their Own Thing," 52-59.

58. Philip Johnson, "Re-building," *New York Times,* December 28, 1978, A, 17; Philip Johnson, "Philip Johnson: Fantastic Architectural Change in U.S.," *U.S. News and World Report,* June 5, 1978, 74-75.

59. Leland Roth, *A Concise History of American Architecture,* New York, 1979, 359.

60. Von Eckardt, "The Defiant Architect," C, 1.

61. Gapp, "Chippendale Architecture," VI, 12.

62. Moshe Safdie, "Letter to Philip Johnson," *Skyline,* August 1, 1978. For a reference to Safdie's remarks on the post-modernist trend in architecture, see Robert Guenther, "Newer Than New?: In Architects Circles, Post-Modernist Design Is a Bone of Contention," *Wall Street Journal,* August 1, 1983, 1.

63. Jencks, *Language of Post-Modern Architecture,* 131.

64. Quoted in Hughes, "Doing Their Own Thing," 59.

65. Gapp, "Chippendale Architecture," VI, 12.

66. Denise Scott Brown, "High Boy: The Making of an Eclectic," *Saturday Review,* March 17, 1979, 54. This discussion is part of a review by Scott Brown of *Philip Johnson: Writings,* Oxford, 1979. See also Martin Filler's review of the book in "Philip Johnson: The Architect as Theorist," *Art in America,* 67, December 1979, 16-19.

67. Scott Brown, "High Boy," 55. Several writers have commented on Scott Brown's remarks regarding Johnson's conversion to post-modernism and his appropriation of the Chippendale motif. See Charles Jencks, "Epigrams on Philip Cortelyou Johnson: (Inspired by His Writings)," *Architectural Design,* August-September 1979, 236; Tom Wolfe, *From Bauhaus to Our House,* New York, 1981, 127. Wolfe exclaimed, "Venturi's partisans were furious. They claimed that Johnson had stolen the idea of the highboy crown and its broken pediment straight from Venturi. . . ." It is interesting to note that one of Johnson's original designs for a Chippendale pediment had a rectangular notch that is almost identical to Venturi's design for his mother's house built in 1962-64 (illustration in Unger, "Tower of Power," 47).

68. Hughes, "Doing Their Own Thing," 59. For a similar remark, see Carleton Knight III, "Post Modern What?," *Builder,* November 1983, 74.

69. Goldberger, "Harbinger," B, 1.

70. *Ibid.*

71. *Ibid.*

72. Goldberger, Harbinger," B, 1. Since Johnson's AT&T plan was first published in 1978, Goldberger has written extensively on the design. His articles from the *New York Times* that are not cited elsewhere include "The New American Skyscraper," November 8, 1981, 68-96; "A Homage to the Skyscraper," April 18, 1982, 29; "City Reaches Pinnacle as Architectural Leader," April 4, 1983, B, 1; "Romanticism Is the New Motif in Architecture," October 23, 1983, H, 1; "Celebrating the Restlessness of Philip Johnson," December 8, 1983, C, 30; "The Intent Was Not to Shock, But to Please," December 25, 1983, 23.

73. Sam Hall Kaplan, "AT&T Building a Tribute to the Corporate Cathedral," *Los Angeles Times,* January 18, 1984, V, 1.

74. Kaplan, "AT&T Building," V, 3.

75. Doubilet, "Not Enough Said," 70. In the same issue of *Progressive Architecture* in February 1984, 98–100, John Jacobus wrote a piece entitled "Philip Johnson: His Work, His Times," in which he asserted that the architect's interest in classical and academic themes could be traced throughout his career. As Jacobus saw it, with the more literal use of historicizing elements in the late 1970s and early 1980s, the AT&T design represented a natural culmination of Johnson's interest in classical architectural forms. John Pastier, "Evaluation: Pennzoil as Sculpture and Symbol," *AIA Journal,* 71, June 1982, 39-43, commented that the AT&T building also reflected Johnson's continuing interest in various design problems that had appeared in some of his earlier buildings. For example, in both his 1976 Pennzoil building and the AT&T tower, Johnson was involved with the question of how a building should meet the sky. As Frank Gehry pointed out, the broken pediment of the AT&T tower was simply a classical reformulation of the split gable design used in the Pennzoil building.

76. Benjamin Forgey, "Towers of Excellence," *Washington Post,* April 17, 1984, C, 7.

77. For additional articles that were published in 1984, see those by Reyner Banham, "AT&T: The Post Post-Deco Skyscraper," and William Curtis, "On Appearing Too Classical," in *Architectural Review,* 176, August 1984, 11-21 and 25-27; and Martin Filler, "High Ruse," *Art in America,* 72, September 1984, 156-159.

BRONX DEVELOPMENTAL CENTER

Bronx, New York

Architects: Richard Meier and Associates

37. Bronx Developmental Center, view from northeast (color plate on page 34)

The Bronx Developmental Center was built from 1970 to 1976 as a total-care residential facility for mentally retarded and physically disabled children of the Bronx community. The project was originally planned for 750 children but after budget cuts, the center was built to accommodate 380 residents, and to serve as an outpatient facility for former residents. The center's program was to enable patients to acquire the skills necessary for independent living. The Facilities Development Corporation, which commissioned the Center for the New York State Department of Mental Hygiene, was created in an attempt to improve the quality of state mental health facilities by hiring talented architects and helping to get their projects through any bureaucratic processes. The building was designed by Richard Meier and Associates.

The Bronx Developmental Center has inspired diverse reactions ranging from the highest praise to fervent condemnation, and has raised questions about what is considered to be appropriate architecture and care for the handicapped. The building received international profes-

sional acclaim and several awards, yet it remained empty as debates over its use raged in court. For some the Center has been considered a symbol of the unfortunate inability of even the best architecture to solve problems that society has not been able to solve.[1]

The complex is located in the North Bronx on a triangular 18-acre site that is part of a campus of hospital facilities. The building is bordered on the east by the Hutchinson River Parkway and on the west by a network of railroad tracks. The decision to preserve an existing wooded area influenced the architects to locate the complex in the northeast section of the site and to situate the main parking area to the west. The complex is best understood as a rectangle in plan, similar to a "U" with the southern end as its base.[2] The main entrance is located on the western side which consists of a long four-story service wing containing administrative offices and educational areas. The western wing is connected to the eastern side of the complex by the southern end, which consists of the larger recreational spaces such as the pool, auditorium, and gymnasium. The eastern side is

38. View from east

39. Southern courtyard

40. Detail of windows

composed of four L-shaped residential buildings. These are stepped back towards the north in response to the triangular configuration of the site.[3]

In the center of the complex are two large outdoor courtyards. These are separated by a four-storied, barrel-vaulted glazed corridor which connects the eastern and western wings. In the larger, southern courtyard there are concrete fixtures such as an open air amphitheater, ramps, and slides. The classrooms, which are located in the western wing, face this courtyard. Since physical therapy is an integral part of the rehabilitation program, the classrooms open onto the courtyard and serve as indoor/outdoor training areas. By contrast, the dominant feature of the northern courtyard is a small training house which serves as an area where domestic conditions are simulated to help residents acquire independent living skills and thus become eligible for outpatient care. The upper courtyard also contains the cafeteria, which projects into it from the western wing and faces a partially roofed dining area. This courtyard is connected at its

northern end by a two-story open corridor that was not glazed due to budgetary limitations. In contrast to the southern end which faces other buildings and is consequently closed, the northern end is open and looks onto a small wooded area.

The center is enclosed in pre-fabricated anodized metal panels covered with a thin reflective aluminum finish. A typical floor-to-ceiling unit consists of three panels, each 11' 6" long, which are placed horizontally, one on top of the other. Window and vent openings were stamped out at the factory and into these openings were placed gasketed windows and louvers for unit ventilators. Normally, panels of this kind are placed vertically on end. However, by placing them horizontally, the architects gained more flexibility of window size, and the varying size of the windows often represents the difference between public and private areas. Classrooms and offices have large horizontal bands of glass while the residential areas have smaller square windows.

The Center has been criticized on many counts, but

41. Residential unit

the majority of the criticism has been elicited by its al- leged unhomelike appearance. The aluminum panels on the exterior, the silver finish, and its sleek surface were criticized on the grounds that a more conventional mate- rial would be more appropriate. Paul Goldberger pointed out that there has been a growing concern that environ- ments for the retarded should be designed in the images of conventional houses in the hope that replicating the environment from which the retarded come will help them in their adjustment.[4] For Goldberger, the Bronx De- velopmental Center is nothing like home — its sleek, austere forms are utterly elegant, but they do not symbol- ize any kind of home.[5] The silver color of the panels and the punched-out, round cornered windows combine to form a highly technological appearance. The complex has been observed by more than one critic to resemble the sides of a ship or a plane. Jurgen Joedicke remarked that the resulting question is then "whether such a puris- tic, technically conceived design is suitable or not for re- tarded patients."[6]

According to Goldberger, there are many features on both the interior and the exterior that help to ease the tension caused by this technological imagery, such as the pastel colors on the interior walls, the graceful propor- tions, and the careful arrangement of living space into small group units. For Goldberger, a sense of unity is created by the round corners of the windows set into the panels, the rounded stair-towers, and the rounded cor- ners of the buildings themselves.[7] He added that many of the residents' rooms look onto a distant highway, and that this view is surprisingly relaxing since "the cars stream by like the flow of a river."[8]

In addition to their unhomelike appearance, the panels have been criticized for other reasons. Mark Ste- vens remarked that, "however beautifully composed the panels on Meier's building — as the light changes so does the coloring — they also shoot light back into one's eyes, giving the building a standoffish air."[9] Rosemarie Bletter suggested that the glare from the reflections of the aluminum panels could be reduced by an ample amount of trees planted in and around the building.[10] Suzanne Stephens said that although the gasketed windows are very effectively integrated into the paneling when viewed from the exterior, this unity is lost when the windows are seen from the interior, where they are imbedded in gypsum board that makes their curved corners seem more obvious.[11] With respect to relations between the exterior and the interior, Stern went so far as to describe them as a Patek Philippe case with a Timex inside.[12]

As Meier explained, the triangular site is located in a "blighted industrial no-man's land," with a highway to the east and railyards to the west. The strategy was to create a four-storied structure that turned in upon itself, thus protecting the children from the external setting.[13] For Joseph Rykwert, the introspective plan is indicated by the courtyards whose vast size and variety of purposes combine to transform them into the squares of a small town. Even the facades facing the courtyard help direct attention to this area, for they are more complex and interesting than the simpler facades of the exterior building.[14] Rykwert observed that part of the program of the school was to establish itself as a small, independent community, totally isolated from its harsh surroundings.[15]

The plan of Meier's Monroe Developmental Center in Rochester, New York (1969–1974), served as a prototype for the Bronx Developmental Center's layout, as Lindsay Shapiro noted. The Monroe plan juxtaposed administrative, educational, and residential areas across large courtyards, and both buildings develop the concept that the therapeutic environment for the mentally retarded should be an enclosed, self-sufficient, and nearly monastic community.[16]

A critic for *L'Architecture d'aujourd'hui* has noted that the arrangement of each unit into a building having four floors sensibly resembles that of apartment houses in the Bronx.[17] In addition, the scale of these residential units is articulated in a simple cellular geometry compatible with the existing residential scale of the Bronx. A critic for *Casabella* has remarked that "this ensures that these buildings remain within the human scale to which the inhabitants are accustomed."[18]

Suzanne Stephens observed how the program related logically to the *parti* of the scheme.[19] The long western wing contains the public areas such as entrance lobby, offices, cafeteria, and classrooms. The more private areas, which include apartment units, small dining areas, and doctor's offices, are situated in the more remote eastern wing. The more widely differentiated purposes of

42. Western wing

43. Southern courtyard

the eastern wing are suggested by the projections in this area of the plan. Ada Louise Huxtable remarked on the skillful control of the progression from public to private space.[20] Rykwert made much of the same point.[21] The progression moves from the lobby and classrooms to the courtyard with its outdoor classroom extensions. Public and private areas are connected by two corridors that cross the courtyards. The two courtyards divide the western spine into two smaller spines, which in turn extend into four residential units. Rosemarie Bletter remarked that this numerical progression from one to two to four occurs with the logic of cell division. The transition from

large to small spaces reflects the social groupings within the building and demonstrates the separation of public from private areas.[22] Even the fenestration signals the difference between large and small spaces. In the courtyards the transition between public and private life occurs most forcefully. Nevertheless, the courtyards, too, have been criticized for their formality. It has been noted, for example, that the concrete forms dominate the natural elements of the greenery. Also, it has been observed that the sleekness of the aluminum skin needs more natural elements to complement it.[23]

Another controversial issue in the design related to matters of safety. Molly Ivins quoted Kay MacHaig, who is a member of the Consumer Advisory Board at Willowbrook, as saying that "the Developmental Center is not a healthy place for anybody to live. . . . It is fraught with safety hazards that are part of the internal design. And some things can never be corrected."[24] The hazards mentioned were a lack of safety glass in some areas, inadequate railings, and what some have called "catwalks." The catwalks, however, have been defended on the grounds that most of them are enclosed, covered bridges, and the two that were not covered were designed exclusively for staff use.[25] In addition to being criticized for open railings and bridges, the Center was also deemed unsafe due to an unguarded drop in the courtyard. In response to these criticisms, the architects have designed wire infill for the railings, terracing for the courtyard, and other necessary adjustments.[26]

Another criticism has been the height of the Center. Since it was built on a relatively small piece of land, the complex is multi-storied, and its four stories pose a problem for the severely handicapped and those in wheelchairs. This matter would not be a concern if only ambulatory residents were selected; however, non-ambulatory patients are the most likely candidates for such residential treatment centers.[27]

Goldberger has remarked that there is no denying that Meier's building is a work of art.[28] Robert Hughes likened its suavely detailed metal walls to the Corbusian machine look.[29] Martin Filler pointed out that both architects have in common a "machine" esthetic that includes elements contrived to look machine-made while actually being hand-crafted.[30] The influence of Le Corbusier's early work is evident in the use of continuous surfaces, solid shapes, and smoothly finished materials. "Its rigorous attention to scale and finish amount to a degree of luxury that has almost vanished from public building since the nineteenth century."[31]

The fact that the building is a work of art has been yet another point of controversy. Some psychologists and parents of the retarded have felt that Meier thought of the building as art for art's sake and that has forced an unhomelike art upon its residents.[32] To this notion Hughes responded that although Meier's architecture is abstract, it is not inhospitable.[33] Goldberger remarked that Meier's purist design vocabulary, used to attain the elegance and refinement characteristic of his buildings, is consistent with the architect's belief that the retarded deserve no less than any other client.[34] Rosemarie Bletter observed that the result is a distinctive look which, according to a survey by Cornell University, makes most of the residents proud to live there.[35] Hans Esser, a medical doctor, has remarked that while an austere environment is not disturbing to the handicapped, a complicated environment which we might find beautiful would be detrimental in that it would cause confusion. On this score, the Center has been found to be good, for in spite of its vast size, its plan is a clear one.[36]

44. Top: a "catwalk"

45. Middle: covered bridge

46. Bottom: detail at southwest corner

47. Swimming pool

48. Living room, residential unit

49. Training "house"

The fact that the Center is a unified institution has caused social critics to consider it to be obsolete; although the building is beautiful, it is still an institution and is therefore another step into the past.[37] These evaluations reflected the recent trend in the care of the mentally retarded to place them in small, homelike settings as opposed to large, dehumanizing institutions. The reasoning behind this attitude is that it will be easier for the retarded to adjust to life in society if they are placed in a more normal environment.[38] Interestingly enough, Meier considered these issues in designing the interior spaces.

Although it was not possible in a large institution to provide facilities for small groups, Meier organized the residential areas into "family" arrangements grouped around a common living room. In addition, he designed a "house" which is located in the northern courtyard as an educational area. This home in the center of a home creates a strong sense of place. As Meier has remarked in an interview with Richard Deems, this was the architect's way of demonstrating that public architecture could indeed be humane.[39] Evidently, he did not succeed in convincing some skeptics.

50. View from northeast

In addition to the trend in de-institutionalizing the re-tarded, it is also currently believed that they should be integrated into the community as much as possible to foster normalization. On this basis the Center has been deemed out of date by virtue of its isolation.[40] Anthony Pinto, who is a member of the Willowbrook chapter of the Benevolent Society for Retarded Children, com-plained that there is no neighboring residential area where a resident can learn how to walk to the corner to buy an ice-cream cone and talk to neighbors on their stoops.[41] To a considerable extent, these factors could not be controlled by the architect; they were the "givens" of the commission. It should nevertheless be said that Meier intended to create a "microcosm world, a sanctu-ary with a strong sense of community."[42] Apropos this is-sue, Rosemarie Bletter added that when seeing this building from the vantage point of its decaying surround-ings, one "may indeed want to question the comparative merit of being outside or inside."[43]

The whole problem of appropriate treatment and an architecture in which to house it came to a climax with the transfer of residents from the Willowbrook State School to the Bronx Developmental Center. Willowbrook is a custodial institution whose residents are incapable of developing independent living skills and consequently will always require full-time care. (Willowbrook received much notoriety in the early 1970s when it was revealed

that the residents were living under inhumane condi-tions.) There was a plan that four hundred Willowbrook residents would be transferred to the Bronx Develop-mental Center. Parents of these residents protested this action on the grounds that the Center was not an appro-priate setting for their children. Abercrombie pointed out that the building will never be used exactly as in-tended.[44] The original intention to provide a center for children who could return to society after some training is clearly reflected in the plan of the complex, which in-cludes a training house.[45] This was not the building to house patients incapable of learning to live indepen-dently.

As is usual in the field of architecture, the Bronx De-velopmental Center had won awards before it was occu-pied. But, as Abercrombie pointed out, its critics have wondered "whether an unoccupied shell should ever be judged excellent architecture."[46] Its honors have included the American Institute for Architects' Honor Award; a Reynolds Memorial Award for distinguished architecture using aluminum; a New York City Club Bard Award; and the American Institute for Architects' Bartlett Award for architecture for the handicapped. All of these honors were awarded in 1977, and in that year Allan Strauss, New York City Club's program chairman, remarked that when the Center received the Bard Award, it represented

51. View from north

the end of an era of vast public construction projects.[47]

State officials agreed that if they had it to do over, they would not build the Bronx Developmental Center.[48] Dr. David Kliegler, deputy director of the Developmental Center, considered the Center's critics unrealistic and explained that in the early 1970s there was money available only for large residential services.[49] Goldberger noted that the architect was commissioned by the Facilities Development Corporation to design a large institution and if by the time the design was realized a different sort of program was preferred, one can only blame bureaucratic delay.[50]

In a review in 1973, Betty Raymond mentioned that architects, designers, administrators, and psychiatrists had agreed that environment is a part of the treatment.[51] In this regard, later critics recognized the positive way that the design on the Bronx Developmental Center addressed its users. Goldberger pointed out the low windows which are almost at floor level, so that even if one is sitting on the floor, one can see outside.[52] Inside, other examples of how the environment stimulates the senses can be found in the use of the forty-seven colors; "vivid ones in public spaces, softer ones in private" were seen "to give further definition and individuality to the patients' experiences."[53] In this regard, the caricature known as the "Steinberg figure," located in the concrete of a courtyard wall, was particularly noted by Abercrom-

bie.[54] In order to prevent a dehumanizing effect, Stephens maintained, "everywhere elements recur that constantly relate to the human dimension and to a system of mathematical proportions."[55] As evidence, Stephens pointed to the use of a 5'9" module for plan and elevations — a measurement derived from Le Corbusier's Modulor.

Comparing the Bronx Developmental Center with similar types of projects financed by public agencies, one cannot fail to remark on its distinctive merits, as Steens suggested.[56] The Bard Award citation said that "everyone can now take pride in the fact that our state government has sponsored such a high level of architectural achievement."[57] Both Filler and Goldberger pointed out that Meier carefully studied the human needs and institutional precedents in preparation for the design.[58] John Hejduk wrote that "to imagine a hospital for mental health like no other hospital — that is a revolutionary act. Revolutionary acts in architecture sometimes produce a masterwork, and that is just what the Meier Bronx Developmental Center is."[59] As such, the building became the focus for a debate about architecture but also about the appropriate treatment for various kinds of retarded people. And the problem remains, as Dr. Kliegler stated, that no one really knows what the best environment for the retarded actually is.[60]

Tana L. Harvey

Notes

1. Ada Louise Huxtable, "The Latest Style Is 'Jeweler's Mechanical'," *New York Times,* December 25, 1977, 27.

2. This notion was taken from an unpublished paper by Steven Manders, "Richard Meier: The Bronx Developmental Center and His Later Projects," Rutgers University, 1983, 2.

3. Rosemarie Haag Bletter, "Recent Work by Richard Meier," *Architecture and Urbanism* (A&U), 64, April 1976, 103.

4. Paul Goldberger, "The Bronx Developmental Center; Is It a Masterwork or a Nightmare?," *New York Times,* May 3, 1977, 43.

5. Goldberger, "A Masterwork or a Nightmare?," 46.

6. Jurgen Joedicke, "Therapie—und Wohngebaude für geistig behinderte Kinder," *Bauen und Wohnen,* 10, October 1978, 409.

7. Paul Goldberger, "Bronx Developmental Center by R. Meier," *Architecture and Urbanism* (A + U), 84, November 1977, 14.

8. Goldberger, "Bronx Developmental Center by R. Meier," 13.

9. Mark Stevens, "Living in a Work of Art," *Newsweek,* May 30, 1977. 60.

10. Bletter, "Recent Work," 103.

11. Suzanne Stephens, "Architecture Cross-examined," *Progressive Architecture,* 58, July 1977, 48. This review is otherwise largely positive, calling the building "clearly a masterpiece."

12. Robert Stern, "Notes on American Architecture in the Waning of the Petroleum Era," *GA Document 1970–1980,* 7. In Stanley Abercrombie, "Bronx Developmental Center," *Interiors,* December 1978, 94, the simile is attributed to James Stewart Polshek.

13. Richard Meier, *Richard Meier, Architect,* New York, 1976, 205. Portions of this statement are quoted in Gianni Mazzochi, ed., "Rieducazione a New York," *Domus,* 569, April 1977, 6.

14. Joseph Rykwert, "The Very Personal Works of Richard Meier and Associates," *Architectural Forum,* 136, 1972, 34.

15. Rykwert, "Personal Works of Richard Meier," 34.

16. Lindsay Stamm Shapiro, "Richard Meier's Architecture of Purity and Possibility," *Artforum,* 16, November 1977, 38.

17. Christian Dupeyron, ed., "Richard Meier: Bronx Developmental Center," *L'Architecture d'aujourd'hui,* 186, August–September 1976, 66. This statement was quoted in Nicolas Silin, ed., "Bronx Developmental Center, New York, 1975," *L'Architecture d'aujourd'hui,* 213, February 1981, 23.

18. G. Milani, ed., "Strategie di Progettazione," *Casabella,* 389, May 1974, 26.

19. Stephens, "Architecture Cross-examined," 44.

20. Ada Louise Huxtable, "A Landmark Before Its Doors Open," *New York Times,* May 8, 1977, 25.

21. Rykwert, "Personal Works of Richard Meier," 31.

22. Bletter, "Recent Work," 103.

23. Stephens, "Architecture Cross-examined," 48.

24. Molly Ivins, "New Center for Retarded Opposed as 'Obsolete'," *New York Times,* May 3, 1977, 43.

25. Ivins, "New Center for Retarded," 43.

26. Stephens, "Architecture Cross-examined," 51.

27. Ivins, "New Center for Retarded," 46.

28. Goldberger, "A Masterwork or a Nightmare," 46.

29. Robert Hughes, "US Architects; Doing Their Own Thing," *Time,* January 8, 1979, 58.

30. Martin Filler, "Modernism Lives: Richard Meier," *Art in America,* 68, May 1980, 125.

31. Hughes, "US Architects," 58.

32. Mentioned in Stephens, "Architecture Cross-examined," 59.

33. Hughes, "US Architects," 58.

34. Goldberger, "Bronx Developmental Center by R. Meier," 10.

35. Bletter, "Recent Work," 102.

36. Goldberger, "A Masterwork or a Nightmare," 46.

37. *Ibid.*

38. Ivins, "New Center for Retarded," 43.

39. Richard Deems, "Richard Meier Comments on the Role of Today's Architecture," *House Beautiful,* April 1978, 87.

40. Goldberger, "A Masterwork or a Nightmare," 46.

41. Ivins, "New Center for Retarded," 46.

42. Stephens, "Architecture Cross-examined," 59.

43. Bletter, "Recent Work," 103.

44. Abercrombie, "Bronx Developmental Center," 92.

45. Huxtable, "A Landmark," 25.

46. Abercrombie, "Bronx Developmental Center," 92.

47. Carter Horsley, "Architecture Awards Honors and Projects," *New York Times,* June 16, 1977, 22.

48. Ivins, "New Center for Retarded," 43.

49. *Ibid.*

50. Goldberger, "Bronx Developmental Center by R. Meier," 14.

51. Betty Raymond, "Health Facilities Brighten Up," *Interiors,* December 1973, 62.

52. Goldberger, "A Masterwork or a Nightmare," 46.

53. Filler, "Modernism Lives," 131.

54. Abercrombie, "Bronx Developmental Center," 94.

55. Stephens, "Architecture Cross-examined," 56.

56. Stephens, "Architecture Cross-examined," 44.

57. Horsley, "Architecture Awards Honors," 22.

58. Goldberger, "A Masterwork or a Nightmare," 46; and Filler, "Modernism Lives," 131.

59. John Hejduk, postscript to Meier, *Richard Meier, Architect,* 238.

60. Goldberger, "Bronx Developmental Center by R. Meier," 14.

EAST BUILDING,
NATIONAL GALLERY OF ART

Washington, D.C.

Architects: I.M. Pei & Partners

52. East Building, National Gallery of Art (color plate on page 35)

The East Building of the National Gallery of Art in Washington, D.C. was designed and constructed under the direction of I. M. Pei and Partners from 1968 to 1978. It is located on the trapezoidal plot of land bordered by the Mall to the south, Third Street to the east, Pennsylvania Avenue to the north, and Fourth Street to the west, where the original gallery is located. Congress had set aside the oddly shaped site for the future expansion of the National Gallery in 1937, four years before the original building by John Russell Pope was completed. Subsequently, there were fitful attempts to realize an eastern extension, which remained unexecuted until funds were provided by Paul Mellon and the commission was given to the Pei office. The building program set forth by the donor, architect, and museum planners included an entirely new structure, the East Building, modifications to what came to be called the West Building, and underground and street-level connections between the two. The underground concourse would house ser-

vice areas, shops, and a restaurant enlivened by a rushing waterfall and several prismatic skylights, visible on a street-level connecting piazza as crystalline sculptural forms and a fountain.

Because of the prominence of both the National Gallery of Art and I. M. Pei, the building program was widely publicized, praised, and criticized. Prior to its opening on June 1, 1978 the East Building designs were treated favorably in the press, even remarkably so in view of later criticism. The early articles, appearing primarily in newspapers and general interest publications, often included statements by J. Carter Brown, the director of the National Gallery, and by David W. Scott, his planning consultant, regarding the specific purposes of the addition. These statements clarified the building program—to provide new exhibition spaces, auditorium space, conservation laboratories, an art history library, slide and photograph archives, and administrative offices. In order to meet the needs of growing numbers of visitors, additional sales areas, dining areas, and large open spaces had to be provided. In order to fulfill its role as a national institution on a conspicuous site in the capital, the East Building was to be suitable in both scale and style, yet accessible and inviting to visitors. After its opening in 1978, however, mixed reviews appeared in unusual abundance in art and architecture journals. Sometimes writers faulted the interior distribution of space, which seemed to favor public gathering places over private display areas; further questions were raised concerning the functional success, the contextualism, the style, and the symbolic content of the new building. On most issues a consensus was never reached, and the original building program was often forgotten.

53. Drawings indicating site plan (a) and development of building design (b-d)

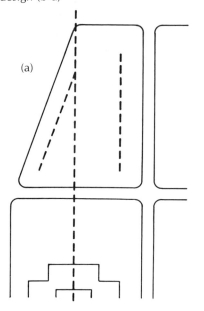

One of the basic challenges to any architect in Washington D.C. is the angularity of the street plan. The difficulties are compounded by zoning restrictions and, in this case, by the need to conform to the monumental scale of neighboring structures. Yet in articles published between the spring of 1977 and the summer of 1978 most of the critics both in the popular press and professional journals considered the East Building a masterful solution. They applauded Pei's design, which met all zoning requirements, provided the maximum number of usable cubic feet, and fully incorporated the difficult geometry of the trapezoidal site.[1] One critic proclaimed that the East Building, like some of Pei's earlier structures, appeared almost as though it had sprung naturally from the earth.[2] Negative judgements soon followed, however, and the fact that the building was carefully designed to fit the site could be considered a flaw rather than a virtue. As one critic phrased it in October 1978, "The architect's reaction to the site difficulty is a kind of 'exaggerated contextualism.' "[3] For another critic writing in January 1979, the unfortunate angles of the site had been accommodated to an obsessive degree and to the detriment of the building as a functioning museum and study center.[4]

The East Building was intended to provide additional exhibition space and space for the new Center for Advanced Study of the Visual Arts (C.A.S.V.A.). Because the building was to serve two functions, the architect divided the trapezoidal site into two parts, forming an isosceles triangle, which was to house the exhibition area, and a smaller right triangle, which was to become the C.A.S.V.A.[5] A gallery-tower rising to a height of 110 feet occupies each point of the isosceles triangle, the three towers organized around a skylit interior courtyard measuring eighty feet above the concourse level. The four levels of each gallery tower are linked vertically by stairways or elevators and horizontally by a mezzanine on

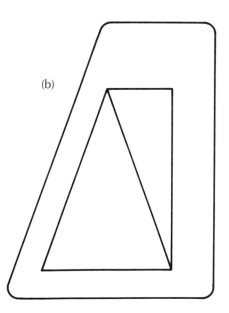

(b)

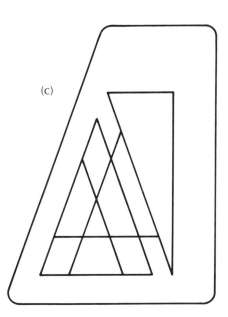

(c)

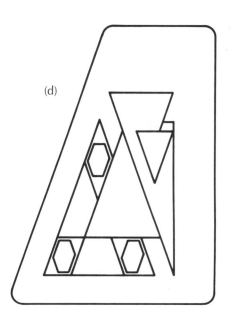

(d)

the second level and a bridge on the fourth level. The eight-story wing of the study center, accessible to the exhibition areas on the first and fourth levels, is built around a central triangular court of the six-story reading room.

The angle formed by Pennsylvania Avenue and the Mall, measuring just under twenty degrees, became the basic theme of the design.[6] The oft-discussed elements of the structure such as the knife-edged 19-degree corner of the C.A.S.V.A. building, the marble pavements, the ceiling coffers, and even the tetrahedronal sections of the enormous skylight that surmounts the interior courtyard of the exhibition area, were derived from this theme. In 1978, summer readers of *Art in America* were enthusiastically urged by one journalist to visit the museum specifi-

cally to enjoy the ". . . acute and obtuse angles [that] are everywhere, amplifying illusions of perspective and cheerfully frustrating one's sense of measurement."[7]

The pervasive triangle was thus accepted as a function of the trapezoidal site in most early accounts. Prior to the June 1 opening date, however, tentative doubts were expressed about a "possible obsession with geometry"[8] apparent in secondary spaces, such as stairwells[9], and in ornamental features, such as the prismatic skylights of the piazza.[10] Later, when the museum opened, the triangular theme was more often criticized for the limitations that it imposed on space and movement.[11] For example, readers of the tabloid *Skyline* were reminded in the August 1978 issue that the triangle is a strongly closed space.[12] There was a clear implication in

54. C.A.S.V.A. Building, central court

55. C.A.S.V.A. Building, 19-degree corner

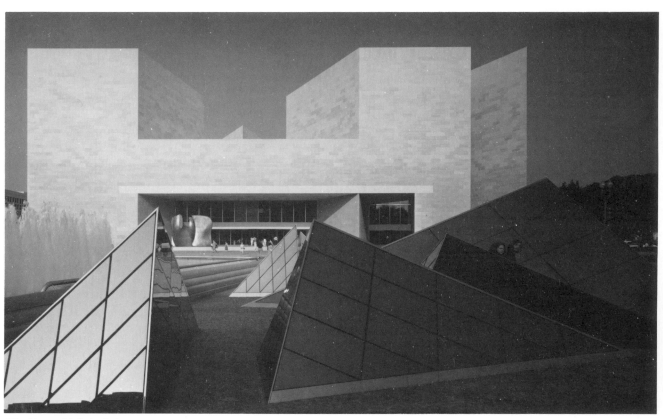

56. Pyramidal skylights

the January 1979 issue of the *Architectural Review* that for an art gallery a closed space was a failed space that made viewing awkward from every angle.[13] In the August 1978 issue of *Connoisseur* another critic complained not of the spatial limitations of the triangular rooms but of the simplistic abuse of the geometric theme which had been employed without regard for associative values that the East Building embodied by virtue of its prominent location and its official function.[14] Yet another reviewer, writing at about the same time for *Art International,* found that precisely because the spaces were created by triangles they were enormously exciting and pleasantly ambiguous.[15]

Recognition of the relationship between the East Building and its architectural surroundings was also cause for comment. A number of commentators believed that respectful homage had been paid to other monuments of Washington by virtue of the dignified scale and material of the East Building and thought that it, like the last piece of a puzzle, fit perfectly into the scheme of the Mall.[16] Yet a skeptic on this point could note "a shadow cast by that very virtue—for Washington's official architecture as a whole is something less than inspiring."[17] On the other hand, not everyone saw a consistency in context: while one commentator cheered for the absence of relationships because of what he perceived as the generally low quality of surrounding buildings, another complained that the trapezoidal building almost ignored its classical surroundings.[18]

On the balance, those who considered the question of context almost unanimously agreed that the Pei addition responded appropriately to the building by Pope. The use of the same Tennessee marble, the continuation of Pope's longitudinal axis through the center of the new exhibition area, the similarity of scale, and the connecting plaza were seen as important elements that related the two structures.[19] Even the smooth surfaces of the new wing were said to be only "a few steps removed from the low relief surfaces of Pope's windowless building,"[20] although even here the opposite view could be taken by a writer who approvingly reported that the new and old parts of the museum seemed unrelated. He contended that the allusions to the neo-classical structure of 1941 were unnecessary and undesirable because of its lack of architectural merit.[21]

Judgments about the interior spaces also varied predictably. In a *Time* magazine issue dated only four days after the official opening, an article stated that the new wing functioned perfectly as a "ceremonial space" for hundreds of visitors, while at the same time providing ". . . the opportunity to contemplate works of art in something akin to privacy. . . ."[22] Nevertheless, within months of the opening, there were visitors who found the building awkward and confusing.[23] Such reactions contrast so sharply at times that, as in other cases, they seem to describe different structures rather than different opinions about the same building.

78

57. Models of East (new) and West (original) Buildings

58. Atrium

The interior courtyard or atrium of the exhibition building, an isosceles triangle carved from the core of the larger exhibition area, aroused particular controversy. Initially the critics proclaimed the lofty space, crossed at various levels by bridges and mezzanines, to be exciting, beautiful and functional.[24] J. Carter Brown had explained that Pei's vast central space should be seen as analogous to the neo-classical rotunda of John Russell Pope's 1941 gallery, where the initial impact was to ". . . lift you by your coat collar out of your stock responses."[25] Pei described the skylit atrium, with its tall intersecting panels of glass, as an extension of the Mall, an indoor public plaza.[26] He designed the space, he says, to accommodate large numbers of museum-weary people, hoping that the excitement of the atrium, a space enlivened by staircases and escalators, balconies and bridges, would encourage visitors to ". . . stay a little longer."[27] Thus the atrium was "designed for a mob scene." "We needed to make the visit a pleasant one," explained Pei, "so we built a circus."[28] Positive judgements on these features were offered primarily by those who acknowledged and accepted as valid the aims of the architect and planners; but there were also those who perceived and criticized the intended qualities of the atrium. Beginning in the autumn of 1978, critics noted with some dismay that the space functioned primarily as a gathering place for waiting visitors and served more to disorient than to reorient those emerging from the peripheral galleries.[29] It was described as a commercialized space and was likened both to a posh suburban shopping mall and to a mass trans-

59. Escalator, stairways, and bridges in atrium

portation terminal.[30] In fact, the very notion that a great deal of money, thought, and square footage had been devoted to a lobby for people rather than to display space for art elicited vitriolic disapproval from a critic who in November 1978, decried its ". . . shocking fun-house atmosphere. . . [its] philistine unseriousness."[31] By March of the following year, another critic had charged that the atrium space seemed hostile to paintings and appropriate only as a receptacle for milling crowds.[32] Disappointed reporters were convinced that the central space overwhelmed the peripheral galleries.[33]

The smaller galleries, located both in the four-storied corner towers and in their connecting links, were yet another subject of controversy. Both Pei and Brown intended the intimate size of the exhibition spaces to be right for a forty-five minute visit, the length of time that they had agreed to be optimum for the public after their museum-research tour of Europe. It was hoped that the location of the galleries, removed from the activity of the central courtyard, would provide viewers with a certain sense of domestic privacy that would enhance their appreciation of the works of art. Finally, by means of movable walls and ceilings, the planners aimed for the degree of flexibility that would properly accommodate a wide variety of temporary exhibitions.[34]

The display areas were initially applauded for succeeding in these ways,[35] yet even early on, a reviewer for the *Washington Post* expressed misgivings about the fact that the galleries occupy only 12 percent of the total space.[36] Others, too, found the rooms small, cramped,

60. View of galleries

61. View of galleries

difficult to locate, and secondary in importance by virtue of their size and location relative to the atrium.[37] Furthermore, the system of vertical and horizontal circulation through the galleries, initially judged "intelligent,"[38] was soon assailed. For two participants in the roundtable discussion published by *Progressive Architecture* in the October 1978 issue, orderly progress through the irregular spaces was deemed difficult and disorienting, traffic patterns seemed without logic, and stairways and walkways seemed often unrelated to the spaces that they served to connect.[39]

A particular problem faced by the architects of museums is the degree to which the building will be seen as serving rather than competing with the art. Predictably,

as few as four months after its opening, critics of the East Building declared with mixed emotions that the building, not the art within it, had become the primary tourist attraction.[40] By early 1979 the East-Building-as-art-object had become a notable topic in the critical literature.[41] Thus, the earliest commentators on the East Building enthusiastically accepted the structure as the outstanding work of art envisioned by its planners, in fact "the most lavish and expensive" holding of the National Gallery.[42] For another writer it was ". . .a magnificent space to move in" but ". : .an ornament, and as vehicle for the display of art . . . only marginally functional."[43] Then, too, there were those who did not think the museum at all attractive. "One of the ugliest buildings in all history," wrote one citizen to the editor of the *Washington Post,* ". . .an angular monstrosity that adds nothing to the Washington landscape . . . [and that] violates the sanctity of the Capitol. . . ."[44] Similar opinions were sometimes expressed in professional journals where the East Building was found weak in design or condemned as a "clumsy giant" that spoiled the formerly pleasant view from the Capitol.[45]

The exterior of the building, to cite a specific example, was considered problematic by critics and architectural historians. One writer acknowledged that the four distinctly different facades of the East Building were justified by the building's dual function, by its relationship to its architectural neighbors, and by the nature of the surrounding streets.[46] Yet he dismissed the Fourth Street facade as lacking in balance and the Pennsylvania Avenue facade as a giant cutout. In reference to the sharp angles of the Mall facade, he proposed that "If the other new architecture on the Mall is Imperial Margarine, as popular adage would have it, then the East Building is cutlery arranged for instant service."[47] During the lively interchange that appeared in *Progressive Architecture* in October 1978, a speaker found the elevations lacking in unity, scale, and meaning.[48] From across the Mall, another critic reported, the exterior appeared to be ". . .a collection of planes and masses in search of a building. . . ."[49] Others objected to the broad planes and sharp angles, finding them clumsy in silhouette and chaotic in overall effect.[50]

Partially to clarify its relationship (or lack of one) to its surroundings, reviewers sought an accurate description of the style of Pei's new building. One critic wrote approvingly that while the building fully respected its neo-classical neighbors in material, height, weight, and mood, it was thoroughly modern, in the spirit of the

62. View from the Mall

63. Aerial view

'70s, but with no "demure evocations of historical style."[51] Other measured judgments considered the structure to be classical in its pure geometry, sparing in its innovations, and appropriately removed from the current battle of modernism versus post-modernism.[52]

Apparently uncomfortable with generalities, however, other advocates searched hard for a definitive stylistic label. The results may have puzzled even conscientious readers. One critic wrote:

> The truly great thing about Pei's achievement is that he managed to make a Classical building that is truly modern. There was no compromising here with Classical orders and stripped-down ornamentation. Rather, Pei went to the geometrical soul of the problem. . . . And yet the modernity of his building resides in the fact that it turns classical axiality on its head, substituting complex, elastic, dynamic conceptions of space for the measured step of classicism.[53]

Another critic suggested that, "One cannot call Pei's design backward-looking; but the East Building is certainly conservative, and in many respects a classical structure, whose visual meaning turns on the idea of established excellence."[54] A third critic stated that the East Building is

> a calm commentary about the commotion, inquiry, and cant that have been heard, these same nine years, about the supposedly limited language of modern architecture. It could not be less modern, actually, or more modern. It could not be less postmodern, as it were, or more. What is "modern" anyway? As Frank Lloyd Wright used to say, "Come on, fellows, let's not concern ourselves with these matters of *taste*."[55]

A fourth critic was equally convinced that "The new east wing of the National Gallery of Art is a building as struttingly 20th century in its design and concept as most official modern structures seem reluctant escapees from the 19th century."[56] A fifth critic described it as a triumph of "late modernism" that "both subverts and transforms the modernist reliance on geometry and technology."[57] The undefined stylistic labels and the ambiguous characterization in some of these assessments tend to obscure their clarity and intelligibility.

The issue of stylistic labels may seem ancillary to an understanding of any building, but when a critic connects social responsibility with architectural style, the issue of style becomes more pressing. A reviewer who complained that the East Building sought "no new directions" in architecture observed that the conservatism of the new wing served to distract the public from its obsession with political and economic difficulties.[58] Yet the opposite view was stated with equal conviction: the "surrealistic exterior" of the building was said to reflect perfectly our national mood of fear and anxiety.[59] The moral responsibility of a building either to mirror public consciousness of its shared fears or to distract it from its generalized anxieties may be a heavy one and hardly an issue to elicit unanimity. Apparently, the East Building was expected by the press to do much more than its planners had thought necessary. Both J. Carter Brown and David W. Scott had clearly stated that the building was intended to provide rooms for temporary exhibitions, study space for scholars, a library, photo archives, staff areas, and space for expanding educational enterprises.[60] Furthermore, they expected that the addition would free the existing building of some of these functions so that it could accommodate new exhibition spaces and other amenities.[61] Their hopes for the building, at least those that appeared in print, were largely of a practical rather than a symbolic nature, while members of the press had loftier expectations. One writer hoped that the stylish new wing of the National Gallery would help to make art seem more "exalted" and to "identify this exalted view of art with our sense of national destiny and purpose."[62] Another writer believed that "The National Gallery should assure visitors that Western culture rests on stable and humane traditions."[63] Yet a third reporter expressed confidence that the East Building had fulfilled this goal: "[The new structure] . . . exemplifies the endurance of humanistic principles and the everchanging possibilities of their manifestation."[64]

Should a building be judged by its ability to fulfill social and symbolic responsibilities assigned to it by critics? Can those critics who have assigned social and symbolic responsibilities to a building judge without considerable bias its ability to fulfill them? Although the symbolic and social functions of the museum may be important facets of its overall success, perhaps success in meeting the purposes assigned to it by planners is an equally important, and certainly a more objective, criterion for judgment.

Marilyn B. Fish

Notes

1. See Ada Louise Huxtable, "A Spectacular Museum Goes up in Washington," *New York Times,* May 22, 1977, 29; and Huxtable, "Geometry with Drama," *New York Times Magazine,* May 7, 1978, 58, where she stated, "The Pei building is all triangular shapes and knife-sharp angles in its matching marble skin. It draws those shapes not from some arbitrary originality, but from its odd trapezoidal site, where Pennsylvania Avenue and Madison Drive converge on the Capitol." Robert Hughes, in "Masterpiece on the Mall," *Time,* June 5, 1978, 62, wrote that the structure is ". . . exquisitely attuned to its site. . . ." During the same month Michael Kernan in "Washington's Cutural Crown," *Horizon,* 21, June 1978, 42, supplied a brief history of the addition and quoted Pei as to the site difficulties and their solutions. An article entitled "East Wing Takes Flight," by Stanley Abercrombie, *Contract Interiors,* 137, July 1978, 68, was a brief positive account in which the East Building was described as a masterful response to a specific site condition. Similarly, the anonymous author of "National Gallery East," *Art Journal,* 137, Summer 1978, 354, described the building as an innovative and brilliant solution to the problem of the site. William Marlin, in "Mr. Pei Goes to Washington," *Architectural Record,* 164, August 1978, 80, gave a positive account of the history of the addition, the goals of its planners, the difficulties encountered in its design, and their successful solutions. James A. Murphy praised the response of the building to the city plan in "P/A on Pei: Roundtable on a Trapezoid, East Building, National Gallery of Art, Washington, D.C.," *Progressive Architecture,* 59, October 1978, 50–51; and Martha McWilliams Wright, "Washington Letter," *Art International,* 22, November–December 1978, 57, applauded the ". . . two triangular buildings . . . cleverly arranged on an odd remnant of land in the shape of a trapezoid."
2. Henry Fairlie, "Washington Diarist: New Museum," *New Republic,* May 17, 1978, 38. "How could one build well (on the awkward trapezoidal site)," asks Fairlie, "Yet how could the building he has now built be anything other than it is?"
3. John Morris Dixon, "P/A on Pei," 50: "The architect's reaction to the site difficulty—the endlessly discussed geometry of the structure—is a kind of exaggerated contextualism."
4. Colin Amery, "Inside the N.G.A.: East Building, National Gallery of Art, Washington," *Architectural Review,* 165, January 1979, 22. He found that the ". . . geometry seems to have taken over. Glancing at the plan one is immediately reminded of the repeating diamond patterns on a pair of golfing socks. . . ." Earlier, in the roundtable discussion "P/A on Pei. . ." in October 1978, Martin Filler had stated that "the pattern created by the East Building's plan might be better suited to a pair of argyle socks. . . ."
5. I. M. Pei, in an interview with Barbaralee Diamonstein, "I. M. Pei—'The Modern Movement Is Now Wide Open,' " *Art News,* 77, Summer 1978, 65. The section of this interview that relates to the East Building sheds considerable light on Pei's view of the educational role of the museum, the site problem, the issue of contextualism, volume, spatial investigation, museum-fatigue levels, and the new museum-going public. For material on the design process, see the exhibition catalogue *I. M. Pei & Partners: Drawings for the East Building, National Gallery of Art—Its Evolution in Sketches, Renderings, and Models 1968–1978,* Adams Davidson Galleries, Washington, D.C.; January 4–February 6, 1979.
6. Marlin, "Mr. Pei Goes to Washington," 84.

7. Franz Schulze, "East Building: Trapezoid Triumphant," *Art in America*, 66, July–August 1978, 58. Schulze found the geometry and other elements of the building generally pleasing.

8. Suzanne Slesin, "Washington's Newest Monument: The Man Who Designed It," *Esquire*, 88, June 1978, 33. Generally writing in favor of the building, Slesin expressed one reservation: "Only in the piazza, with its ungenerous fountain and pointy skylights, which jut out of the fan-shaped granite cobblestones do we feel that the work is too mannered, the obsession with the geometry too relentless." The article summarized J. Carter Brown's contribution, explained the choice of I. M. Pei & Partners, and described the site solution. Slesin concluded: "The East Building is an architecture buff's dream. Pure geometry—easy to read, neatly done. Classical, innovative. Clear, wonderfully disorienting."

9. Paul Goldberger, "New Washington Gallery a Palace," *New York Times*, May 30, 1978, C, 25. Characterizing it as a minor problem, Goldberger pointed out that "the building's insistent geometry . . . occasionally becomes a bit obsessive, as in the case of the stairwells in the study-center wing that rise not straight but along an angle, making it difficult to ascend comfortably."

10. Slesin, "Washington's Newest Monument," 33.

11. Schulze, "East Building," 63; Patrick Pinnell, "Piranesi in Washington," *Skyline*, August 1, 1978, 2; Amery, "Inside the N.G.A.," 22; and Filler, "P/A on Pei," 52, who found the "irregularly shaped galleries . . . (to be) confusing and disorienting, making orderly progress through them difficult. . . ."

12. Pinnell, "Piranesi in Washington," 2.

13. Amery, "Inside the N.G.A.," 22.

14. Christian Otto, "Washington—A New Center for the Arts?," *Connoisseur*, 198, August 1978, 324.

15. Wright, "Washington Letter," 57.

16. Huxtable, "A Spectacular Museum," D, 29; Goldberger, "New Washington Gallery," C, 3; Benjamin Forgey, "The Maturing of the Mall: A 'Noble Building' Shaped Largely by Its Site," *AIA Journal*, 67, June 1978, 39; Marlin, "Mr. Pei Goes to Washington," 80. Even a year later, Paul Goldberger pointed out that Pei may have rejected both the current classicizing fashion and strict modernist anti-contextualism, yet succeeded admirably in relating the East Building to its architectural environment ("The Winning Ways of I.M. Pei," *New York Times Magazine*, May 20, 1979, 124).

17. Schulze, "East Building," 62.

18. See respectively, Murphy, "P/A on Pei; Roundtable," 50–51; and Amery, "Inside the N.G.A.," 22.

19. Huxtable, "A Spectacular Museum," 29; Marlin, "Mr. Pei Goes to Washington," 84–86; Dixon, "P/A on Pei," 50.

20. Dixon, "P/A on Pei," 50.

21. Murphy, "P/A on Pei," 50–51.

22. Robert Hughes, "Masterpiece on the Mall," 62.

23. Dixon, "P/A on Pei," 52; Filler, "P/A on Pei," 52. Stephens, "P/A on Pei," 51, alleged a lack of spatial legibility, an illogical flow of movement throughout the building, and a lack of visual recession resulting from the use of triangular spaces. William Allen, "Inside the N.G.A.: East Building, National Gallery of Art, Washington," *Architectural Review*, 165, January 1979, 22, found the building confusing and badly illuminated. For Hugh Adams, "The Museum as Art Object," *Art and Artists*, 13, February 1979, 39, the exhibition galleries are "not apparent at first glance." Rather they are "tucked away . . . in fly type towers, in little hexagonal rooms, reached by tiny twisty stairs." Much of the art is "stashed away in a witty, inefficient, and hideously expensive use of space."

24. Huxtable, "A Spectacular Museum," 1, 29–30; Forgey, "The Maturing of the Mall," 38–41; Marlin, "Mr. Pei Goes to Washington," 79–92; Schulze, "East Building," 50–63; Russell Lynes, "National Gallery's New Building Is Triangular Triumph," *Smithsonian Magazine*, June 1978, 46–55; Forgey, "An Exhilarating Triumph in Washington," 58–62.

25. J. Carter Brown quoted by Paul Richard, "Monumental Modern," *Washington Post*, May 21, 1978, G, 2.

26. I. M. Pei quoted by Barbaralee Diamonstein, *American Architecture Now*, New York, 1980, 150. Pei discussed the social responsibility of architecture, the role of the museum in society, and specific goals for the East Building in this interview.

27. Quoted in Diamonstein, *American Architecture Now*, 149.

28. Pei quoted by Lynes, "National Gallery's New Building," 47.

29. Amery, "Inside the N.G.A.," 22. Donald Canty, "Building as an Event: I. M. Pei & Partners' East Building, National Gallery of Art, Washington," *AIA Journal*, 68, Mid-May 1979, 109, found the central space somewhat disorienting but generally fulfilling Brown's vision of it.

30. Amery, "Inside the N.G.A.," 22; and Filler, "P/A on Pei," 52, respectively.

31. Richard Hennessy, "Type and Progeny; Recent Monu-

mental Architecture," *Artforum*, 17, November 1978, 70, found the East Building ". . . an utterly Victorian building . . . confused and confusing. . . ." It is characterized by ". . . structural incoherence . . . a striving for effects which quickly turns pompous. . . . The roof plus the rest of the building represents a shotgun marriage of two utterly opposed construction techniques. . . . A Brobdingnagian budget has made it possible to torture the stone of the East Building into knife-edged precision. At first amazing, this ultimately disgusting craft has been made an end in itself, pursuing an object that could have been better and more easily made in cast concrete."

32. Paul Richard, "East Building Revisited," *Washington Post*, March 11, 1979, L, 1, 6. Since his commentary of the previous year, Mr. Richard discovered two major flaws, first in "the exhibition function of its central hall" and second in "the short supply of galleries provided with changing, natural light."

33. Jo Ann Lewis, "The National Gallery of Art, East Building," *Washington Post Magazine*, May 21, 1978, 24, expressed one reservation in an otherwise positive review: "Only after considerable looking around do you discover that no painting galleries are in evidence, and it is the curious fact of this building that they are not." See also Richard, "East Building Revisited," L, 6.

34. Pei in Diamonstein, "The Modern Movement," 67. Brown reiterated his concern for domestically scaled galleries in *Architectural Digest*, 40, January 1983, 24–30; and in *National Geographic*, November 1978, 680–701.

35. Forgey, "An Exhilarating Triumph in Washington," 62; Marlin, "Mr Pei Goes to Washington," 85.

36. Lewis, "The National Gallery of Art," 25.

37. Dixon, "P/A on Pei," 55; Allen, "Inside the N.G.A.," 29–30; Amery, "Inside the N.G.A.," 22; Adams "Museum as Art Object," 39. See also Manuela Hoelterhoff, "Three New Museums That Make No Sense," *Wall Street Journal*, April 2, 1982, 23.

38. Forgey, "An Exhilarating Triumph in Washington," 59.

39. Filler, "P/A on Pei," 52, and Stephens, "P/A on Pei," 55.

40. Filler, "P/A on Pei," 54; Kernan, "Washington's Cultural Crown," 46.

41. Amery, "Inside the N.G.A.," 22; Adams, "Museum as Art Object," 39.

42. See Grace Glueck, "Washington's Bold New Showcase For Modern Art," *New York Times*, May 7, 1978, D, 1. Also see Douglas Davis, "Tale of Two Triangles," *Newsweek*, May 22, 1978, 67; and Lewis, "The National Gallery of Art," 1.

43. Adams, "Museum as Art Object," 39. Oddly, this remark was published only two months after Pei's East Building received the Gold Medal of the AIA. The accompanying citation says that the East Building "achieves a sensitive balance between works of art and the art of architecture." See the comments in *AIA Journal*, 68, January 1979, 15.

44. Letter to the editor, *Washington Post*, March 29, 1978, A, 21.

45. Amery, "Inside the N.G.A.," 22.

46. Otto, "Washington—A New Center," 324.

47. *Ibid*.

48. Stephens, "P/A on Pei," 50.

49. Canty, "Building as an Event," 50.

50. Otto, "Washington—A New Center," 324; Dixon, "P/A on Pei," 50; Canty, "Building as an Event," 106.

51. Schulze, "East Building," 56.

52. See respectively, Slesin, "Washington's Newest Monument," 34; Marlin, "Mr. Pei Goes to Washington," 92; and Huxtable, "A Capitol Art Palace," 58.

53. Forgey, "An Exhilarating Triumph," 62.

54. Hughes, "Masterpiece on the Mall," 62.

55. Russell Lynes, "National Gallery's New Building," 46, characterized the building as "struttingly 20th century in its design and concept . . . a structure as unconventional as it is elegant. . .,made of the finest materials put together with craftsmanship of very uncommon refinement. . . ."

56. Marlin, "Mr. Pei Goes to Washington," 84.

57. Douglas Davis, "Tale of Two Triangles," 66. Davis delighted in the magnificent simplicity of the triangle as the governing principle. He found the building to be ". . . a triumph of 'late modernism,' " flexible, welcoming, and unintimidating, with an appeal to both popular and esoteric tastes. Davis quoted Pei extensively and discussed the details of such features as the foundations and the veneering.

58. Carter Ratcliff, "Modernism for the Ages," *Art in America*, 66, July 1978, 53.

59. Hennessy, "Type and Progeny," 69.

60. J. Carter Brown, in *National Geographic*, 684, carefully described the demands of the site and program and their respective solutions.

61. David W. Scott, "Plans and Programmes—the National Gallery's East Building," *Connoisseur*, 178, December 1971, 265, offered a clear explanation of the need for the addition and a description of the site, followed by information concerning materials, allocation of interior space, and funding.

62. Hilton Kramer, "Going beyond the Edifice Complex," *New York Times Magazine*, May 7, 1978, 63, characterized the East Building as ". . . a place that makes art itself seem important and even exalted. And because this is our *National* Gallery, located in the seat of power and itself a quasi-governmental institution, it has the effect of identifying this exalted view of art with our sense of national destiny and purpose. This is something that no other art institution is in the position to achieve to the same degree, and it is achieved here with the requisite display of authority and elegance—both in the design of the building and in what has gone into it. Entering the great hall of the East Building, one is made to feel a tremendous sense of confidence in the culture and civilization it symbolizes. It is a thrilling experience, and I suspect that it will fill the hearts of all but the stoniest skeptics with a feeling of pleasure and pride for a long time to come." William Marlin, "Pei Ranks High Among Great Architects," *Christian Science Monitor*, January 12, 1979, 17, identified the East Building as "a symbol of architecture's relationship to the bedrock beliefs and basic identity of the American people."

63. Ratcliff, "Modernism for the Ages," 52.

64. Wright, "Washington Letter," 57.

Governor Nelson A. Rockefeller
EMPIRE STATE PLAZA
Albany, New York

Architects: Harrison and Abramovitz

64. Empire State Plaza (color plate on page 36)

The long history of the Governor Nelson A. Rockefeller Empire State Plaza, popularly called the Albany Mall, the South Mall, or more simply the Mall, was from its inception destined for controversy. The Albany Mall was conceived in 1962 and built between 1965 and 1979 in Albany, New York. In 1969 Joe Picchi, a writer for the *Times-Union* (Albany) predicted that a graduate student from the 1980s contemplating a history of the Mall would find faded clippings revealing the Mall's greatly increased cost, the impasse and eventual compromise between Mayor Corning and Governor Rockefeller over financing, the constant criticism by comptroller Arthur Levitt, the never-ending conflicts among contractors, and the inflated cost of the Cultural Education Center.[1] However, Picchi did not predict that the monument would be so much debated in architectural circles. From its early

planning stages it has been laden with nicknames such as "St. Petersburg-on-the-Hudson," "Halicarnassus on the Hudson," "Brasilia in Downtown Albany," and "the Nelson Rockefeller Pyramid," to name a few, while at the same time it has also been hailed as "a noble symbol of state government," and "one of the most brilliant, beautiful, efficient and electrifying capitals in the world."

The Governor Nelson A. Rockefeller Empire State Plaza consists of ten buildings set on a six-story platform. The ten buildings include four Agency Buildings, the Swan Street Building, and the Legislative Office Building on the west side; the Justice Building, the Meeting Center, and the Tower Building on the east side; and the Cultural Education Center at the southern end. The platform, measuring 1,700 feet by 600 feet, raises the Albany Mall above the surrounding city and is the base for

65. View of the platform, with two Agency Buildings and the "Egg"

nine of the ten buildings. The platform houses a concourse of cafeterias, shops, auditoria and meeting rooms, parking garages and mechanical equipment; it is connected to the Cultural Education Center by a series of steps which bridge the street that separates the platform and this building.

Set between the encircling buildings on top of the platform are a series of three reflecting pools and an ornately patterned pavement. The reflecting pools and the pavement traverse the long length of the platform connecting the elegant nineteenth-century State Capitol with the Cultural Education Center. Anchoring the interior of the west sector of the Albany Mall are the twenty-three-story Agency Buildings whose design matches that of the Tower Building on the southeast sector of the platform. Each Agency Building consists of a marble-covered core and a three-sided office area, faced with marble and glass strips, cantilevered from the core. The strips hide

any appearance of individual stories. The design of the forty-four-story Tower Building on the eastern side of the Mall is similar to the Agency Buildings, but the offices are wrapped around a diamond-shaped core and both components are faced with the glass and marble strips.

Among the five remaining structures, three are the only buildings of the Albany Mall designed by other architects, albeit in close association with Harrison and Abramovitz and in accordance with the overall design scheme for the Mall. These three buildings are the Swan Street Building (architects: Carson, Lunden, and Shaw), the Justice Building (architects: Sargent, Webster, Crenshaw, and Folley), and the Legislative Building (architects: James and Meadows and Howard). The design of each is similar and there are elements of each which relate to the larger whole. Each building is sided with piers set in alternating sequence, parallel and perpendicular to the building facade. The Meeting Center and the Cultural

66. Cultural Education Center

Center are probably more controversial considering both their design and their function. The Meeting Center, more commonly known as "The Egg," sits on the eastern end of the platform. The only curvilinear structure on the platform, the Meeting Center houses two auditoria, one seating 500 people and the other 950 people. The eight-story Cultural Educational Center rests on its own platform and is connected to the main platform on the mall by steps. This building houses the Archive Center, the New York State Library, and the New York State Museum.

Although Governor Nelson A. Rockefeller (Republican Governor of New York State from 1959 to 1973) claimed the inception of the Albany Mall was motivated by needs for ever-increasing office space and for reversing the gradual deterioration of downtown Albany, many writers convey quite a different story.[2] The more commonly told anecdote describes a visit by Princess Beatrix

of the Netherlands to Albany in September 1959, when the Governor became embarrassed by the squalor of some parts of downtown Albany.[3] We do know that in 1961, Govenor Nelson A. Rockefeller appointed the Temporary State Commission on the Capital City, naming Lieutenant-Governor Malcolm Wilson as Chairman. In 1963 the Temporary State Commission on the Capital City and the Subcommittee on Albany-Capital Harbour submitted their report. This commission and subcommittee proposed to revitalize downtown Albany's decaying core by locating all future State office functions and future growth within the heart of Albany. They presented four "concepts" which would provide both the sites for State offices and a way of revitalizing the downtown core. The accepted concept, which was presented at this time, was titled "The South Mall."[4]

The site chosen for the South Mall lies to the west of the Hudson River, bordered on the east by Eagle Street

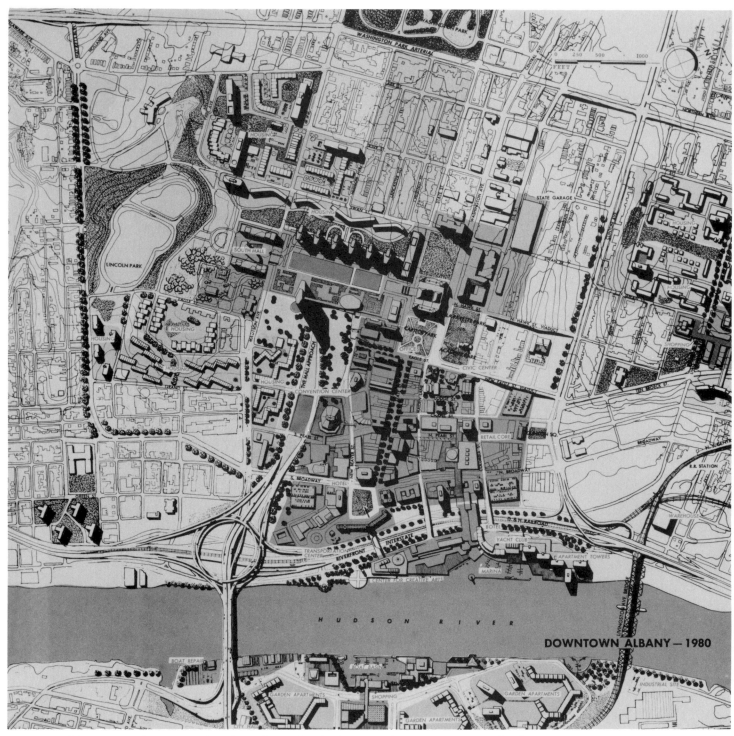

67. Map of downtown Albany reproduced in *Albany/Plan for the Capital City*, a 1963 report by the Temporary State Commission on the Capital City. Projected new construction to be completed by 1980 is indicated, including residential, retail, and convention facilities; in 1980, almost none of the proposed construction had occurred.

and on the west by Swan Street. Occupying 98.5 acres, the South Mall area extended from the State Capitol to the Governor's Mansion and was locally know as "the Gut."[5] Taking official action, the State Superintendent of Public Works filed appropriation maps claiming the land for the State on March 25, 1962. This action would eventually lead to the displacement of approximately 3,000 households, 9,000 residents, and 350 small businesses.

It wasn't long before the action was disputed. On March 26, 1962 Mayor Erastus Corning II issued a statement to the Temporary State Commission on the Capital City. He considered the action hasty and saw it as a violation of the human rights of the 3,000 families inhabiting the area. Mayor Corning felt that all the residents should be relocated slowly into alternative housing before any of the land was cleared.[6] He sued the State to have the land acquisition declared illegal, but on June 29, 1962, the courts ruled in the State's favor and demolition for the South Mall project began July 11, 1962. On August 30, 1962 Mayor Corning announced that the city had withdrawn its opposition to the State's South Mall program after he reportedly found a law whereby the city would not lose tax monies.[7]

Residents of the South Mall area had varied reactions to the project. For some, "The South Mall project is a good thing. All these slums need to be torn down"; yet for another, "I just can't see taking everything away from the poor people. Rockefeller should go drop dead. If only we could get a poor man in office, one who knows our hardships. . . ."[8]

Another consequence of displacement may be seen in the case of the Cathedral of Immaculate Conception, its parishioners, and survival. The Cathedral, having escaped demolition, still stands on the corner of Eagle Street and Madison Avenue. Its spires rise against the newly defined skyline, which is dominated by the imposing forms of the Albany Mall. Although the Cathedral escaped destruction, the surrounding demolitions brought with them the removal of several hundred parishioners and their financial support.[9]

Mayor Corning's concern for alternative housing for the 9,000 residents being displaced by the South Mall marked the beginning of a long battle over the issue. On April 3, 1962 the State Division of Housing opened the South Mall Redevelopment Site Office to answer inquiries by residents and owners of South Mall property, and ultimately hoping to provide a relocation service. At this time James W. Gaynor, State Housing Commissioner, reported that the State did not intend to move any families from the South Mall site until it had relocation housing available for displaced families.[10] Harry A. Vodery, the Albany regional director of the National Association for the Advancement of Colored People, spoke out against both the city and the State and their actions regarding the Mall area. Vodery maintained that "had the Mayor used half as much energy in fixing up the city and building the much needed housing as he is fighting the state, the

mall situation might not have happened."[11] Vodery reported that survey results showed that while the black population in Albany doubled over eleven years, the available housing declined.

On February 1, 1967, Albany newspapers announced that construction of residential housing in the South Mall was scheduled to start in the fall of 1967. The housing was to provide approximately 440 apartment units for low and middle income families. The projected housing was to occupy a 9.2 acre site east of the Mall bound on the west by Eagle Street, on the south by Madison Avenue, and on the north and east by the mall's arterial approaches.[12] In August 1967, the plans were revealed and the design was hailed for its emphasis on the human element.[13] The apartments would be costly for the State to maintain while the residents would be paying a low rent. This aspect of the design was ridiculed, and it was even suggested that the State charge luxury rents for these apartments.[14]

On February 3, 1969, Governor Rockefeller announced that he was scrapping plans for the proposed South Mall Housing Project. The announcement claimed that the earmarked money, $18.4 million, would be banked for future use by the Housing Authority.[15] Three months after this announcement the city revealed alternative plans for housing. These plans also met with serious opposition to the point where one resident indicated that "the poor are 'serving warning' they've been promised so much but so little has been done since 1963 when the Mall site was cleared."[16]

Why Mayor Corning and the State Housing Authority abandoned the uprooted residents in their difficult situation was frequently asked. In 1969 W. David Gardner observed that once the Mall's financial package had been worked out, the Mayor and others involved did not press the need for new housing for displaced residents. Gardner noted that while nothing was done for the residents, the "slum lords," apartment owners, and those who owned businesses or their own homes in the area were paid generously for their holdings.[17] After an attempt to use the already cleared and partially built land,[18] the 9.2-acre South Mall Housing Project Site was eventually made into a parking lot.[19] The promised but never built housing project continued to be and remains today a bone of contention.

In Mayor Corning's March 1962 address to the Temporary State Commission on the Capital City, he emphasized two major objections to the South Mall project: 1) the violation of the displaced residents' human rights; and 2) the loss of tax revenues which would be necessary for providing municipal services to the South Mall complex.[20] Almost immediately, several suggestions were made regarding the possibilities for financing the Mall without the city losing tax revenue. The Albany Chamber of Commerce recognized the feasibility of private interests constructing buildings in the South Mall and leasing them back to the State. The Chamber of Commerce felt that such a plan would provide the State with economical office facilities without increasing bonded indebtness and the city with the tax revenues necessary for maintaining police, fire, water, street, and other services.[21] M. Perry Chapman, a planner from Rochester, New York, suggested that the State could restore the lost tax base by providing convention facilities, theaters, hotels, and shopping spaces to be built and maintained by the private sector.[22]

The loss of tax revenues to the city of Albany was only one problem with which Governor Rockefeller had to contend when working on a way to finance his project. The normal procedure, which is furnished by the State Constitution, Article 7, Section II, would have required Rockefeller to submit the project to the State Legislature.[23] The state voters would then have had to approve a bond issue which would provide funds for the project to the State. This process would have been time-consuming and would have brought risk of voter disapproval and proved to be unattractive to Rockefeller.

In 1964 Mayor Corning developed an alternative financing plan. The details of this plan provided that the city would sell the bonds to build the complex. The State would then occupy the building under a lease-purchase arrangement. After a specified period of time when the bonds were retired, the State would take over ownership of the complex.[24] The city's debt limit would not allow the Mall's $300 million price tag, however, and alternative bond financing was sought.[25] Of the two remaining sources of funding—the county or the State Teacher's Retirement Fund—the county's financing of the project was more acceptable because the interest rate was lower.[26] On May 11, 1965, an agreement was signed with the details of the financing package worked out including provisions to pay back lost taxes to both the city and county. This particular agreement met with disapproval, and Arthur Levitt (Democratic State Comptroller from 1955 to 1979) was notably absent at the ceremonies for the signing of the financial agreement. He issued a statement saying he had to approve the document but that his approval did not extend to the financial policies.[27]

With the laying of the cornerstone in June 1965, construction on the South Mall project began, and the originally anticipated costs began to rise. In 1967, Walter McQuade reported that the price, originally slated at $400 million, could escalate to nearly $1 billion.[28] Rockefeller defended the high cost of the project by claiming that the South Mall "may turn out to be the greatest thing to happen to this country in 100 years," and he repeated a similar sentiment in Senate Confirmation Hearings on his nomination as Vice-President of the United States in 1974: "We are ending up with what is going to be undoubtedly the most beautiful urban development in the United States."[29]

Arthur Levitt criticized the building program that was compressed into too short a time period in an inflationary era and maintained that this project, in addition to all other construction programs, intensified the pattern of over-spending and over-borrowing. Levitt stated, "The

symptoms of the disease are now upon us: unreliable estimates, lack of normal competition, escalation in cost, rising interest costs, and a heavy financial burden which will grow with each year."[30] Rockefeller defended his decision to let all contracts at once: "If we had stretched out the contracts for these buildings, there would have been a five-year delay and a hundred-percent rise in the costs."[31]

The use of space was also criticized as both inefficient and costly. In 1971 Eleanore Carruth published statistics indicating that out of 3,562,000 gross square-feet of space only 1,665,000 square-feet was usable as office space.[32] In 1976, Paul Goldberger offered a reason for the small percentage of usable space as compared to gross space. He wrote that efficiency in much of the complex was "put aside in favor of architecture, or in favor of what someone thought was architecture."[33] Evidently, the planning of office space for the Mall was inadequate. On January 26, 1975, the New York Times noted that the State still needed a half-million square-feet in private office space after the Albany Mall was complete.[34] With respect to costs, Eleanore Carruth supplied very detailed statistics. She stated that the average production cost in New York City for usable office space was $35 per square foot, whereas at the Albany Mall the production cost for usable space in the office buildings ranged from $120 to $230, and averaged more than $150 per square foot.[35]

The extravagant use of space and money received mixed reviews from other sources. The most favorable reactions came from those who had offices in the Mall. Judge Fred A. Young stated, "There's a lot of luxury I'll tell you. . . . But I don't think there's waste when you figure this thing is built to last 100 years after we've gone."[36] John C. Bryon, a civil engineer in the Office of General Services, maintained that "the construction cost is not that high, considering today's inflation and the cost of other major projects. . . ."[37] Others were indifferent to its price. Assemblyman Mark A. Siegel commented, "I have to admit I've become a closet mall freak. . . . I wouldn't buy it for $2 million, but since it's there, it's nice. . . ."[38] The immense amount of Vermont Pearl and Georgia Cherokee marble is often cited as one of the extravagances.[39] In 1972 it was considered the largest single undertaking being constructed in the nation.[40] In the Building Stone News, in 1972, it was noted that by using marble as an exterior finishing material, New York State would receive hundreds of years of service from the Albany Mall. It was praised for being a beautiful, sound and durable natural stone, and considered to be the most economical material that could have possibly been chosen for this project.[41] In 1979 marble slabs became "dangerously loose" on the Cultural Education Center and on the Swan Street Building, and the Office of General Services at the Albany Mall was in the process of suing both the architectural firm and construction company for the Swan Street Building for faulty design and workmanship.[42]

Throughout the Albany Mall's conception, planning, and construction, Nelson A. Rockefeller considered the Mall to be the start of Albany's revitalization. The role of the Mall as a factor in revitalizing downtown Albany is impossible to measure as there are no adequate statistics on this subject, but this issue has received a great deal of attention from the press since the announcement of the plans for the "South Mall Project" in 1962. Early on, in April 1962, it was predicted that the small businessman would become victim of relocation, as it is difficult to replace an already-established market.[43] It was noted by a planner for the city of Rochester that in order for the Mall to be a key factor in revitalizing downtown Albany, facilities would have to operate for more than the eight-hour working day.[44]

Contrary to the high hopes of State and city officials, planners, and those responsible for the South Mall Project, many businessmen who were left in areas adjacent to the project began to fear negative effects, especially the loss of established clientele, shortly after construction had begun. In 1968, three years after construction of the Mall began, one businessman said that until the completion of the Mall, it would be a matter of survival, and he added, "As for me, I don't know if I'll make it."[45] In another article in December 1968, business was described as ranging from "holding on" to "at its worst," and many merchants were disappointed that construction was not moving at a faster pace.[46] Although such negative feelings prevailed, there were high hopes that with the completion of some of the Mall's buildings, business would pick up.[47]

Officials from the Office of General Services, the office responsible for the design and construction of the Mall, continued to reassure community groups that the project "has to enrich the community in general."[48] Many officials predicted that in the long run the Mall would be the key to "a rosy future" in Albany.[49] In 1971 Carl E. Touhey, then president of the Albany Area Chamber of Commerce, claimed that "Before the last brick is set, the furor and criticism will come to a dead silence and we will strut like peacocks, telling visitors from throughout the world that we built the South Mall."[50] Amidst the negative feelings of the local businessmen and the high hopes of the State and city officials, less biased viewers made their own comments. William Farrell, a writer for the *New York Times,* found the Mall to be "an extravagant colossus" and felt it substantially contributed to the decline of the city's downtown shopping area."[51] It is interesting to note that in the years around 1970, the Albany Mall had few friends who were not government officials. In the early 1970s the buildings began to open. By the official dedication of the Mall on November 21, 1973, the Swan Street Building, the Justice and Legislative Buildings, as well as the Tower Building, were occupied.[52]

In March 1974, the *Knickerbocker News Union-Star* ran a series entitled "After the Mall . . . What Will It Mean for Albany?." This series attempted to evaluate the

68. View from south

effects of the Mall on the downtown business and residential communities. When this series was written, eight of the ten buildings were completed and a majority of the 11,000 employees had moved in. The last article in the series summed up what the problems had been all along and why the downtown area had not been revitalized to the levels of earlier expectations. What had been lacking, said Robert G. Fichtenberg, was an overall plan. Downtown Albany should have been redeveloped as a thriving business and convention center in phases, along with the development of the Mall.[53] It was noted in the first article of the series that finding a businessman who then saw the Mall as the salvation of the downtown area was nearly impossible.[54] Due to lack of planning, many storeowners moved their shops out of the downtown area to suburban shopping centers in order to survive.[55] The shoppers and businessmen questioned the policy that let the stores leave in the first place.[56]

Not all the sentiment was negative. Fred Rosenblatt, owner of a commercial office building, was convinced of the eventual success of downtown Albany. He felt that the energy crisis and the concentration of State employees in the downtown area would influence many to move into the downtown area to live, and that the residents would want to shop and eat downtown.[57] City officials and planners began to work on a transportation system which would move people in the Mall at the top of the hill to the business district at the bottom of the hill, a trip which few ventured on their lunch hour. Some of the ideas looked into were moving sidewalks and escalators or small buses.[53] (To my knowledge such a transportation system has never been developed.)

By the mid-seventies financial issues concerning the Albany Mall were quelled in the press, and more positive predictions appeared once again. In 1973, Commissioner of the Office of General Services, General O'Hara predicted, "The whole Mall has been like a crocus trying to get up from under the winter snow. Now it's blossoming and, in five to seven years, there'll be nothing but glowing praise for it."[59] To the extent that this became true, part of the credit is owed to community activists.

In 1970, Harold Rubin, president of the Center Square Association, the oldest neighborhood association in Albany, wrote to Rockefeller asking for the creation of a special zoning district which would surround the Mall.[60] It was not until July 1972, when McDonalds planned to build a restaurant across from the southeast corner of the Mall, that the state began to take action. At this time Harold Rubin asked the Albany Board of Building and Zoning Appeals to delay approval of the restaurant until a development plan was devised for the area. The Center Square Association was concerned about the long-range effects which McDonalds might have on the area immediately west of the Mall. Rubin explained, "No matter what you think of the Mall architecturally, it's certainly unique. We feel that the area to the west of it should be preserved as a reminder of Old Albany, free from neon lights and such eating places."[61] The Committee on the South Mall Environs was appointed in late 1972 by Governor Rockefeller. This committee aimed to serve the concerns of the State, the city, and the residents for the surrounding neighborhood. On October 1, 1973, the Committee presented its report to Governor Rockefeller and Mayor Corning. The report presented very specific recommendations for zoning, building types, heights and materials, and the general appearance of each of the defined neighborhoods. The committee worked on the premise that the South Mall and its environs were quite different in form and function, and recommended that the historic neighborhoods, properly conserved and rehabilitated, could be used to "provide an ideal foil for the monumental impact of the mall complex."[62]

In 1974, Richard J. Patrick, Albany City Planning Director and Co-Chairman of the Committee on the South Mall Environs, stated, "The theory is that the Mall should be like the Acropolis, monumental and self-contained. . . . I know this sounds corny but the fact is the Mall shouldn't have imitators."[63] The idea of the Mall being like the Acropolis comes from the 1962 report made on the South Mall Project by the Temporary State Commission on the Capital City and the Albany-Capital Harbour Subcommittee. This early committee wrote that "Government can be thought of as an 'idea' and as a 'business.' The 'idea' of government belongs on an acropolis."[64] The 1962 committee felt that its acropolis should have the qualities of a focal civic shrine, should dominate the work-a-day city, and should express the qualities of dignity, drama, and permanence inherent in the "idea" of government.[65]

The design of the Albany Mall has been praised and criticized for both its aesthetic and symbolic qualities. Not long after the Temporary State Commission on the Capital City and the Albany-Capital Harbour Subcommittee released the preliminary designs, the South Mall Project design was criticized. In September 1963 James

Burns writing for *Progressive Architecture* called the proposed South Mall Plan an "exercise in architectural pop art."[66] He described the buildings as "half a cantaloupe sliced on a bias" (the Meeting Center) and "forms of cubistic coition" (the four Agency Buildings and the Tower Building). The proposed Arch of Freedom (which would have stood where the Cultural Education Center now stands) was described as "a croquet wicket with avoirdupois" and the proposed Convention Center as "an upside-down orange half from a Kraft salad." Neither of these buildings were built.

Both Albany newspapers, the *Times-Union* and the *Knickerbocker News,* reacted to this notice with fury.[67] The articles are basically the same, and both writers maintained that James Burns, who was not an architect, was too critical of the "Culpable Parties," which Burns named as "architects Wallace K. Harrison, George A. Dudley and Blatner and Williams, plus that would-be architect Governor Nelson A. Rockefeller."[68] When Jan Rowen, editor of *Progressive Architecture* in 1963, was interviewed, he explained that "most serious people in the profession take a strong exception to it [the South Mall]."[69] The "unrepentant Mr. Burns," when interviewed for the *Times-Union* article, said a design competition should have been held and "designs architecturally better and more suited to such a project" would have been produced.[70]

To our knowledge, the architecture of the South Mall was not reviewed again until after the model went on display in the State Capitol in June 1969. T.H. Littlefield, an art critic for the *Times-Union* in 1969, compared the architecture of the South Mall to the 1933 Century of Progress Chicago World's Fair.[71] Littlefield compared the Cultural Education Center to the Golden Temple of Jehol, Chicago, and the Toltec Temple, Xochicalco; the Meeting Center to the Perisphere at the New York World's Fair of 1939; the Agency Buildings to the general exhibits group on Lake Michigan; the Tower Building to the Federal Building Towers of 1933; and the Swan Street Building facade to the Century of Progress's Hall of Science. In a later article, Littlefield referred to the architectural style of the Mall as Albany Baroque, and he advocated visiting the Mall while under construction as its most worthwhile visual image.[72]

Littlefield was not the only critic who thought that the architectural style predated its conception. Kenneth Evett, writing for the *New Republic* in 1973, described the buildings as overly conspicuous skyscrapers or monumental low-rise buildings. The monumental low-rise buildings "present a sampling of modern architectural cliches" designed in a "quasi-classical, quasi-brutalist style."[73] A staff member for the *New York Times* suggested on March 15, 1974, that "The mall itself, a circa 1910 Beaux-Arts dream in Pop-up Futurama style, is something that many find more surreal than stately."[74]

Writing two years later, in 1976, and again in 1977, Paul Goldberger was more adamant about the outdated design of the Mall.[75] He wrote that the mall complex was

69. View from south with the four Agency Buildings. The nineteenth-century State Capitol Building is at the end of the Mall.

not a vision of the future but one of the past: "The ideas here were dead before they left the drawing board." He argued that every design decision emerged "from an out-dated notion of what modern architecture, not to men-tion modern government, should stand for." Goldberger noted that while many of Wallace K. Harrison's earlier designs were once considered progressive, the later de-signs had grown increasingly conservative. Goldberger found the buildings to be pompous, empty, and banal. The images which the buildings represent—"one part Buck Rogers to two parts warmed-over classicism"—held no real meaning, reported Goldberger.[76]

Among those who favored the architectural design were State officials and the architect Wallace K. Harri-son. John Bryon, Director of the South Mall Construc-tion, commented that the architects used a design which would "withstand the test of time." "Look around," he continued, "you won't see any 'trendy' architecture that will soon be dated."[77] Wallace K. Harrison also defended his design: "When talking about the Mall, you're talking about something that has been carefully studied, a culmi-nation of 50 years in design."[78]

Many critics of the Mall have found its most notable feature to be its aesthetic and symbolic links to fascist ar-chitecture. As mentioned earlier, the symbolic intent of the South Mall Complex was outlined by the 1962 com-mittee, but the intent seems not to have been clear to all viewers. Wolf von Eckardt was the first to associate the symbolic nature of the Mall with fascist architecture. In 1970, von Eckardt discussed psychiatrist Jules H. Masser-man's ideas of "Ur-defenses." Masserman said that the "Ur-defense" most prevalent among rulers is the delusion that their name and person will be immortalized in their indestructible granite monuments. Masserman cited Mus-solini's "Foro Mussolini" and Franco's "Valley of the Fallen" as recent examples.[79] This is an interesting con-cept in view of the renaming of the "Empire State Plaza" to the "Governor Nelson A. Rockefeller Empire State Plaza" on October 6, 1978. In 1979, Martin Filler gave a brief history of the Mall and its controversies and criti-cized the absence of a relationship between the buildings and the site at all levels. Filler claimed, "the scheme is such a naive hodgepodge of barely digested design ideas," and cited such predecessors as Yamasaki, Breuer, Le Corbusier, Oscar Niemeyer, and Albert Speer.[80] In his book, *The Shock of the New*, Robert Hughes classified the Albany Mall as "The International Power Style of the Fifties," a style that descended from fascism and nazism.

Hughes wrote that the Mall was designed for and expressed the centralization of power. He continued, "one could see any building at the Albany Mall with an eagle on top, or a swastika, or a hammer and sickle; it makes no difference to the building."[81]

These evaluations were harsh by any standard. The controversial past and present of the Empire State Plaza is a complicated story involving politics and social concerns, financial considerations, aesthetic evaluations, and a ponderous period of construction. These aspects of its history did not always interrelate happily. However, it should be noted that although the design and cost of the Mall were targets of considerable and sustained criticism during the planning and construction stages and for a short time after its official dedication, very little has been written about its more recent life as a functioning complex of offices and public spaces. At this writing, the office buildings seem to fulfill their roles as an environment for the workaday operation of various state agencies. The cost of creating sumptuous surroundings—the omnipresent marble sheathing, for example—is but an issue of the past to State and other workers and the visiting public, who now simply enjoy moving about the rich interiors.

In recent years the Mall has become something of a tourist attraction, drawing many thousands of visitors. Cultural events and exhibitions, permanent and temporary, are promoted through the Convention and Tourism Administration Office located in the Mall. By such efforts, the Mall has become a focal point for bus tours of central New York State; and travel sections of many regional newspapers, along with New York City's *Daily News,* have run feature articles on the Mall. Even some of the past controversies about the Mall have been usefully appropriated for promotional purposes. For example, a booklet prepared by the New York State Office of General Services proudly emphasizes the cost of the facility, touting the mall as "A $1 billion tourist attraction open to the public free of charge."

In 1981, Carol Herselle Krinsky noted that the Mall had become popular with local residents for a number of reasons.[82] It has encouraged architectural rehabilitation and gentrification. New businesses have moved in to do a brisk trade where the older merchants had closed during the period of construction. In the summer there have been concerts and other events held on the platform area; in the winter there has been ice-skating. There has been art on the Mall, as well as in the State Museum. William Kennedy, longtime resident of Albany, and winner of the Pulitzer Prize for his writings on the city, supported these observations with statistics in 1983, which showed the heavy usage of the Mall and its facilities.[83] These statistics include the following facts: 1) 800,000 people pass through the museum in the Cultural Education Center annually; 2) 405,000 used the convention facilities in the Mall in 1981; 3) 60,000 people came to the Youth Theater's production in the Egg; 4) 60,000 people attended performances of the national dance and drama companies which performed at the Egg; 5) 50,000

70. Crowds gather on the Mall

visitors guided themselves through the Mall; 6) 98,757 visitors took a guided tour of the capitol and the Mall; and 7) 40,000 people annually jam into the Mall plaza for Fourth of July fireworks.

Whether the Empire State Plaza has met all of the lofty goals and expectations set for it will no doubt continue to be a matter of speculation. At present, said Krinsky in 1981, "the Mall is something to which residents can point as being distinctively theirs, as being new, as being clean, and as being a sign that someone cared to make their city noticeable."[84] Ultimately, these qualities may mean more to people who use the architecture than any exalted theories of aesthetics or issues of taste. While some find Governor Rockefeller's vision disturbing, said Krinsky, others "will remember that a work of architecture does not have to be good to be popular, or to be tolerated, or to be promoted, or to be important. People do not always apply moral standards to its evaluation; they can like things of which they do not approve."[85]

Maria Pellerano

Notes

1. Joe Picchi, "New Look at Albany's South Mall Project, New Model Details Scope of Change in City's Future," *Times-Union* (Albany), June 15, 1969, E, 1–2.
2. Edward Swietnicki, "Rocky Tells of Mall Start," *Knickerbocker News,* January 20, 1972. This article reports on Governor Rockefeller's speech to the Albany Chamber of Commerce at their annual meeting on the Mall's conception. A description of the deterioration of Albany may be found in Paul Goldberger, "The Space Age Comes to the Empire State," *Horizon,* July 1977, 62. Goldberger credited Rockefeller with realizing that the State played a role in Albany's decline. Especially important was the gradual move of the state offices to a suburban office campus three miles from the State Capitol under the administrations of Thomas E. Dewey and Averell Harriman.
3. The details of the Princess Beatrix story were reported most fully in Joe Picchi, "Future Queen was 'Mother' of

71. Fireworks over the Mall at night

South Mall," *Times-Union*, February 1, 1980. This story was first mentioned in Richard L. Madden, "For Albany: A Major Face Lifting," *Herald Tribune*, December 20, 1964. Many other writers have conveyed this story in their articles since this early date. Wolf von Eckardt, "Rocky's Monumental Error, or the Billion Dollar Misunderstanding," *New York*, April 20, 1970, 29, reported that Rockefeller was embarrassed when he escorted Princess Liliane de Rethy (the second commoner wife of King Leopold III of Belgium) through Albany in 1963.

4. The Temporary State Commission of the Capital City and the Subcommittee on Albany-Capital Harbour, *Interim Report: Albany Capital Harbour*, 1962, 2–3. The revised report of 1963 was presented in a slipcase covered with a reproduction of G.P. Seurat's *A Sunday Afternoon on the Island of La Grande Jatte*.

5. See William Kennedy, "Everything Everybody Ever Wanted," *Atlantic Monthly*, May 1983, 78–81, for a good description of "the Gut" before it was cleared. He focused on the locally "famous" personages. He also included a bit of history about the Mall, its funding, and legislation.

6. Erastus Corning II, "Text of Corning Statement to State," *Knickerbocker News*, March 27, 1962. In this statement, Corning criticized the plan for its lack of consideration of the residents living in the area, for the anticipated loss of tax revenue to the City of Albany, and for the economic loss which would result from unemployment caused by displaced business.

7. Dick Weber, "Cheers Greet Surrender on Mall, Voices of Approval Drown Out Worried Comments of Mall Residents," *Knickerbocker News*, August 31, 1962. In reference to this law, Edward S. Conway, Albany

County Republican Chairman stated in this article, "The Mayor obviously referred to Section 545 of the Real Property Tax law which was effective April 4, 1962 after being passed by the Republican Legislature and signed by Governor Rockefeller as part of his program."

8. Weber, "Cheers Greet Surrender."

9. Jack Pietro "Mall Forcing Cathedral to Fight for Survival," *Times-Union*, October 14, 1968.

10. Dick Weber, "State Promises Homes for Residents of Mall," *Knickerbocker News*, April 3, 1962.

11. "Albany Aims to Halt Housing, NAACP Official Charges," *Knickerbocker News*, May 4, 1962, A, 4. Vodery also reported that eleven percent of the housing available to black people had been torn down, burned or declared unusable.

12. "South Mall Housing Set," *Knickerbocker News*, February 1, 1967.

13. "The Mall's Futuristic Housing" (editorial), *Knickerbocker News*, August 2, 1967.

14. "Luckiest Tenants in the World" (editorial), *Times-Union*, October 8, 1968. The anonymous writer claimed that the monthly cost to the State would average $453.90 per month, while the tenant would only pay approximately $67.38 per month. The writer suggested that if a rent proportionate to the cost of the apartment were charged, the housing officials would have plenty of tenants, thus relieving the already burdened taxpayer. (The high cost of this housing was attributed to its proximity to the South Mall and the general feeling that the housing project should conform to the architectural theme of the Mall; see Joe Picchi, "South Mall Housing Project: Expensive for Many Reasons," *Times-Union*, October 20, 1968, B, 1,8.)

15. Roy Neville, "City Perplexed at Housing Back-Down," *Times-Union*, February 5, 1969, 3. Rockefeller declared the expenditure for housing to be "way out of line." Martin Filler in "Halicarnassus on the Hudson (The Governor Nelson A. Rockefeller Empire State Plaza)," *Progressive Architecture*, 60, May 1979, 106, noted that the total cost for the housing project would have been one-percent of the total cost of the entire South Mall Project.

16. Roy Neville, "Housing Sites Create Jungle, Residents Say," *Times-Union*, May 14, 1969. The major criticisms of the alternative housing plans pointed out that high-rise projects tend to be "concrete jungles"; that sites were all planned for the extremes of the city where living is considered undesirable; that such plans would perpetuate the ghettos; and that the citizens should have more input in the choice of sites. This article also reported that when residents attempted to meet with State officials regarding the abandonment of the South Mall Housing Project, someone told them it was none of their business.

17. W. David Gardner, "Mister Rockefeller Builds His Dream House," *Ramparts*, September 1969, 36. In this article, Gardner focused on the financial aspects of the Mall. He also discussed the displacement of residents and the housing which was never provided to them.

18. In August 1970 the Albany Housing Authority had approved the sale of part of the 9.2-acre tract to be used for church-sponsored middle-income housing for the elderly. This sale was first reported in John Mc-Loughlin, "Albany OKs Mall Land Sale for Middle Income Housing," *Times-Union*, August 18, 1970. This sale never came to pass, but the Capital Area Council of Churches, with help from the State Division for Housing and Community Renewal, built South Mall Towers, a pair of high-rise apartment houses for senior citizens on South Pearl Street just above Madison Avenue. This was reported in "The Mall's Neighbors, Some Fear It as a Trap, Others Hope It Will Give the Area New Life," *Knickerbocker News Union-Star*, March 7, 1974, B, 1.

19. Mark Libbon, *City of Marble: A Look Into the Empire State Plaza*, Albany, 1977, 9. The *City of Marble* is a twenty-one-page booklet independently published by Mark Libbon and sold at local Albany newsstands. In an interview for Robert Basler, "He Sees Cracks in the 'City of Marble'," *Knickerbocker News*, July 22, 1977, Libbon described the book as a history and guide to the Mall.

20. Corning, "Text of Corning's Statement to State."

21. "Albany C. of C. Hails Agreement on Mall," *Knickerbocker News*, August 31, 1962.

22. M. Perry Chapman, "A Planner Writes on Mall Project" (letter to editor), *Times-Union*, September 18, 1962. He also suggested that the city build a civic auditorium which would promote convention activity and cultural endeavors.

23. See Libbon, "City of Marble," 7.

24. First reported in Madden, "For Albany: A Major Face Lifting."

25. "The Mall: Too Much Delay" (editorial), *Knickerbocker News*, February 18, 1965.

26. Dick Weber, "Mall Financing Problem," *Knickerbocker News*, January 20, 1965. The interest that the county would charge was then 3½ percent whereas the interest on the State Teacher's Retirement Fund would have been 4½ to 4⅝ percent.

27. Doc Rivett, "Work to Start Soon South Mall Pact Signed," *Times-Union*, May 12, 1965, 1, 7. In the same month comptroller Levitt wrote: "Such financing is not only a circumvention of moral constitutional procedures, but it is necessarily more expensive than financing through the direct issuance of full-faith-and-credit obligations of the State of New York. True, the latter method is slower and more uncertain, because it requires the approval of the People. But this is exactly what the framers of the constitutional provision intended: deliberation in the incurrence of debt, with review and consent by popular referendum." Cited in Samual Bleeker, *The Politics of Architecture: A Perspective on Nelson A. Rockefeller*, New York, 1981, 195.

28. Walter McQuade, "New York Rebuilds Its Capital," *Fortune*, May 1967, 173.

29. Joe Picchi, "Rocky·Defends His Mall As 'One-in-a-Century,' " *Times-Union*, January 29, 1971; and James E. Underwood and William J. Daniels, *Governor Rockefeller in New York: The Apex of Pragmatic Liberalism in the United States*, Westport, Connecticut, 1982, 208.

30. Von Eckardt, "Rocky's Monumental Error," 29.

31. Picchi, "Rocky Defends His Mall."

32. Eleanore Carruth, "What Price Glory on the Albany Mall?," *Fortune*, June 1971, 95.

33. Paul Goldberger, "The Albany Mall: Cliches of Modern Architecture," in *On The Rise*, New York, 1983, 158. This review originally appeared in the *New York Times*, July 2, 1976. In 1977 Paul Goldberger noted that Nelson Rockefeller's fondness for major and costly construction projects dated back to the 1930s when he worked with his father John D. Rockefeller, Jr. on the construction and management of Rockefeller Center, New York City (Goldberger, "The Space Age," 62). Goldberger also cited the specific extravagances of the buildings on the Mall.

34. Linda Greenhouse, "Albany Mall's Space Inadequate for State Workers," *New York Times*, January 26, 1975, 41.

35. Carruth, "What Price Glory," 95.

36. Frances X. Clines, "Legislators Pick Art for the Mall Group Selecting the Works Is Avoiding Abstracts," *New York Times*, March 26, 1972, 52. In 1977 Paul Goldberger noted that many employees evaluated the Mall in terms of amenities for their daily routines, such as underground parking space, the convenient location of coffee and snack areas to work spaces, or the lack of stores for shopping at noontime (Goldberger, "The Space Age," 67).

37. Harold Faber, "After 15 Years, Downtown Albany's Empire State Plaza Is Completed," *New York Times*, May 28, 1978, 42.

38. Stephen R. Weisman, "Albany Mall Is Enjoyed by Friend and Foe Alike," *New York Times*, June 24, 1976, 35.

39. Libbon, "City of Marble," 2.

40. Willy Amheim, "A Pictorial Report: Albany's South Mall Complex Moves Toward Completion Stage," *Building Stone News*, July 1972, 7.

41. Amheim, "Pictorial Report," 7.
42. See Sheila Rule, "Albany Aide Cites Supplier as Marble Falls from Mall," *New York Times*, April 22, 1979, 59; and Eric Freedman, "State Sues 2 Firms for Flaws at Mall," *Knickerbocker News Union-Star*, August 7, 1979. The State was suing for $25 million in damages plus interest from New York City architectural firm of Carson, Lundin and Thorson, and $28 million plus interest from Penn York Construction Corp., the successor to Foster-Lipkins Corporation, of Long Island.
43. Weber, "State Promises Homes." James W. Gaynor, State Housing Commissioner, made these observations regarding the predicament of the small businessman.
44. Chapman, "A Planner Writes on the Mall Project."
45. Swietnicki, "Mall Affects 'Inner City'," *Knickerbocker News*, June 20, 1968, C, 2. Swietnicki compares what would eventually be the Albany Mall to Brasilia.
46. Ed Manogue, "South Pearl Businessmen Bank on the Mall," *Times-Union*, December 8, 1968, E, 1. The general tenor of this article was negative as many businessmen were close to failing. A florist who had been in downtown Albany for sixty years said, "This is the worst business has ever been here. Even during the depression, business wasn't as bad as this."
47. Manoque, "South Pearl Businessmen," 2.
48. "Employment Factor Stressed in Schodack Talk, Mall Impact Many-Sided Club Told," *Knickerbocker News*, February 7, 1969. When questioned further, the official said it was difficult to predict what the specific benefits to communities in the area would be.
49. Ralph Thompson, "Rocky Says Albany Has a Rosy Future and He'll Stay on Til Mall Is Done," *Times-Union*, January 12, 1971.
50. Thompson, "Albany Has A Rosy Future."
51. William E. Farrell, "Albany Mall Reveals High Price of Renaissance Downtown Declining as New Steel and Marble Rises," *New York Times*, February 15, 1971, 44.
52. This is when Governor Rockefeller renamed the complex the Empire State Plaza. The official dedication scheduled for October 1974 was rescheduled by Rockefeller, who resigned as Governor on December 11, 1973 with one year left to his term. Information from Libbon, "City of Marble" 17–21.
53. Robert G. Fichtenberg, "Albany's Symphony in Marble A Commentary; Mall: the Gamble May Stem from Blight," *Knickerbocker News Union-Star*, March 12, 1974.
54. "The Mall: Will It Fulfill Its Promise?," *Knickerbocker News Union-Star*, March 5, 1974, A, 10.
55. "Treading Water in Downtown Albany," *Knickerbocker News Union-Star*, March 6, 1974, B, 1. In this article it was reported that Sy Solomon, owner of Solomon's Furs, had moved out of his downtown store in 1972, and relocated in Colonie, a suburb of Albany, and that he was still unable to sell his empty store in downtown Albany.
56. "Mall Views Change as Buildings Grow from 'Tragedy' to 'Asset'," *Knickerbocker News Union-Star*, March 8, 1974, B, 1.
57. "Treading Water in Downtown Albany,"1.
58. "From 'Tragedy' to 'Asset'," 1.
59. M.A. Farber, "Albany Mall Proves Dazzling to Inhabitants," *New York Times*, January 25, 1973, 43.
60. Linda Greenhouse, "Mall Neighbors in Fight to Preserve Charm," *New York Times*, February 20, 1974, 39.
61. John McLoughlin, "Hamburger Stand by Mall Is Opposed," *Times-Union*, July 7, 1972.
62. Joint City/State Committee on the South Mall Environs, "Report on the Committee of South Mall Environs," 1973, 3.
63. Greenhouse, "Mall Neighbors in Fight," 39.
64. Temporary State Commission, "Interim Report," 4.
65. Temporary State Commission, "Interim Report," 4.
66. "Cacophony of Forms in New Capital," *Progressive Architecture*, 44, September 1963, 70. James Burns's authorship of this article is revealed in a review by Michael Pilley, "Scrap All Mall Plans, Says Magazine Writer," *Times-Union*, September 27, 1963.
67. Pilley, "Scrap All Mall Plans," and William Ringle, "Now They're Picking on Our South Mall," *Knickerbocker News*, September 26, 1963, A, 1–2.
68. "Cacophony of Forms," 70.
69. Ringle, "Picking on Our South Mall," 1.
70. Pilley, "Scrap All Mall Plans."
71. T.H. Littlefield, "Spirit of Chicago Fair Pervades South Mall Architecture," *Times-Union*, June 15, 1969, E, 3.
72. T.H. Littlefield, "Where Do We Go From Here," *Times-Union*, February 8, 1970, 1.
73. Kenneth Evett, "The Albany Mall," *New Republic*, February 1973, 23. The monumental low-rise buildings which Evett referred to are the Justice, Legislative, and Swan Street Buildings. The skyscrapers he referred to are the Tower and the four Agency Buildings.
74. "State Capital," *New York Times*, March 15, 1974, 32.
75. Goldberger, "The Albany Mall: Cliches," 159; and Goldberger, "The Space Age,"65–66.
76. Goldberger, "The Space Age," 71.
77. Doug de Lisle, "Architect Hotly Defends His Project," *Sunday Record* (Albany), August 1, 1976.
78. De Lisle, "Architect Hotly Defends His Project."
79. Von Eckardt, "Rocky's Monumental Error," 26.
80. Martin Filler, "Halicarnassus on the Hudson (The Governor Nelson A. Rockefeller Empire State Plaza)," *Progressive Architecture*, 60, May 1979, 106. This article includes photographs by Ezra Stoller.
81. Robert Hughes, "The Faces of Power," *The Shock of the New*, New York, 1981, 108.
82. Carol Herselle Krinsky, "St. Petersburg-on-the-Hudson: The Albany Mall," *Art the Ape of Nature*, ed. Moshe Barasch and Lucy Friedman, New York, 1981, 785. Comparing the Albany Mall to St. Petersburg, the second city of Imperial Russia, Carol Herselle Krinsky presented a comprehensive article on the Mall. She described its physical features, its legislative and financial history, the ethical issues involved, and its aesthetic value. The notes provide a good bibliography.
83. Kennedy, "Everything Everbody Ever Wanted," 88.
84. Krinsky, "St. Petersburg-on-the-Hudson," 785.
85. *Ibid.*

72. Top: Gehry House (color plate on page 37). View of entrance front on 22nd Street
73. Bottom: Gehry House backyard

100

GEHRY HOUSE

Santa Monica, California

Architects: Frank O. Gehry and Associates

The critical fortunes of the Gehry House began in mid-1977, when Frank and Berta Gehry bought a nondescript two-story house on the southwest corner of Washington and 22nd Streets in Santa Monica, California. The previous owners had covered the exterior walls with asbestos shingles painted a shade of pink that is not remarkable in Southern California, and the living quarters had been converted into a so-called mother-daughter combination, with a separate entrance, a second kitchen, and a full bath upstairs. The Gehrys re-converted the house to a single family dwelling and enlarged it on three sides with the addition of an angular sleeve of corrugated metal, glass, and exposed wood framing. To the original 2100 square feet of the house, some 800 square feet were added to the ground story and 680 square feet of deck at the second level. The work was completed to the design of architect/owner Frank O. Gehry between January and September 1978.

Along the entrance front on 22nd Street, the pink building is sheathed by a plane of corrugated metal that is broken by the insertion of the front door and pierced by windows on either side of it. The fact that one window is glazed and the other unglazed introduces an ambiguous distinction between enclosed and unenclosed space and that impression is enhanced by the spatial volumes defined by chain link over the doorway. The strong sense of layering reappears under the apex of the roof on the lateral walls of the house, where a window has been cut into the asbestos siding to reveal the wood framing; and within that glazed reveal, a single pane with a hinged sash has been inserted. In this manner, the notion of additive layering in some areas is contrasted to other sections of the house where successive layers of the building are peeled back and revealed. These ideas and the ambivalent sense of enclosure are also suggested in the large but irregular shape of the prominent window on the front right side of the house, where one side pane overlaps the other to blur the neatness of the corner and where there are no calmly horizontal or stately vertical edges.

Along Washington Street the corrugated sheath is again interrupted where a bay window for the new addition seems to have been wedged askew. The force of its

74. View of opening in corrugated wall on Washington Street

apparent dislocation is expressed in the bent and seemingly broken net of chain link above the glazed volume, and in the need to cut a level, operable window on the metal sill. Outside the kitchen, a picket fence chatters its way down the edge of the property, past the house and a trapezoidal "window" opening into the backyard. The opening frames a desert cactus in the yard like a desolate still life. And from the yard the entire scheme is revealed as a stage set: the corrugated metal, a thin wall, is backed with plywood and propped up by 2 × 4s, as is the cactus.

The house opens to the backyard through a row of simple glass doors that stand just beyond the old confines of the house, encasing and memorializing it. Inside, the structure of the older house has been selectively stripped of its plaster walls and ceilings to reveal the

75. Skewed window

76. Kitchen

wooden framing of studs and joists. In some areas where the architect sought to expose and preserve sections of wood lath underneath the plaster, the strips were too rotted to save and had to be replaced by fresh ones.

The kitchen runs from the front to the back of the new addition, with eating areas at both ends. It is paved with black asphalt, and a hose is used to clean the floor. (There are two drains in the middle of the space.) The kitchen paving is at grade level, whereas the level of the rest of the house was left on its original foundations several steps higher. The original windows on this side of the house were preserved *in situ;* they separate the living room from the new kitchen and frame the views from one space to the other. Because the ceiling height remains constant between the old and new areas, the lower floor of the kitchen provides an airy work space that is brightly lit by the skewed cubical window. The fact that the sill of this window is some six feet above the ground permits almost complete privacy from the street, while the cube window admits a maximum amount of light and dramatic views of the tall trees along the property line.

The paradoxical aspect of the remodeling is that Gehry's interventions preserved the old house almost entirely and even restored it to the extent that it was made a single family dwelling as originally constructed. In remodeling it as a primary residence for his family, Gehry concocted an ambitious formal relationship of framed views between the old and new building. At times this relationship is lovingly nostalgic; at other times it is more contentious. For the casual observer, however, the most prominent aspect of the house is the extensive use of such unlikely materials as corrugated metal and chain link, and the display of so much raw carpentry and such protrusive glass edges.

The first printed criticism of the house appeared just months before completion, in an article by John Dreyfuss in the *Los Angeles Times* in July 1978, when neighbors must have realized how the finished building would look.[1] The statements of the neighbors quoted in the article were of various sorts: some claimed to understand the design, while others did not; among those who liked the building, all had been treated to a tour of it, whereas those with objections to it seemed to have judged the

77. View from Washington Street

building only by its exterior. A man a few doors away described the house as "antisocial" and intentionally designed to offend. "It's a dirty thing to do in somebody else's front yard," he complained. Another resident saw the house as an imposition of "a piece of art on a quiet neighborhood that we may or may not like to live with." Others did not pretend to know what the architect's intentions were—they simply objected to the way the house looked. One person labelled the house a "monstrosity" and claimed to speak for the whole block.

The fact is that most of those who saw the building inside and out (Gehry gave informal tours) came away with a new appreciation of it. Called by a distressed citizen, the mayor of Santa Monica inspected the house to determine that it complied with city codes and came away a convert. "A masterpiece," she professed, "I love it."[2] A member of the city council was less enthusiastic. Having toured the house after receiving a complaint, the council member concluded that it would be "a nice house to live in, but not to look at"—an assessment that is less remarkable for its candor than for its solomonic gesture to political expediency.

Despite local opinion, Dreyfuss predicted that the house would attract national attention. He also pointed out, as so many others would, that a visit was necessary to begin to appreciate Gehry's intentions. Aware of the perspectival tricks in the composition, of the use of industrial materials and exposed studs as sculpture, and of the surrealistic implications involved in viewing the old house through openings in the new one, Dreyfuss praised "this strange, exciting, thought-provoking build-

ing of highly sophisticated beauty."[3]

A month after its local debut in print, the Gehry House was discussed again in the *Evening Outlook* (Santa Monica) where again the general impressions of the public remained negative.[4] One neighbor called the house an "eyesore" that was out of character with its surroundings and refused to see the interior. A more curious neighbor hoped to tour the inside but remained skeptical of Gehry's rumored intention to have the house look unfinished: "I hardly think that's fair," she said, "If it would ever look completed, I might get used to it."[5] Obviously affected by the tenor of the criticism levelled at the unfinished building, Gehry reasserted the seriousness of his intentions, the desire of his family to live there, and his hope that the neighbors would accept the house once they saw it in its finished state. The *Evening Outlook* article described the feeling at 22nd Street and Washington as "intense," while also reporting that half-a-block away, a resident hadn't heard of the issue, didn't know the people involved, and hadn't seen the house.

Dreyfuss's prediction that the Gehry House was destined for national attention proved correct. Within three months the house reached a broader public in an article by Paul Goldberger in *New York* magazine in the fall of 1978. The notice was an exhibition review devoted to Gehry's work, especially the architect's house.[6] Goldberger observed a metaphorical significance in the angular juxtapositions of forms that so strongly suggest colliding elements and jumbled composition; he recognized in these motifs an allusion to the juxtaposition "between physical forms and between conceptual ideas of what a

78. Bedroom

79. Living room

building can be." Thus, Gehry's apparent nonchalance and lack of conventional finish "plays at being far more primitive than it truly is." For Goldberger, the rugged finishes provoked a reconsideration of the elemental aspects of composition.

These observations might have answered the objections of the neighbors in Santa Monica but probably would not have satisfied them. More important, Goldberger saw ideas in the house that were purely formal in nature. In essence, he drew a contrast between these ideas and the work of architects more involved with historical quotation or popular imagery, and saw in Gehry's work a closer alliance with a tradition of abstraction.

Not all reviewers were as responsive as Goldberger to the display of Gehry's works. In the tabloid *Skyline,* Steven Harris insisted that the compositions were "based on nothing more complicated than the primacy of orthogonal organization, at least when verticality is assumed to be the norm."[7] In his view the instability suggested in these compositions lacked a static context against which they could be measured and thus fell short of the achievements of the great Russian constructivists. If it was reminiscent of Duchamp or Schwitters, the Gehry House nevertheless lacked "specific internal references." And while the use of chain link related to other architects' use of vernacular elements, "the ability to transcend the mundane through specific references to architectural elements is absent." In sum, the Harris review brought to bear a sequence of preconceived standards and found it lacking. Within four months the simple inability to appreciate Gehry's intentions had been catapulted from a Santa Monica neighborhood to the East Coast and echoed in the jargon of architectural

theory. As Philip Johnson was later to say of the Gehry House, "It's so far out of normal expectation that it defies traditional criticism."[8]

By 1979-80 the reputation of the Gehry House had spread to a national and international audience and captured the imagination, if not the universal affection, of professionals and non-professionals alike. In the United States, references and pictures appeared in *Time* magazine in January 1979 and in *People* two months later.[9] By 1980, local newspapers all over the country carried stories about the house.[10] The Southern California Chapter of the American Institute of Architects awarded the house a Citation in 1979, and the national AIA gave it an Honor Award in 1980.[11] And in the same years the "dedicated" art and architectural journals in America followed with major critical pieces, occasionally "scooped" by the foreign architectural press from Tokyo to Italy that rushed its coverage of Gehry's house and his other works into print. On this evidence, it can apparently take less than six months for a building to become nationally famous, and less than eighteen months to gain substantial international attention.[12]

One of the striking features of the critical literature on the Gehry House is the degree to which later discussion had been anticipated by the architect's statement published in the *International Architect* in 1979.[13] In that statement Gehry's intentions in establishing a dialogue between the old and new house were made clear. The "freshness" of the dialogue was to be maintained by preserving an unfinished appearance in the deployment of colliding forms and the raw treatment of materials. By "editing" views of the old house through surviving doors, windows, and framing, an element of surrealism was in-

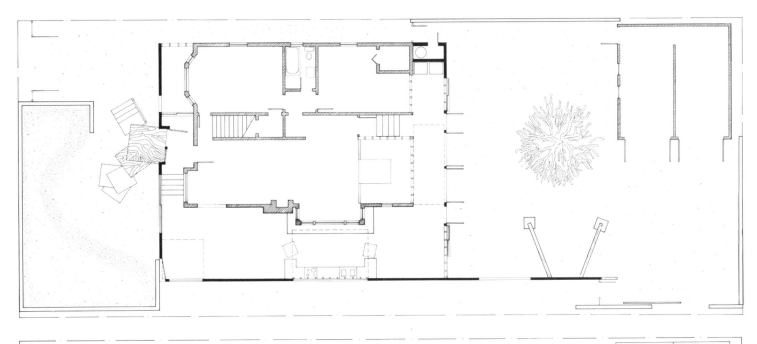

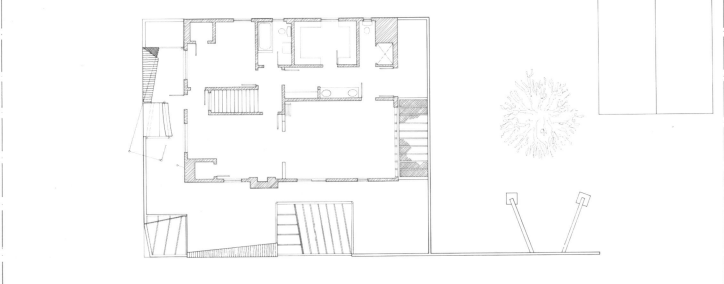

80. First floor plan

81. Second floor plan

troduced. This effect was intentionally enlivened by layering the additions to create ambiguous readings of interior-exterior relationships. Nostalgic imagery was introduced through abstract forms such as the chain link sections on the roof that, Gehry admitted, may have been inspired by playground backstops. The notion of using common building materials to create art objects was made explicit by Gehry's mention of artists like Rauschenberg, Serra, Andre, and Judd, who had influenced him[14]

To some degree the architect's own assessment must have contributed to the critical opinions about the house, but a larger portion of the credit must be due to the architecture itself. Over and over, the critics repeated that photography could do no justice to the house but rather emphasized its most abrasive characteristics without communicating any of the warm, homelike, and traditional atmosphere conveyed by a visit.[15] But misgivings about the ambience and misunderstandings based on photographs hardly explain the objections of some commentators to what seemed like a new language of form.

In *Progressive Architecture,* for example, Suzanne Stephens was disturbed by the mixing of art and architecture:

The combination of a system of elements that belong distinctly to art and one that belongs to architecture creates the basic split—and consequent malaise. As a mixed-media work, the

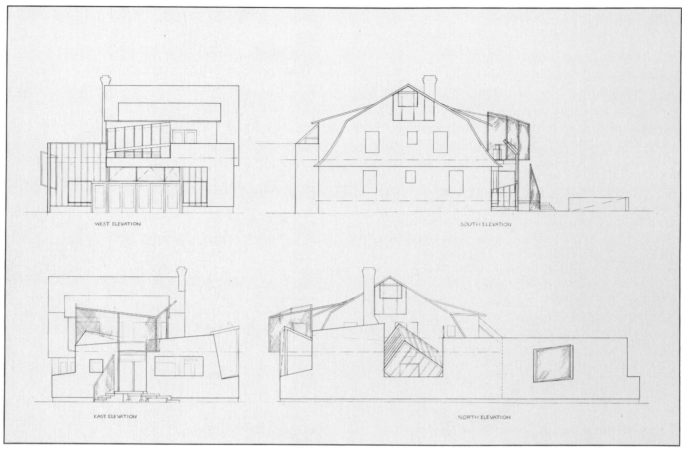

82. Elevations

melding of forms creates neither a work of art nor a work of architecture, and thus becomes contrived. . . . By appropriating modern art's abstracted relationships and nonobjective qualities for a habitable dwelling, Gehry violates the basic premise of modern art, that it be about art and its own process.[16]

Stephens went on to suggest that the principles of modernist architecture—"principles like open plan, expressed structure, and so on"—provided a conceptual and physical coherence that the Gehry House lacked. "Without acknowledging the difference between use put to the vocabularies of art and architecture," she claimed, "we are left with an amalgam of art parts and architecture parts."[17]

The notion that the house was an assemblage of art parts was an early and persistent theme in the literature. Although he gave it an award, Helmut Jahn described the Gehry House as "a pure piece of art, and in its methods and techniques falls short of total integrated architecture."[18] In a discussion with Kenneth Frampton reported in *Art in America* (June 1980), Gehry responded to the charge that his work was "subversive" and "anti-architectural" with the comment that he considered his own work to be too architectural.[19] In a conference on "Art and Architecture: A Changing Relationship," Gehry's point of view was clear from the title of his address:

"What's the Difference What You Call It."[20] In Gehry's view,

> an artist . . . has a material problem to solve, he has a visual problem to solve and he personally expresses himself with materials within a confine and I think architecture is the same. The confines are different—we have political issues, we have social issues, we have technical issues. . . . We are having great arguments now about whether architecture is art, who is an artist, who is an architect and what the differences are. I have been in a few of those debates and it always ends up that the difference is the architect is willing to put a toilet in his structure.[21]

In the July 1980 issue of the *Architectural Review*, which carried a survey of his recent work with a text by Barbara Goldstein, the review began by heralding Gehry as "one of a handful of architects in the United States who can unabashedly and truthfully describe himself as an artist."[22] Evidently, this reviewer found no difficulty in reconciling art and architecture, artist and architect in one person and his buildings. Goldstein emphasized the contrived aspect of a design process that included stripping a wall and rebuilding in such a way that its insulation and wooden lath were left to show. While mocking the usual preoccupations with fine finish, Gehry had also glorified the construction process, and Goldstein concluded that "his work is art, and it is ironic in nature."[23]

Among those critics who were most concerned as to whether the formal qualities of the house lay more in the province of art or architecture, the question of its associative imagery was largely unexplored. But the notion that the house design contained associative, some say specifically Jungian, content persisted in the comments of many critics. Hodgetts had alluded to this matter in a brief *Skyline* notice, and others brought up the issue repeatedly. For Hodgetts, the house "resonates with memorials to the American life style: if one cooks in the driveway, it's because that's what used to happen on Saturdays in the summer; if the living room feels like an attic, it's because it's probably more fun to be up there anyway; if the terraces end in backstops, you can at least play catch."[24] This is the way he explained, respectively, the asphalt kitchen floor, the living room with exposed joists, and the wild assembly of chain link deployed on the upper story. Goldstein described the kitchen as "an old fashioned room which is surrealistically suspended in the memory of a school yard." "The kitchen," she suggested, "seems to rest on an asphalt playing field, with a chain link sports structure floating above."[25] Pastier suggested that the house could be discussed from many points of view as art, architecture, or mere curiosity, but that it should also be considered "as a manifestation of nonlinear logic, visual symbolism and the Jungian collective unconscious."[26] Pastier shied from this task, but pointed out that the complex interior spaces bear equally complex inner meanings. Pastier concluded that the Gehry House was an especially appropriate place for Frank and Berta Gehry's two little boys "for it is a timeless incarnation of all the houses that children have imagined in their dreaming and their playing in attics, and even on the first visit it gives one the inexplicable feeling of having been there before."[27] By shearing the walls of shingles and plaster, Pastier suggested, Gehry "also laid bare part of his soul, and part of ours as well."

To such an analysis, and the architecture that inspired it, Wolf von Eckardt was quite impervious. He likened Pastier's commentary to the proverbial emperor's new clothes and the architecture to "a well-stocked lumberyard viewed through a telescope."[28] As to Pastier's notions about nonlinear logic, visual symbolism, and the collective unconscious, von Eckardt was utterly dismissive: "they did this sort of thing some 65 years ago in Zurich and called it Dada." But the issue persisted in the discussion of Gehry's work. Morgenstern, writing in the *New York Times Magazine* in 1982, claimed the house to be "autobiographical in a loose, metaphorical way . . . and in a literal way, too."[29] He quoted Gehry's sister Doreen Nelson on this point:

> Here's this flat sheet of metal outside and Frank saying, "I've parted it for you so you can come in." And what's inside is our grandparents' house in Toronto on Beverly Street, with the

83. Kitchen and skylight

dark stairway leading up to the bedrooms. When Frank bought that pink house, he did a transformation not only on the house but on himself. He put all this stuff around it to present himself as a new person, but an *old* new person who's still connected to where he came from and who he was.[30]

The occasion for von Eckardt's comments was the publication of the AIA Honors Award in 1979. The jury comment indicated that the Gehry award had been the most controversial given that year and that the jury had been particularly concerned about the fact that the house "was out of context with the immediate neighborhood."[31] But even that conclusion could be open for debate, depending on one's definition of context and neighborhood. Before the house was completed, the neighbors were complaining publicly that the house was "out of character with this part of the neighborhood."[32] In Gehry's view there was no unity to the architecture in the area to begin with.[33] On the other hand, Gehry had argued less convincingly that he had tried to be "contex-

84. Backyard facade

85. Chain link on second floor

tual" by building out to the allowable setback lines.[34] He also claimed that "the most important things on the street are the sky and the trees and the whole house is built to help emphasize them."[35] In fact, reflections of the surroundings are amply mirrored on the windows seen from both the exterior and the interior, and Gehry is particularly proud of the way he adjusted the corner window of the house to produce a reflection of the kitchen ceiling lights at night: the reflections on the glass line up perfectly with a street lamp seen through the window on the corner of Washington and 22nd Streets.[36] To some extent the issue of context is a matter of semantics, and Goldberger stated the issue most clearly when he wrote that "The house makes none of the gestures toward relating to context that architects have come to employ in recent years and laymen have tended to prefer all along."[37] Goldberger even considered the house a dangerous model to follow: "A dozen of these within sight of each other would put at end to any environment."[38]

Semantic issues aside, another question is whether the Gehry House was understood as a fitting statement in Los Angeles and Southern California, to whose architecture it may or may not have specific or conceptual affinities.[39] With the garden wall propped up by 2 × 4s and part of the entrance front treated as a similar screen, the critics' allusions to the Hollywood movie set were inevitable.[40] Stephens suggested that the garden side of the house, with its rectilinear wood and glazed surfaces, bore some similarity to the California Case Study Houses of the 1950s.[41] Filler, who described an "authentic sense of place in California," suggested that the Gehry House fuses two strains of California architecture, the hand-crafted wood tradition and modern technological imagery.[42] Pastier likened Gehry's work to Simon Rodia's Watts Towers: "Simon Rodia used beer bottles, crockery and sea shells as cladding for his backyard castle, and Gehry has used chain-link fencing, utility grade plywood and corrugated sheet metal for his."[43] The architect has suggested that his work is a commentary on Los Angeles in its energy and its suggestions of impermanence. Elsewhere Gehry described the context of Los Angeles as a banal environment with "bits and pieces of industrial buildings and freeways" and corrugated metal and stud framing: "I have just regurgitated it in another personal way."[44] For Knobel, the collection of unlikely materials in the Los Angeles streetscape makes Gehry's works fitting and analogous to the disparate nature of the city, "secure in its odd juxtapositions of the plain, vulgar, and elegant."[45] Obviously, there has been more than one way to understand this vocabulary of forms and that understanding has clearly depended on individual perceptions of the architecture and the ambiance in Southern California.

What, then, was perceived to be the intention of the rugged materials in Gehry's house? For Goldstein, they represented a comment on second-generation suburban buildings of Los Angeles, where small houses are successively demolished to build larger ones, and where scaffolding and corrugated iron are common to the process of architectural "face lifts."[46] For Stephens, the use of these materials "summons painful remembrances of the built environment the profession has not been able to control."[47] According to Jayne Merkel on the other hand, the exposed carpentry and industrial materials were domesticated: by keeping them natural, exposed, and in the domestic context, "Gehry tames them whether he wants to or not."[48]

On the subject of materials, Gehry has said, "I'm not a chain-link freak. I'm horror struck at the stuff. But somebody must like it because they're making an awful lot of it. . . . I mean, if the culture makes all this baloney, why not use it?"[49] But Gehry is a little inconsistent in explaining his use of such materials. On one level, he claimed, they are "more of a commentary on our world in which that particular kind of wire is made in great abundance and absorbed by the culture and denied by the culture because many people don't like it."[50] In another instance, he explained the use of such materials as a means "to explore ways of keeping construction costs down by using less expensive materials more inventively."[51] Elsewhere he likened the use of cheap raw materials for aesthetic purposes to the work of artists "to show that it is important to use readily available materials and to suggest that you can make beauty out of it, just like Rauschenberg does in his art."[52] He elaborated on this point in another interview: "I think when we look at the achievements of a Donald Judd or a Carl Andre we're seeing a vision of what many other disciplines are going to come to terms with. And by this I mean the recognition of humble materials, among other things. . . . These materials have a real vitality and honesty —and they're cheap."[53] To *U.S. News and World Report*, Gehry spoke of the affinity with Warhol's soupcan paintings, where the use of common cultural artifacts alters the way we look at things.[54]

The strong shapes of the house and Gehry's open admission of influence from various artists has inspired the critics to categorize the house variously as surrealist, minimalist, pop, perceptual, conceptual, brutalist, mod-

ernist, and post-modernist. Regarding the inspiration of the house itself, Gehry claimed an affinity with Magritte: after finishing the house, he saw a Magritte painting with a huge house inside a room, and although he didn't remember it, he concluded that he must have seen it before.[55] More recently, Gehry's architecture has been considered minimalist by Shapiro, who wrote of Gehry's ties to minimalist, conceptual, and process art.[56] The minimalist qualities were further discussed by Gilbert-Rolfe, who identified two aspects by which Gehry's architecture would qualify for the term. In short, Gilbert-Rolfe proposed that minimalism deals with clarity rather than reduction and that its effect depends upon an object turning "into more than itself."[57] For him, these concepts accurately described the Gehry House.

Gilbert-Rolfe's comments were occasioned by what he assumed was a more general tendency to interpret Gehry's architecture as post-modernist, but his assumption is not borne out in the balance of the critical literature, which seems to be as certain that Gehry's house is not post-modernist as it is that the house is not modernist. Goldberger was tentative in his categorization, claiming that Gehry's ability to craft abstract objects out of ordinary materials allied him "more to the modernist tradition of abstraction than to the currently developing post-modern world of cultural symbol."[58] For Filler, too, Gehry's apparent disinterest in historicism and surface decoration clearly separated him from the ranks of post-modernism.[59] On the other hand, Goldstein maintained that the work "questions both the dominance of function and the well-ordered aesthetics of 'modern' architecture."[60] That Gehry is not a modernist is a point that Philip Johnson argued when he said that "in the heyday of Modernism, when we had to do it like Corbusier or not do it at all, Frank would have been totally ignored."[61] Charles Jencks, who coined the term post-modernism in architecture, evidently did not think Gehry fit that description in 1980, and termed his work late modern.[62] Within two years, however, Jencks had apparently reconsidered and discussed the Gehry House under the rubric of "Post Modern Space." He suggested that Gehry had "developed a complicated Post-Modern space with a *Late-Modern use of industrial materials*" (Jencks's italics).[63] Ryder captured the other side of the dilemma when she pointed out that it was much easier to determine what the house isn't—conventional, modern, or post-modern—than to specify what it is.[64] Susan Doubilet probably spoke for many when she suggested that Gehry's work was "too personal to be categorized as either modern or post-modern."[65]

It is clear from this review of the literature that in matters of both terminology and perception, the critics have not reached general agreement and have been unable to understand the Gehry House within the confines of existing categories of style and meaning. Is the Gehry House successful architecture? The answer in the critical literature depends on the yardstick by which success is measured. To the uninitiated, the house was said to look like "a bunkhouse for the Plasmatics."[66] To Conroy, it "looks from the outside as though some energetic children had built it out of demolition-yard left-overs," a characterization strikingly similar to von Eckardt's "well-stocked lumberyard viewed through a telescope," and to Filler's "lumberyard vandalized by a rampaging teen-ager."[67] A writer for the *Boston Globe* concurred with the early reactions of the neighbors: "I probably wouldn't want him on my block either."[68] Stephens remarked on its "outrageous appearance."[69] And at the AIA convention where Gehry was given an award for the house, Bruce Graham—architect of the tallest building in the world, the Sears Tower in Chicago—asked him if he was "serious."[70] Elsewhere, and with disarming and potentially misleading simplicity, Gehry summed up his view of the house:

> What I did with this house is plain R & D—research and development. You can't take chances or risks with a client because you're playing with other people's money. So I have to do such R & D work on my own time and with my own money. What's happened is that suddenly everyone thinks that everything I do now is like this house. That's rubbish. This is simply where I practice.[71]

While it is true that much of Gehry's work is not "like this house," his style is distinct and it, like the Gehry House, continues to elude the critics.

Tod A. Marder

Notes

1. John Dreyfuss, "Gehry's Artful House Offends, Baffles, Angers His Neighbors," *Los Angeles Times,* July 23, 1978, 24–25.
2. Dreyfuss, "Gehry's Artful House," for this and the following quotation.
3. Dreyfuss, "Gehry's Artful House," 24.
4. Will Thorne, "House That Gehry Built Stirring Up SM Controversy," *Evening Outlook* (Santa Monica), August 22, 1978.
5. This reaction may have been sponsored by Gehry's comments in the Dreyfuss article about the aesthetic value of tentativeness rather than finished appearances. This is the first mention of an objection to the unfinished quality of the design which is, of course, an objection that cannot have been levelled fairly until the architect's intentions were fully known or the building

completed. The *Evening Outlook* mentioned that the house had been under construction for eight months and was within two weeks of completion.
6. Paul Goldberger, "California Corrugated," *New York,* October 23, 1978, 99–100. The article was a review of the exhibition of Gehry's work at P.S. 1 in Long Island City.
7. For this and subsequent quotations in this paragraph, see Steven Harris, "202 Frank Gehry," *Skyline,* November 1978, 2.
8. Interview in "Building of the Quarter, The Gehry House, Per Voco," *Archetype* (England), 1, Summer 1979, 23. In the same volume see the contribution of William Ted Georgis, "Interview: Frank Gehry," 10–11.
9. Robert Hughes, "Doing Their Own Thing, U.S. Architects: Goodbye To Glass Boxes and All That," *Time,* January 8, 1979, 52–58; and Sally Koris, "Renegade Frank Gehry Has Torn Up His House—and the Book of Architecture," *People,* March 5, 1979.
10. See, for example, Paul Goldberger, "A House Slipcovered in Metal," *New York Times,* May 17, 1979, C, 6; Jo Werne, "Architects Clash on 'Morality' of U.S. Designs," *Miami Herald,* October 28, 1979, H, 20; John Dreyfuss, "Gehry: The Architect as Artist," *Los Angeles Times,* November 7, 1979, IV, 8; Thomas Hine, "A Careless Design Carefully Done," *Philadelphia Inquirer,* January 13, 1980; Sarah Booth Conroy, "The Remodeled American Dream, East and West," *Washington Post,* May 20, 1980, D, 12; Jayne Merkel, "It's Just a Colonial Turned Outside-In," *Cincinnati Enquirer,* August 3, 1980, E, 8.
11. See "1979 Design Awards," *Los Angeles Architect,* December 1979, for the Citation. On the same occasion the jury of Ron Herron (London), Helmut Jahn (Chicago), and Esther McCoy (Los Angeles) gave the more prestigious Award to Gehry's Mid-Atlantic Toyota Office interiors. The national AIA Honor Award was reported in *Skyline,* May/June 1980, 9; and Wolf von Eckardt, "The Good, The Bad and the Tricky," *Los Angeles Times,* July 18, 1980, V, 16.
12. Among the foreign publications not cited elsewhere in these notes, see Susan Doubilet, "Gehry Wraps Old Homes in New Ideas," *Globe and Mail* (Canada), March 27, 1980; "Une Maison Qui Joue l'Ouverture," *Maison Française* (France), March 1980, 76 ff.; "Casa Gehry, Santa Mónica, California," *Arquitectura* (Spain), May/June 1980, 56–59 (largely taken from the article in *Archetype,* Summer 1979); "Selearchitettura," *L'Architettura* (Italy), 426, July 1980, 426–427; "A New Wave in American Architecture: Frank O. Gehry," *Space Design* (Japan), 5–8, July 1980, 5–15; Roseanne Robertson, "Frank Gehry: Small Buildings Getting Better and Better," *Sydney Morning Herald* (Australia), June 23, 1982; Malvina E. Bush, "Arquitecto Vanguardista Cuyos Edificios Provocan Controversias Feroces," *Hombre* (Venezuela), March 1983; "Architects Own Houses of the World," *Toshi-Jutaku* (Japan), 8307, July 1983, 80–83.
13. The text by Gehry is at least as extensive as any subsequent commentary. See "Frank Gehry's Suburban Changes: Architect's House in Santa Monica, 1978," *International Architect* (England), I, 1979, 34–46.
14. Gehry's commentary in "Frank Gehry's Suburban Changes," 34–46.

15. See, for example, the comments of Jaquelin Robertson, who admitted going to the house filled with skepticism, discovering it to be "a very, very pleasant place to be in," and leaving it "feeling very excited" (interview in "Building of the Quarter," 24). Among those who discussed the traditional and homelike character of the house, see Goldberger, "A House Slipcovered in Metal," C, 6; Martin Filler, "Eccentric Space: Frank Gehry," *Art in America,* 68, June 1980, 116–117; Tim Street-Porter, "The Outside-In House: An Experiment in Architecture," *Belle* (Australia), 41, November/December 1980, 135–136; and Goldberger, "Genius or Eccentric," *New York Times Magazine,* April 15, 1984, 70.

16. Suzanne Stephens, "Out of the Rage for Order," *Progressive Architecture,* 61, March 1980, 85.

17. *Ibid.*

18. "1979 Design Awards," *Los Angeles Architect.*

19. Filler, "Eccentric Space," 112–114. Of the buildings under discussion (the Gehry House was not), the architect claimed that he "wanted to give them a different kind of objecthood," although he denied seeing them as pieces of sculpture.

20. Christopher Knight, "Can Architects and Artists Work Together?," *Los Angeles Herald Examiner,* March 8, 1982.

21. Frank Lowe, "Issues of Architecture" (interview with Frank Gehry), *Communique* (Australia), September 1982, 10.

22. Barbara Goldstein, "Frank Gehry," *Architectural Review,* 168, July 1980, 27.

23. Goldstein, "Frank Gehry," 32.

24. Craig Hodgetts, "LA House Hot Stuff," *Skyline,* April 1979, 12. According to Hodgetts, "John Soane may have been the last architect to cultivate such an overtly mnemonic style, or to allow his work to become so obsessively nostalgic. . . . Even Charles Moore, at first glance the preeminent eclectigenarian of our time, has little of the curatorial finesse or wry appreciation that characterize the way Gehry has preserved a tattered shag in one room, or a scrap of particularly evocative wall paper in another." In 1979, Ryder also wrote of images of childhood nostalgia embodied in the design (Sharon Lee Ryder, "Brutally Frank," *Residential Interiors,* November/December 1979, 60).

25. Barbara Goldstein, "In California Un Oggetto Architettonico," *Domus,* 599, October 1979, 9. See the later discussion by Goldstein, "Frank Gehry," 32, where she expressed the same ideas.

26. John Pastier, "Of Art, Self-Revelation and Iconoclasm," *AIA Journal,* 69, May 1980, 169.

27. Pastier, "Of Art, Self-Revelation," 172.

28. Von Eckardt, "The Good, the Bad and the Tricky," V, 16.

29. Joseph Morgenstern, "The Gehry Style," *New York Times Magazine,* May 16, 1982, 60.

30. Doreen Nelson in Morgenstern, "The Gehry Style," 60.

31. See *Skyline,* May/June 1980, 9; also reported in Conroy, "Remodeled American Dream," D, 12.

32. Thorne, "House That Gehry Built."

33. Conroy, "Remodeled American Dream," D, 12, quoted Gehry: "I worried a lot about the morality over what I was doing in the neighborhood, but there really isn't any unity to the architecture—there's everything, Spanish, cottage, multi-family." By this time, the objections of the neighbors had partially subsided due to the publicity the house had received. According to Conroy, Gehry reported that some of the neighbors expressed pride in the house and brought their friends to see it: "I'm a two-block hero to the children," Gehry said.

34. Stephens, "Out of the Rage," 82: "By building the house to the allowable setback lines, Gehry claims to be 'contextual,' although many would argue that contextualism involves more than conforming to building lot patterns."

35. Thorne, "House That Gehry Built;" Gehry in "Frank Gehry's Suburban Changes," 36.

36. See Gehry's comments in "Frank Gehry's Suburban Changes," 38; and the discussion by Jeremy Gilbert-Rolfe, "Frank Gehry's Setting for *Available Light*" (album notes), *Available Light,* The Museum of Contemporary Art, Los Angeles, 1983.

37. Goldberger, "A House Slipcovered in Metal," C, 1, 6.

38. Goldberger, "A House Slipcovered in Metal," C, 6. Jaquelin Robertson had a similar reaction (interview in "Building of the Quarter," 24).

39. For a contribution to the semantic battle fought on this front, see the comments of Lindsay Stamm Shapiro, "A Minimalist Architecture of Allusion: Current Projects of Frank Gehry," *Architectural Record,* 171, June 1983, 115. If Gehry is a regionalist, she maintained, it is in the region of what architect Kazuo Shinohara termed "naked architecture." For my view of the concept of "regionalism" in recent California architecture, see Marder, "California Counterpoint," *Arts Magazine,* 58, October 1983, 8.

40. These allusions were preceded by Gehry's references to stage sets in "Frank Gehry's Suburban Changes," 38, 42, 46.

41. Stephens, "Out of the Rage," 85.

42. See Filler, "Eccentric Space," 111–112; Martin Filler, "Breaking the Rules and Getting Away With It," *House and Garden,* 152, September 1980, 146–153, 200; and the related discussion by Jean-Louis Cohen, "Charles Eames, Frank O. Gehry—La Maison Manifeste," *Architecture Movement Continuité* (AMC, France), 54–55, June/September 1981, 77–84.

43. Pastier, "Of Art, Self-Revelation." 171.

44. Frank Israel, "Frank O. Gehry's California Framework," *Gentlemen's Quarterly,* December 1981, 45; and, for the Gehry quotation, Lowe, "Issues of Architecture," 10.

45. Lance Knobel, "Frank Gehry—Los Angeles: Links in a Context of Fragmentation," *Architect's Journal* (England), 176, December 22–29, 1982, 31.

46. Goldstein, "In California Un Oggetto Architettonico," 9.

47. Stephens, "Out of the Rage," 81.

48. Merkel, "Colonial Turned Outside-In," E, 8.

49. Quoted in Morgenstern, "The Gehry Style," 58.

50. Quoted in Lowe, "Issues of Architecture," 9.

51. Quoted in Israel, "Frank O. Gehry's California Framework," 45. Gehry had articulated the same views with specific reference to his house as early as 1978: "The use of materials has to do with a sense of the need to explore inexpensive building. This is a time of less. Today people cannot afford to build the way they used to

and I think it behooves the architect to find new ways to help teach people." Quoted in Thorne, "House That Gehry Built."

52. Quoted in Anne Gilman, "Architects Who Live By Their Designs," *Los Angeles Magazine,* February 1981, 172.

53. Quoted in Peter Carlsen, "Designing the Post-Industrial World," *Art News,* 80, February 1981, 83–84.

54. "Today We Have a Kind of Free For All Architecture" (interview), *U.S. News and World Report,* May 30, 1983, 54.

55. Reported in Conroy, "Remodeled American Dream," D, 1. For Gehry's thoughts on surrealism in his architecture, see "Frank O. Gehry," *New Art Examiner,* 10, June 1983; and "Interview: Frank Gehry," *Transition* (Australia), February 1983, 23–24.

56. Shapiro, "Minimalist Architecture," 114. Shapiro was discussing Gehry's current (1983) projects, but she had already used the term in connection with the house in 1979 (interview in "Building of the Quarter," 28). In the same collection of interviews, Gebhard asserted that the house made stronger reference to the "high art world of minimal sculpture and painting" than to architecture ("Building of the Quarter," 25).

57. Gilbert-Rolfe, "Frank Gehry's Setting for *Available Light.*"

58. Goldberger, "California Corrugated," 100.

59. Filler, "Eccentric Space," 112.

60. Goldstein, "Frank Gehry," 32.

61. Quoted in Morgenstern, "The Gehry Style," 66.

62. A photograph of the famous kitchen window appears in Charles Jencks, *Late Modern Architecture and Other Essays,* New York, 1980, 39. The applicability of Jencks's term late modern had been previously announced in 1979 in "Building of the Quarter," 10.

63. See Charles Jencks, *Architecture Today,* New York, 1982, 214 ff., where the house appears in the chapter on "Post Modern Space" and not in the chapter on "Late Modern Space." Jencks asked, "Is it ad hocism, Late-Modernism, Post-Modernism, punk, the "cheapskate" aesthetic (another Gehry claim), cutouts a la Moore, sadomasochism, accidentalism—or even 'architecture'? Labels are hard to apply, partly because too many fit."

64. Ryder, "Brutally Frank," 58, continued, "It is the quintessential house in drag, appearing to be what it is not, while at the same time being all the things it pretends not to be: a conventional house dressed up in the clothing of another genre."

65. Susan Doubilet, "Remember Post-Modern?," *Skyline,* May 1980, 8.

66. "Best Iconoclastic Building," *L.A. Weekly,* September 17–24, 1982, 24.

67. Conroy, "Remodeled American Dream," D, 12; von Eckardt, "The Good, the Bad and the Tricky," V, 17; Filler, "Breaking the Rules and Getting Away With It," 148.

68. Robert Campbell, "Architecture," *Boston Globe,* September 12, 1982, B, 2.

69. Stephens, "Out of the Rage," 81.

70. Merkel, "Colonial Turned Outside-In," E, 8.

71. Gilman, "Architects Who Live," 171.

THE J. PAUL GETTY MUSEUM
Malibu, California

Architects: Langdon · Wilson · Mumper
Architectural consultant: Stephen Garrett
Historical advisor: Norman Neuerburg

86. The J. Paul Getty Museum, entranceway (color plate on page 38)

. . .The public should know that what they will finally see wasn't done on a mere whim or chosen by a committee delegated for such a task; it will simply be what I felt a good museum should be, and it will have the character of a building that I would like to visit myself. . . .I realize that our new building will be an unusual one and that architecture of this nature is not being done in our day and age.[1]

J. Paul Getty, *Los Angeles Times*,
September 16, 1973

Since 1954, J. Paul Getty had used a wing of his Malibu ranch house as a repository for his growing art collection, and by 1968 Getty began to consider an expansion in the form of a public museum. At first, the plans for expansion took the form of an additon to his home. Later, he developed the idea of a separate edifice on the Malibu property. Several proposals were considered for the museum, including a re-creation or partial reproduction of his Sutton Place Tudor mansion in Surrey, England; a replica of the Villa dei Papyri in Hercula-

neum, Italy; and even a scheme combining the exterior of the villa with the interior of Sutton Place.[2] In April 1970, Getty decided to recreate the villa that had been buried in A.D. 79 by the eruption of Mount Vesuvius, and partially excavated in the mid-18th century by the Swiss engineer and archaeologist Karl Weber. The excavator's notes and reconstructed plans served as a prototype for the museum, which also derived many features from other buildings from the ancient cities of Herculaneum, Pompeii, and Stabiae.[3] Although Getty was in England during the museum's construction, he personally approved and examined every design element, down to the last mosaic tile.[4] Architect Stephen Garrett acted as his liaison and architectural consultant and later served as director of the museum. Norman Neuerburg, a scholar of ancient Roman architecture, worked as historical advisor, making five trips to Italy for the project. Under the direction of Langdon and Wilson, an architectural firm based in Los Angeles, construction began in December 1970. Emmet L. Wemple and Associates landscaped the grounds. On January 16, 1974, the museum opened to the public.

Getty's 65-acre property is located on a panoramic site overlooking the Santa Monica Bay, a site not unlike those chosen by the wealthy owners of ancient villas overlooking the Bay of Naples. In true California fashion, however, the museum must be reached by automobile from the Pacific Coast Highway; because of the complaints of neighbors regarding crowding and parking, pedestrians are prohibited and a reservation system is required for all visitors.[5] The modern world falls behind as the visitor passes through the imposing entrance gate and ascends the driveway paved in simulated Roman paving stones recreated in poured concrete. Due to the steep slope of the valley and in keeping with Roman tradition, the museum was built on a podium structure. This provides space for the visitors' garage and for receiving, storage, conservation, an auditorium, and various offices. Steps and an elevator rise from the garage to the main peristyle, which is composed of an open loggia with columns made of the reinforced concrete necessary for earthquake resistance. At the Villa dei Papyri this end of the peristyle was closed, but here it is open to afford the visitor a broad view of the Pacific Ocean through the surrounding eucalyptus trees. The peristyle extends 300 feet to the museum portals. Three sides of the peristyle use the Doric order, while the taller Corinthian order is employed for the facade on the front of the museum to accommodate the greater height of the entrance.[6] Following the Roman villa tradition, the peristyle garden defines the major axis of the building. A secondary axis runs through the atrium, a west porch, and the east and west gardens. The gardens, the atrium, and the peristyle were landscaped and planted in accord with the visual and literary evidence of their ancient Roman counterparts.[7] The careful craftsmanship in the construction and decoration of the building may be judged in the side bays of the main peristyle, created by real and illusionistic architecture.[8] The bay divisions are echoed in the terrazzo floors and indicated by strips of mosaic in meander patterns. Successive bays have windows alternating with trompe l'oeil paintings including columns, wainscotting, and garlands in illusionistic space. The many subtle variations and alternations in decoration combine in typical Roman fashion so that no two bays have the same details. Among the many examples of fine marble work is the Hall of Colored Marbles, which contains recut marble from fourteen ancient sources as well as marbles recently cut from ancient quarries.

Getty's fascination with the Villa dei Papyri evidently dated back to 1912, when at the age of twelve he made his first visit to Herculaneum. His preoccupation with Roman antiquity is manifested in his book, Collector's Choice, published in 1955. In one chapter he gives a fanciful account of the villa within the context of a romantic story involving Lucius Calpurnius, the owner of the Villa dei Papyri in Roman times. Lucius Calpurnius is described as the richest man in Pompeii, and he possesses an impressive art collection that includes the Lansdowne Herakles, which of course is now part of the Getty collection. Not surprisingly, some have observed

"more than a trace of self-portraiture" in this fantastical account.[9] Getty was nevertheless knowledgeable and pragmatic enough to recognize the impossibility of creating an exact facsimile of the ancient villa; the most he could do was to try to insure the archaeological correctness of the whole and its parts wherever possible.[10] Yet questions about the authenticity of the new museum and comparisons with fantasy architecture were raised from the moment that Getty's "Invitation" to the new building was published, giving rise to the so-called "plastic flower controversy."[11]

In the first of a number of Los Angeles Times articles, the art critic Henry Seldis wrote, "D.W. Griffith and Walt Disney would turn green with envy if they were to see what J. Paul Getty hath wrought. Purist archaeologists and art historians will no doubt turn purple. . . . "[12] John Pastier, the architecture critic for the Los Angeles Times, later suggested that

> . . . the worst failing of the museum is as a piece of architecture and archaeology. It is a faithful reproduction of nothing that ever existed, re-created by inappropriate technologies and frequently lacking in basic design judgement.[13]

Pastier claimed that inappropriate models from various sources had been combined "in a manner that often negates their nature and purpose or creates an incongruous appearance."[14] Ignoring what little is known of the Villa dei Papyri, Pastier complained, the design had moved interior walls, sections of the plan were shifted, and one section of the ancient villa was omitted. Pastier criticized the second floor as guesswork because no information on the elevation of the Villa dei Papyri remains.[15]

Responding to Pastier's accusations, Getty's consultant for archaeology, Norman Neuerburg, defended the building as a legitimate scholarly adaptation. He argued that modifications due to site restrictions were justified inasmuch as the same sort of changes were also made in ancient villas. Dr. Neuerburg questioned Pastier's credentials as an archaeolgist and reasserted the legitimacy of the museum's architectural sources and conception.[16] In Neuerburg's articles and interviews, where the models for features at the Getty are discussed, he reminded readers that many preconceived ideas about Roman art and architecture are not substantiated by the evidence.[17] As one supportive critic wrote, people who think of Roman antiquity as "aged marble archaeological ruins will be dazzled by the vibrant, even gaudy, colorful lively scenes. . . . And they will realize, perhaps for the first time, that ancient Rome was not a colorless environment."[18] Yet other critics continued to call the paintings in the peristyle "too vivid" and "too harsh, too bold," and even suggested that perhaps they were intended to fade.[19] According to Neuerburg, the colors used are actually more subdued and less typical of ancient frescoes than the ones he originally submitted for Getty's approval.

87. Aerial view. Rendering by David Wilkins

88. Drawing made in Florence, Italy for the Getty Museum of an inlaid marble pavement design. Collection: Archives of the J. Paul Getty Trust

89. View of fountains from west porch

Neuerburg wrote extensively about the museum's construction, its archaeological precedents, and its details, as well as the reasons for necessary deviations from ancient prototypes.[20] Regarding the main vestibule of the museum, Neuerburg explained that the intricate floor and wall patterns were popular in the late 1st century B.C., especially at Herculaneum, and that the excavation reports repeatedly refer to the large quantities of marble removed from the Villa dei Papyri, much of which is now in the Naples Museum. The walls contain recut ancient marbles and pieces recently taken from ancient quarries. The pavement pattern derives from the House of the Deer in Herculaneum. The illusionistic ceiling painting of grape tendrils is inspired by a fragment from the House of the Orchard in Pompeii. Deviations from the ancient models in plan and execution were required by the site, the special needs of the museum, building codes, modern construction methods, and Getty's preferences, but archaeological accuracy was maintained wherever possible. In deference to the changes and scholarly interpolations from ancient models, however, Neuerburg referred to the building as "a recreation rather than a reproduction."

The majority of commentators and critics have agreed that a great deal of research went into the design of the building and, according to some, the museum's authenticity is precisely what differentiates it from the same Hollywood extravaganzas to which other critics liken the Getty.[21] Despite the accuracy of the archaeology, the precision of the result—correct or not—left many critics cold. This seems to have been the case where Pastier complained that the building lacks "fidelity to the spirit of the original" due to its rigid symmetry and the machine-made feeling of the whole.[22] In response, Neuerburg contended that the irregular outline of the Weber plan was only the result of a later remodeling of the Villa dei Papyri and that formality and axiality were important characteristics of Roman architecture.[23] Several other critics voiced complaints about the pristine results of an archaeology too well executed. Grace Glueck describes the carefully researched and recreated details as fussy, and the outcome as "overwrought 'restoration' that invites comparison with the worst excesses of Colonial Williamsburg."[24] Noting the grandeur and theatricality of the building, others make the inevitable associations with a Hollywood movie set.[25] In this regard the museum's contextuality with Southern California has been suggested by several critics: in a town that has a restaurant in the shape of a derby hat, why not have a museum in the shape of a villa?[26] Gebhard suggests that the Getty Museum relates to Southern California architecture by the fine line it rides between reality and illusion, but whether this is a positive or negative factor varies with each critic.[27]

Questions of the museum's authenticity or contextuality apart, is the Getty in good taste? The critics have attacked the taste of the patron and criticized the aesthetics of its ancient Roman models. Thus, while some authors

90. Entrance vestibule

pointed to the scholarship and craftsmanship that accompanied the construction as an answer to accusations of the gaudiness of an "Easter egg color scheme," other commentators found the Getty tacky, whether accurate or not, and found the repetition of ancient Roman "over-indulgences" questionable.[28] Even staunch defenders of the museum comment on the bright colors and lavish marbles: according to Pastier, Neuerburg stated: "no one ever accused the Romans of good taste."[29] To the same criticism, Getty had a blunt response: "If you don't happen to like Roman villa you won't like the museum."[30]

Other journalists responded positively to the inten-

tions of builder and building. *Los Angeles Times* columnist Jack Smith found the museum a stimulating way to escape into ancient history and found it easy to "surrender to the illusion."[31] With the exception of scholars and art students, most visitors, according to Smith, will decide whether or not they like the Getty before even entering the museum proper: ". . . it will just be a question of whether we are enchanted by the structure; whether we buy it."[32] Joseph Morgenstern, writing for *Art News*, found the atmosphere of the museum relaxing and inviting. For him the Getty is ". . . about as far from forbidding and as close to unassuming as an Imperial Roman

91. Design for the mural decoration of a bay in the peristyle court. Rendering by David Wilkins. Collection: Archives of the J. Paul Getty Trust.

villa can be. It's a residence of the gods, but happy gods, hospitable gods."[33] A Canadian correspondent found the Getty a tasteful oasis "centuries rather than 17 through-way miles removed from burgeoning, brassy, Los Angeles. . . ."[34] A visitor with expectations of the "gross and anachronistic" was disappointed by the Getty; hoping for some "incongruities on the order of San Simeon," instead she found an appropriate and tasteful reconstruction.[35]

The predominant fuctional issue concerning the Getty museum centers on the extent to which the building competes with the art. Getty did not consider this a problem. Regarding the Greek and Roman art collection, he states:

> What could be more logical than to display it in a classical building where it might originally have been seen? . . . Since it is an accepted part of both American and European museums to include period rooms for furniture and paintings and to build a complete setting, an environment as they sometimes call it, to give the feeling of what it all would have looked like together, why not do it for Greek and Roman sculpture? But instead of a room or two, we are doing a whole building.[36]

Getty applied a similar sensibility to the furniture and painting galleries: "I like a museum to be intimate and friendly. I do not get as much pleasure from a series of neutral galleries in which one sees a row of paintings or a row of statues as I do when they are placed in an appropriate setting."[37] In the rooms devoted to paintings and decorative arts on the second floor, intimacy is created through the use of rich wall coverings and period room settings. Getty's position was clear; works of art are best displayed in an environment similar to the one for which they were created.

On this matter, predictably, there was notable disagreement. Charles Jencks found the museum "very sympathetic to the antiquities displayed."[38] Other critics maintained that a replica of a classical building was particularly appropriate because, besides the ancient Greek and Roman holdings, most of Getty's collection consists of classicizing art from the Renaissance through the Neoclassical periods.[39]

Those commentators who disagreed felt that the museum is not sufficiently neutral and therefore competes with the art work.[40] Noting a paradox, the Art Journal states: "The villa seems real—yet we know it is not. The works of art are real—yet they don't seem to belong. What Roman patrician would display fragments and damaged pieces . . . ?"[41] Thus, whether the Getty is considered supportive of the art or detracting from it remains debatable, depending on the visitor's preference. According to Neuerburg, "It's a matter of philosophy. Is a work of art supposed to speak for itself in a sterile surrounding, or should it be in·a setting which complements it?"[42]

The relationship between the second floor galleries and the rest of the museum is also controversial. The departure from the villa environment on the upper level is considered by many to be anachronistic or destructive of the carefully created illusion formed below.[43] Less typically, the upper galleries are praised as a refreshing change: a different subject and a different environment.[44] The wallpaper has been criticized as distracting and even labeled "bordello-red."[45] But many find it appropriate for the Renaissance and Baroque paintings galleries, as well as the period rooms, citing the Frick and other museums as well regarded precedents.[46]

In retrospect it should also be said that critics' opinions on the appropriateness of the environment often seem to depend on their understanding of the collection. Those who perceived the majority of Getty's collection to be antiquities believed that the setting is appropriate. Garrett pointed out that the largest volume of Getty's collection is Greek and Roman art and maintained that a Roman villa is a logical setting.[47] Paul Goldberger, who primarily discussed the French furniture and European paintings in the collection, considered their display in a replica of an ancient Roman villa to be a "silly" idea.[48]

Early on, William Wilson had criticized the display of contemporary replicas of ancient mural paintings and recasts of ancient bronzes, claiming that the museum requires the visitor to distinguish "reconstruction from reproduction from restoration."[49] Reyner Banham also opposed the museum as a setting that clashes with rather than complements its holdings, but for a slightly different reason.[50] Suggesting the overall air of scrupulous research, he conceded that "Neuerburg, I am sure, can quote chapter and verse for every triglyph, bucrane, niche and astragal. . . . " But Banham complained that the disparity between the sparkling new condition of the museum and the worn antiquities strikes a discordant note:

> Far from looking at home, they look lost. The setting deprives them of their residual life and

makes them look like junk, in contrast with the mummified completeness and high finish all around them. The missing noses, toes, fingers which were their warrant of antiquity and authority now make them look worn and discarded. You wonder what they're doing in a smart new motel like this.[51]

For Banham, the building is out of keeping with the "nouveau riche decadence" associated with what he considered to be comparable architecture, such as Caesar's Palace in Las Vegas. Of the Getty he said:

> The erudition and workmanship are as impeccable and absolutely deathly as this kind of pluperfect reconstruction must always be . . . no blood was spilled here, no sperm, nor wine, nor other vital juice.[52]

Clearly each critic has a different perception of historicizing architecture, as well as ancient Roman art and life!

Such comments as the one quoted raise the question of how the Getty museum should be judged as a work of contemporary architecture.[53] In the *Los Angeles Times*, Pastier judged the museum "frequently lacking in basic architectural design judgement."[54] For him, the museum's overall spirit is one of "pretentious sterility," its effect "awkward and far removed" from the original intention of recreating a Roman villa; in short "the building is a bad piece of work esthetically and functionally." In *Progressive Architecture*, the long-time California critic Esther McCoy praised the Getty for its grand space, and for its ability to function well as a museum. She described the natural sequence formed by the use of courtyard and atrium components, where open and covered spaces interweave naturally from enclosure into sunlight, providing good circulation and restful gardens as a welcome complement to the museum.[55] The layout of the museum is also commended by other journalists who note how it surrounds the inner peristyle, allowing for a non-directional flow in the museum. Thus the visitor is not compelled into a one-way, start-to-finish traffic pattern, which is viewed by some as an unfortunate aspect of museum design.[56]

Henry Hope Reed, a contemporary architect and prominent member of the Classical America group, praises the museum's craftsmanship and the beauty of its classical vocabulary: "What the J. Paul Getty repeatedly underscores is the visual abundance made possible by the classical. It is a cornucopia of all arts awaiting anyone who is willing to accept the lessons of the past."[57] Reed was impressed with the Getty's ability to incorporate the environment, and wondered why there are not more classical colonnades, porticoes and courtyards in Southern California. Other critics have also noted the appropriateness of the site — like the Villa dei Papyri, located on the Bay of Naples, the museum enjoys a Mediterranean climate, adding considerably to its appeal.[58]

For better or worse, it may well be true that the ulti-

92. Inner peristyle garden with replicas of ancient bronzes

93. Peristyle garden and pool

mate critical success of the J. Paul Getty Museum depends less on its archaeology or its qualities as a functioning museum than upon our perceptions about its character and validity as 20th-century architecture. Getty's intentions were stated simply: "I thought it worthwhile to create one building in the Roman tradition. The Greco-roman buildings that remain have had hard usage during the last couple of thousand years."[59] But the consensus of many critics seems to have been that over $17 million might have been spent on something "of and for our own times."[60] The issue — whether or not there is a correct architecture for our times — is not new. Similar controversies, for example, surrounded John Russell Pope's classical buildings of the 1930s in Washington, D.C.: the Jefferson Memorial and the National Gallery of Art.[61] Critics have complained that " in this 'enlightened' day and age, to reconstruct a 1st century B.C. villa from Herculaneum in Malibu, California, is a show of plebian bad taste."[62] On the other hand Charles Jencks even celebrates the implication of the use of modern technology and our new abilities of simulation: "Through our reproduction techniques (xerox, film, synthetic materials) and our specialized archaeologies (in this case archaeological and landscape specialists), with our technologies of air-conditioning and temperature control and our structural capabilites (of putting the whole thing over a parking garage) we can do what the 19th-century revivalist couldn't."[63] Does an architectural language relate exclusively to one period of history? Is it unethical to use architecture from another time period for contemporary building?

For the historian and critic David Gebhard, these questions have a clear answer.[64] Since all architecture borrows heavily from past forms, he maintained, designing becomes a matter of consciously or unconsciously choosing a period from which to select a prototype. Ancient architecture is no more or less justifiable as a model than more recent architecture:

> . . . Even if a case could be made that ethics and design are somehow related, why is it reprehensible to employ distant forms of the past, rather than borrowed forms of the near past?

Gebhard claimed that the museum had answered the question: To whom am I addressing myself? "Its answer is not to the high elite, nor to the professional art critic or historian. It has addressed itself — and successfully so — to a lay audience."[65] The variety of its attractions — historical, architectural, horticultural and artistic — frees the museum from the "typical dreary" syndrome. In short, Gebhard saw the controversy as a conflict between the interpretation of elite and popular taste: " . . . the nouveau riche atmosphere of Rome, its predilection for the garish, loud and opulent does not appeal to the taste of a high art critic today. . . . "[66] Comparing the museum with popular California attractions such as the Hearst Castle, Knott's Berry Farm, and Forest Lawn, Gebhard notes,

94. South porch

> The distance which exists between the ideology and the imagery of these popular monuments and those of the high culture elite tragically illustrates the chasm which has existed throughout the whole of the 20th century, between the imagery of the avant-garde, high art elite, and the vernacular imagery preferred by the majority of our society.[67]

For Gebhard, writing in 1974, the Getty Museum had succeeded as popularizing architecture. For Jencks, writing three years later, the museum was an avant-garde design — in a word, post-modern. Considering the span of architectual choices available, Jencks wrote, " . . . the Getty Museum is a passable, if unintended example of Post-Modern building, commendable for its pluralism and opening of choice but neither brilliant nor especially moribund."[68] Earlier, in 1975, Goldberger had implied a similar attitude, commending the pleasant atmosphere of the Getty as a sign of the movement away from "arrogant heavy modernism."[69] At this point, of course, the issues of interpreting the architecture and weighing its success become indissoluably mixed. In *Esquire* magazine in 1977, Joan Didion distinguished the popular appeal of the museum architecture from the "embarassment" it causes the "informed."[70] The discomfort, she thought, may also be the result of the fact that ancient art in the museum does not look the way we would have preferred to see it. Thus, the "learning" throughout the building is "unremittingly reproachful." Ancient marbles were not dusty and broken but were opulent reminders of power; ancient murals were not originally mellow-hued but were brightly colored "as if dreamed up by a mafia don." An antiquity in this context "depresses many people, strikes an unliberated chord." As a result, wrote Didion, "The Getty tells us that we were never any better than we are now and will never be any better than we were, and in so doing makes a profoundly unpopular statement."

Similarly, Banham discounted Gebhard's claims for the Getty as a lay person's museum. "Whatever the erudite likes of Gebhard may say," protested Banham, "this is, very definitely, high art. What makes it despicable, despite its virtue, is that it is 'failed' high art."[71] Clearly, Banham's judgement is based on the conception of reconstructed antiquity, while Gebhard's analysis is based on the museum's demonstrable appeal.

In a preview of the museum for the *Los Angeles Times*, William Wilson predicted that "L.A. intelligentsia, paranoid about our town's reputation as Kitsch City and the Plastic Paradise" will add this to their list of tacky expensive Southern California monuments.[72] Although the collections are excellent, he suggests no one should take the building seriously: "Campier sensibilities who love playful theatrical artifice will delight in it as the funniest folly since the Assyrian Rubber Factory. The First Real Plastic Museum." In *Westways* magazine, Smith summarized local skepticism, "Here was Los Angeles, trying to rise above its comic image as one vast breakaway movie set, where nothing was what it seemed to be and now our richest patron had built a sandcastle for his second childhood and set us back 2,000 years."[73] Aware of such negative opinions, Smith elsewhere confessed, "Ever since I had turned into the stone road I'd been nervous. I was afraid I was going to like it and I knew I shouldn't"[74]

Banham claims that "Gettybashers" have directed most of the criticism at the patron himself, "the last of the big looters, balancing his collection on top of a cliff that might have been better left as nature intended it."[75] The fact is that many critics flatly consider the museum an egotistical "whim" or a "rich man's fantasy."[76] *Los Angeles Times* critic Wilson wrote that "the Getty outstrips any exisiting monument to expensive, aggressive bad taste, cultural pretension and self-aggrandizement, south of Hearst Castle."[77] In an interview for *Finance* magazine, Garrett said that Getty's reasons for building the museum included tax considerations, philanthropy, and "a certain amount of ego."[78] In subtly veiled or bolder tones, critics suggested that the villa was built to augment Getty's imperial aspirations, including associations with the Roman Emperor Hadrian."[79] Another critic noted, "The J. Paul Getty Musuem will be a museum of and by, if not entirely for, J. Paul Getty."[80]

There is another side to this story, for many commentators have considered Getty's endeavor in a more generous light. The museum has been called "an impressive gesture of one man's largesse to the artistic commonwealth of all men," and the high quality of the art and the no-admission-fee policy is seen by many journalists as a generous contribution to the quality of Southern California culture.[81] Preferable to the anonymity of "caverns" such as the Vatican, the Metropolitan Museum of Art, or the Louvre, the personal stamp of the patron is to many an admirable quality. Although the Getty Museum was never intended as a home, like that of the Fricks or the Gardners, it has had for some visitors a sense of private property gone public.[82] John Russell Taylor in the *London Times* suggested a motive somewhere between pure egotism and selflessness for building the museum.[83] Taylor stated that the museum is indeed a rich man's dream and likens it to the romantic, Victorian vision of antiquity as seen in the museum's painting *Spring* by Lawrence Alma-Tadema: the museum is, according to Taylor, "a vast monument to the same sort of 1910ish taste." He differentiates the Getty Museum from the wild eclecticism of other romantically classical buildings, such as Hearst Castle, by virtue of archaeological accuracy and stylistic consistency represented in the design of the villa. Taylor pointed out that if Getty does not exactly invite us into his home, "he does something more self-revealing: he invites us into his mind to share his fantasies.[84]

Ruth Wilford Caccavale

Notes

1. J. P. Getty, "Getty Museum Invitation from the Collector," *Los Angeles Times,* September 16, 1973, CAL, 1. The contents of this article appeared in various American and foreign newspapers. In the Getty Museum *Guidebook*, Getty's decisions are presented as if made by a group of trustees; see L. Cristin ed., *Guidebook: The J. Paul Getty Museum,* Los Angeles, 1975, 8. New Jersey, 1976, and an extensive obituary by A. Whitman, "J. Paul Getty Dead at 83, Amassed Billions from Oil," *New York Times,* June 6, 1983, 1. For the scheme combining the villa exterior with the interior of Sutton Place, see P. Failing, "The $1,000,000,000 Art Museum," *Art News,* 80, November 1981, 84.
3. For further information on the Villa dei Papyri, see D. Comparetti and G. de Petra, *La villa ercolanese dei Pisoni, i suoi monumenti e la sua biblioteca,* Turin, 1883 (republished by Centro Internazionale per lo Studio dei Papiri Ercolanesi, Naples, 1972); J. J. Deiss, *Herculaneum: Italy's Burned Treasure,* New York, 1966; C. Waldstein and L. Shoobridge, *Herculaneum; Past, Present and Future,* London, 1908. Recently, R. Gore, "The Dead Do Tell Tales at Vesuvius," *National Geographic,* May 1984, 557–613, published an illustration of the museum to clarify the appearance of the ancient building.
4. D. Shaw, "J. Paul Getty's Dream Museum: Critics Pan It, Public Loves It," *Smithsonian,* May 1974, 31.
5. P. Goldberger, "Getty Museum's Roman Styling, Once Criticized, Draws Crowds," *New York Times,* August 26, 1975, 38.
6. For more on this matter, see N. Neuerburg, *Herculaneum to Malibu: A Companion to the Visit of the J. Paul Getty Museum Building,* Malibu, 1975.

121

7. Cristin, *Guidebook,* 19. For a description of the gardens and their ancient prototypes, see J. D'Andrea, *Ancient Herbs in the J. Paul Getty Museum Gardens,* Malibu, n.d.; J. Irby, "Architects Complete $500,000 Landscape," *Palisadian-Post* (Pacific Palisades), May 2, 1974; and A. Elliot, "J. Paul Getty's Legacy: What Is in Store for the Garden of the Billionaire's Whim," *Horticulture,* November 1977, 10–13.

8. This is noted by many reviewers, such as D. Meilach, "Malibu's Getty Museum: It's Big, New, Controversial," *Sun-Times* (Chicago), April 21, 1974. The museum has been honored with awards for its craftsmanship in several media including tilework, landscaping, and marble installations. See "Tile Work on Getty Museum Wins Four Top Annual Awards from Ceramic Tile Institute," *Building News,* January 18, 1974; "Area Landscapers Win Honors," *News* (Camarillo, California), November 29, 1974; D. Haley, "J. Paul Getty Museum: Malibu's Awe-Inspiring Treasury of Arts," *Masonry Industry,* July 1974, 2–8.

9. J. R. Taylor, "Mr. Getty's Invitation to Share His Fantasies," *Times* (London), May 25, 1974. A similar idea was expressed earlier by D. Davis, "Welcome to Gettyland," *Newsweek,* January 28, 1974, 84.

10. In the foreword to the Museum *Guidebook,* Getty stated, "I believe that the ancient Roman proprietor would find the peristyle garden in the Museum very close to the one at Herculaneum. And even though there are some changes, I believe he would recognize the floor plan of the main level "(Cristin, *Guidebook,* 6). See also Shaw, "Getty's Dream Museum," 31.

11. E.g., W. Wilson, "A Preview of Pompeii-on-the-Pacific," *Los Angeles Times,* January 6, 1974, CAL, 44; "Roman Villa Is Recreated on Coast to House Getty Art Collection," *New York Times,* January 17, 1974, 1–3; Shaw, "Getty's Dream Museum," 30; D. Gebhard, "Getty Museum: Is It 'Disgusting' and 'Downright Outrageous'?," *Architecture Plus,* 2, September-October 1974, 56–61.

12. H. Seldis, "What J. Paul Getty Hath Wrought in Malibu," *Los Angeles Times,* September 16, 1973, CAL, 60. The *Los Angeles Times* articles were frequently quoted by later writers, and Neuerburg complained that "Unfortunately, their comments were picked up around the world and repeated by other equally unimaginative people. The public, fortunately, doesn't pay too much attention to what critics say. . . . It seems that this was something the public was ready for, even if the 'establishment' wasn't." Quoted in N. Neuerburg, "Building the J. Paul Getty Museum—A Personal Account," *Classical America,* 4, 1977, 72. For more opinions and views of the public, see "Getty Museum" (letters to the editor), *Los Angeles Times,* September 30, 1973, CAL, 12.

13. J. Pastier, "Architecture: What Getty Hath Wrought," *Los Angeles Times,* January 28, 1974, IV, 1.

14. Pastier, "What Getty Hath Wrought," 5.

15. Weber's plan indicates stairs, but the extent of any second floor structure is unknown. The criticism of the upper floors was largely about the treatment of the interior walls. Completely departing from the Roman theme, they are covered with silk damask paper and house the European paintings and decorative arts. See D. Waldron, "A Billionaire Makes His Dream Come True," *New York Times,* November 3, 1974, V, 11; and M. Royer, *Newport News and Mesa News* (Newport Beach, California), June 1975.

16. N. Neuerburg, "The Getty Museum" (letter to the editor), *Los Angeles Times,* February 24, 1974, IV, 8. Neuerburg had received a Ph.D. in ancient art from the Institute of Fine Arts, New York University.

17. "Roman Villa is Recreated on Coast," 1–3. The reaction of some visitors indicated how necessary this education was.

18. H. von Breton, "Major West Coast Mecca—J. Paul Getty Museum Opens," *News-Press* (Santa Barbara), January 13, 1974; Goldberger, "Getty Museum's Roman Styling," 38.

19. R. Reilly, "Getty Museum in Malibu, A Mecca for Art Lovers," *San Diego Union,* February 24, 1974. Other critics and visitors have acknowledged the museum as a unique educational opportunity. See, for example, J. Smith, "What Getty Begat in Malibu," *Westways,* November 1974; D. Hodson, "Europe in Malibu" (letter to the editor), *Westways,* January 1975. Getty was also interested in teaching from this classical reconstruction, and he justified the construction of his building by the fact that it would give visitors the unique opportunity to see what an ancient Roman villa would have looked like. Said Getty, "There is I believe, no other place in the world where one can go to see such a building in any state except ruins; as one now sees them in Pompeii. There are replicas and imitations of ancient public buildings, but none of a private structure—so this one should prove a unique experience." (Letter to the editor, *Los Angeles Times,* April 19, 1973, CAL, 60.) He also expressed this opinion in T. Lambert, "J. Paul Getty Defends His Museum" (interview), *Los Angeles Times,* February 14, 1974, IV, 1.

20. See N. Neuerburg, "The New J. Paul Getty Museum," *Archaeology,* 23, July 1974, 175–181; Neuerburg, *Herculaneum to Malibu: A Companion to the Visit of the J. Paul Getty Museum Building,* Malibu, 1975; and Neuerburg, "Building the J. Paul Getty Museum—A Personal Account," 54–73.

21. "Public Museums," *Art Journal,* 35, Summer 1976, 414–418.

22. Pastier, "What Getty Hath Wrought," 5.

23. Neuerburg, "The Getty Museum," IV, 8.

24. G. Glueck, "Getty Museum Is a Hit with Visitors," *New York Times,* May 28, 1974, 34.

25. For example N. Mathews, "Getty's Museum Collection: 'Like a Hollywood Set'," *Tracy Press,* (Tracy, California), March 6, 1974; and S. Eichelbaum, "Getty's Highbrow Disneyland," *Examiner* (San Francisco), January 31, 1974.

26. This reference is to the recently demolished Brown Derby Restaurant, which was built in 1926. For similar points, see S. Slobojan, "A First-Century Roman Villa Lies Hidden in California," *News* (Detroit), January 20, 1980; F. Reinsch, "The Getty Museum: A Roman Villa in Disney County," *Patriotic Ledger* (Quincy, Massachusetts), January 4, 1974, 1–2; and "Public Museums," *Art Journal,* 35, Summer 1976, 416.

27. Gebhard, "Is It 'Disgusting'?" 57–59.

28. J. Kutner, "Getty Museum's Art Indulgence," *News* (Dallas), July 1, 1975.

29. Quoted in Pastier's reply to Neuerburg's letter to the editor, "The Getty Museum," *Los Angeles Times,* February 24, 1974, IV, 9. For still more letters to the editor, see "Museum Critics," *Los Angeles Times,* March 31, 1974, HOM, 9.

30. Getty quoted in Shaw, "Getty's Dream Museum," 31.

31. J. Smith, "Nice Having Done Business. . . ," *Los Angeles Times,* June 14, 1976, IV, 1. For similar opinions, see "Rome in Malibu," *Los Angeles Magazine,* February 1974; P. Cullen, "Speaking of Art," *The View* (Sierra Madre, California), March 21, 1974; "The J. Paul Getty Museum," *Designers West* (Los Angeles), April 1974; and H. Lowe, "Los Angeles," *Star* (Montreal), November 19, 1977.

32. Smith, "What Getty Begat in Malibu." Authors presenting similar ideas include: P. Schneider, "Pompeii sur Pacifique," *L'Express* (Paris), July 22, 1974; and B. Winters, "Getty Museum Works Despite Its Critics," *Baltimore Sun,* June 30, 1975.

33. J. Morgenstern, "Getty's Little Palace in Malibu," *Art News,* 76, March 1977, 72.

34. Lowe, "Los Angeles."

35. N. Friedenn, "Museums," *Playboy,* August 1974, 30–31. The reference is to William Randolph Hearst's "castle" in San Simeon, California.

36. Getty, "Getty Museum Invitation," CAL, 60.

37. Getty, "Getty Museum Invitation," CAL, 60. Getty reiterated this point of view in the interview by T. Lambert, "J. Paul Getty Defends His Malibu Museum," 1. For more information on the issue of museum architecture, see P. Goldberger, "What Should a Museum Be?," *Art News,* 74, October 1975, 33–38; and H. Searing, *New American Art Museums,* New York, 1982.

38. Jencks, "Don't Panic," *Architectural Review,* 163, February 1978, 84. This opinion had also been expressed by S. Eichelbaum, "Getty's Highbrow Disneyland," *Examiner* (San Francisco), January 31, 1974.

39. U. Eco, "Vi Scrivo da Pompeii (California)," *Espresso* (Italy), November 2, 1975. For a description of Getty's collection, see B. Fredericksen, *Masterpieces of Painting in the J. Paul Getty Museum,* Malibu, 1980; *The J. Paul Getty Museum Guidebook,* sixth edition, Malibu, 1983; G. Wilson, *Decorative Arts in the J. Paul Getty Museum,* Malibu, 1977; C. C. Vermeule and N. Neuerburg, *Catalogue of the Ancient Art in the J. Paul Getty Museum,* Malibu, 1973; and the seven-part series of articles by S. Garrett, J. Frel, B. Fredericksen, J. L. Bordeaux, G. Wilson, and H. Sorensen, "The J. Paul Getty Museum," *Connaissance des Arts,* 274, December 1974, 120–124; 275, January 1975, 56–63; 276, February 1975, 84–88; 277, March 1975, 52–59; 278, April 1975, 80–87; 279, May 1975, 106–113; and 280, June 1975, 90–97.

40. For example see Pastier, "What Hath Getty Wrought," IV, 1; Shaw, "Getty's Dream Museum," 30; and Goldberger, "What Should a Museum Building Be?," 38.

41. "Public Museums," *Art Journal,* 35, Summer 1976, 418.

42. N. Neuerburg quoted in "The Getty Museum: Malibu's Roman Villa," *Evening Outlook* (Santa Monica), March 9, 1974.

43. J. Smith, "What Getty Begat in Malibu."

44. C. van der Weyde, "Getty Museum" (letter to the editor), *Los Angeles Times,* May 1, 1974, II, 6. Another reviewer, also in the minority, wrote that the second

level "eliminates any disorientation that could be caused by walking from a Roman villa into an 18th century sitting room" (S. McGrew, "The Getty Museum," *Southwestern Art* (Austin, Texas), February 1974).

45. According to this author, the wallpaper would look better as backing for "nude barmaids painted on velvet than for classical Greek sculpture" (E. Edwards, "The World's Richest Museum Stands Aloof on Its Olympus," *Herald* (Miami), August 12, 1979). As there is no classical sculpture in the wallpapered rooms, and contrary to the article's title, the museum sits in a canyon, one has to wonder about such opinions. There were knowledgeable people who opposed the wallpaper, such as Fredericksen, Getty's curator of paintings (Wilson, "A Preview of Pompeii-on-the-Pacific," CAL, 48; "Roman Villa Is Recreated on Coast," *New York Times,* January 17, 1974).

46. See, for example, a response to E. Edwards "The World's Richest Museum," by E. Riley, "No Nude Barmaids" (letter to the editor), *Herald* (Miami, letter to the editor), September 25, 1979.

47. Garrett interviewed by Failing, "The $1,000,000,000 Art Museum," 84. This viewpoint is encountered again in L. G. Wilson, "Meubles Merveilleux in Malibu," *Interiors,* September 1974, 82.

48. Goldberger, "What Should a Museum Building Be?," 38. The main level, with some administrative offices, contains fewer galleries than the second floor, but more galleries are devoted to the classical collection than to either paintings or decorative arts. The silk damask wallpaper was recently removed from most of the European painting galleries. When the new Getty museum is constructed in Brentwood, all but the antiquities will be displayed in the new location, and the second floor of the older museum will be renovated to incorporate it into the Roman villa atmosphere. These changes will dispel criticism over the appropriateness of paintings and furniture in this setting.

49. Wilson, "A Preview of Pompeii-on-the-Pacific," CAL, 44. The replicas Wilson referred to are located in the courtyards and gardens, clearly separated from the art collection.

50. R. Banham, "Lair of the Looter," *New Society,* May 5, 1977, 238.

51. *Ibid.*

52. Banham continued: "No one ever puked in the pool or pissed in the fountains. Nor will they—custodians hover, like thought police," (Banham, "Lair of the Looter," 238.)

53. See McCoy, "Report from Malibu," *Progressive Architecture,* 55, July 1974, 33; Gebhard, "Is It 'Disgusting'?," 56–61; Goldberger, "Getty Museum's Roman Styling," 38; Banham, "Lair of the Looter," 238; and Jencks, "Don't Panic," 83–85.

54. Pastier, "What Hath Getty Wrought," IV, 1; and Pastier, "The Getty Museum," IV, 9.

55. McCoy, "Report from Malibu," 35. See also S. Slobojan, "A First Century Roman Villa."

56. P. Cullen, "Speaking of Art," *View* (Sierra Madre, California), April 18, 1974. The unity of the entire complex was also praised in "Public Museums," 414–418.

57. H. H. Reed, "Roman Villa in Malibu," *Skyline,* May/June 1980, 16–17. The summer after the new museum

opened, a new line of furniture was introduced that was inspired by the Getty's classical collection. See ''Dr. Norman Neuerburg and the Getty Museum," *Ameritone Reports* (Long Beach, California), 1974; and M. Hoffman, "Home Decor Now Reflects Influences of Getty Villa," *News* (Wilmington, Delaware), October 7, 1974.

58. "Public Museums," 416; B. Deane, "Getty Art Museum Built for Laymen," *Tribune* (Tampa), October 26, 1980; and Wilson, "Meubles Merveilleux in Malibu," 82.

59. Getty quoted in Cristin, *Guidebook*, 6.

60. J. Smith, "Doing as the Romans Did," *Los Angeles Times*, May 8, 1974, IV, 1. For similar opinions see A. Hoyt-Johnson, "Museum Critics" (letter to the editor), *Los Angeles Times*, March 31, 1974, HOM, 9: Morgenstern, "Getty's Little Palace in Malibu," 72; and Jencks, "Don't Panic," 83–84.

61. Gebhard, "Is It 'Disgusting'?," 59. Goldberger, "Getty's Museum's Roman Style," 38.

62. Elena Karina Canavier continues: "These same people do not, however, object to a work of art from the same period, or any other, being wrenched from its original surroundings and impaled upon the wall of a modern museum or caged in a glass display case"; See "The New Getty Museum," *Artweek*, April 6, 1974, 1.

63. C. Jencks, *The Language of Post Modern Architecture*, New York, 1977, 95. See also, Jencks, "Don't Panic," 83.

64. Gebhard, "Is It 'Disgusting'?," 59. Jencks, "Don't Panic," 83, also raised this issue and mentioned other contemporary revivalist architects including Henry Hope Reed, John Blatteau, and Quinlan Terry.

65. Gebhard, "Is It 'Disgusting'?," 59.

66. Gebhard, "Is It 'Disgusting'?," 61. The museum had already been labeled a "monument of the pop environment," due to its popularity. See also G. Glueck, "Getty Museum Is a Hit with Visitors," *New York Times*, May 28, 1977, 34.

67. Gebhard, "Is It 'Disgusting'?," 61.

68. Jencks, *The Language of Post Modern Architecture*, 95.

69. Goldberger, "What Should a Museum Building Be?," 38.

70. Didion continued, "Something about the place embarrasses people. The collection itself is usually referred to as 'that kind of thing,' as in 'not even the best of that kind of thing,' or 'absolutely top-drawer if you like that kind of thing,' both of which translate 'not our kind of thing' " ("Getty's Little House on the Highway," *Esquire*, March 1977, 30).

71. Banham, "Lair of the Looter," 238.

72. Wilson, "A Preview of Pompeii-on-the-Pacific," CAL, 44, wrote that the less sensitive, "campier sensibilities who love playful theatrical artifice will delight in it as the funniest folly since the Assyrian Rubber Factory. The First Real Plastic Museum."

73. Smith, "What Getty Begat in Malibu." This idea also appeared in Glueck, "Getty Museum Is a Hit," 34; and Schneider, "Pompeii sur Pacifique."

74. Smith, "Doing as the Romans Did," IV, 1.

75. Banham, "Lair of the Looter," 238,

76. Von Breton, "Major West Coast Mecca;" C. Foley, "Getty's Herculean Folly," *Observer* (London), January 13, 1974; H. J. Seldis, "What J. Paul Getty Hath Wrought in Malibu," CAL, 60; "Museum Classical: An Oil Baron Has Created a Senator's Dream in Malibu," *Building Design and Construction*, September 13, 1974; Taylor, "Mr. Getty's Invitation," May 25, 1974. It is ironic in this context that Getty never saw his new museum. Although he intended to retire in Malibu, Getty died in England on June 6, 1976, two-and-a-half years after the museum had opened to the public.

77. Wilson, "A Preview of Pompeii-on-the-Pacific," CAL, 44.

78. M. T. Harris, "Billionaire's Bauble: The Getty Museum Has a Style of Its Own," *Finance*, May 1975.

79. In a biography of Getty, his friend and legal advisor, Robina Lund, claimed that Getty fancied himself as the reincarnation of the Roman Emperor Hadrian. The other person that Getty considered a kindred spirit, according to Lund, was William Randolph Hearst, the builder of San Simeon Castle, to which the Getty Museum is frequently compared. Lund quoted Getty as saying that ''Hadrian, Hearst and I are alike—we all liked things on a grand scale. Palatial buildings, fine pictures, gold and silver plate. . ." (R. Lund, *Getty: The Stately Gnome*, London, 1977, 148–149). The building of the museum was offered as support for this hypothesis, since it was "patterned after Hadrian's villa at Herculaneum." This is incorrect: Hadrian was emperor (A.D. 117–136) after the Villa dei Papyri was buried by the A.D. 79 volcanic eruption.

80. Reinsch, "A Roman Villa in Disney Country."

81. J. P. Nugent, "What? A 'Proper Museum' That Isn't Boring?," *Los Angeles Times*, June 1976; and H. Seldis, "It's the Collection That Counts," *Los Angeles Times*, January 17, 1974, IV, 8; Reinsch, "A Roman Villa in Disney Country."

82. See W. Billick, "Getty Museum" (letter to the editor), *Los Angeles Times*, September 30, 1973, CAL, 12; Wilson, "A Preview of Pompeii-on-the-Pacific," CAL, 44; C. Kang, "Dramatic Malibu Debut for New Getty Museum," *Herald-Examiner* (Los Angeles), January 17, 1974; M. Irvine, "Herculaneum at Malibu," *Financial Times*, January 28, 1974; F. Wight, "The Romans, the Regency, and J. Paul Getty," *Art News*, 73, February 1975, 55. Garrett suggested that part of the museum's popularity is due to people's curiosity about Getty, but ". . . if they came here expecting to see Getty's dining room I fear they are, in part, rather disappointed" (quoted in B. Polson, "The Getty Museum; Hardly a Case of Robbing Peter to Pay (J.) Paul," *Washington Post*, January 12, 1975). Since Getty's death and the announcement of his will, Getty's serious interest in the museum is unquestioned. Even Henry J. Seldis, one of the more outspoken critics of the new museum, admitted that "in the final analysis, Getty proved to be a generous patron rather than the world's most miserly billionaire;" see "What Getty's Death Means to the Museum," *Los Angeles Times*, January 20, 1976. In Lund's biography of Getty, he was quoted as having said, "I would like to be remembered as a footnote in history, but as an art collector, not a money-laden businessman!" (Lund, *Getty,* 12).

83. J. R. Taylor, "Mr. Getty's Invitation."

84. Taylor was probably responding to Getty's "Invitation," in which he stated, "I would like every visitor to feel as if I had invited him to come and look around and feel at home" (Getty, "Getty Museum Invitation," CAL, 1).

HOUSE VI

Cornwall, Connecticut

Architect: Peter Eisenman

95. House VI (color plate on page 39)

House VI was designed and built in Cornwall, Connecticut by the architect Peter Eisenman between 1972 and 1976. It was intended as a weekend house for Suzanne and Richard Frank, an architectural historian and a photographer, respectively, whose principal residence is in New York City. Before House VI, the Franks lived in a small schoolhouse which still stands along the driveway near the entrance to the Cornwall property. When they made their decision to build a new structure as opposed to renovating the old, they approached Peter Eisenman, whom they had met some years earlier.

Eisenman, always a controversial figure in the architectural community, was then known as much for his role as educator, author, and critic as he was for his architecture.[1] He had founded the Institute for Architecture and Urban Studies in New York in 1967, and his own designs had received broad publicity with the inclusion of his House I and House II in the collaborative book *Five Architects,* published in 1972.[2] House III, often cited as his most successful built work, was completed in 1971, but it is House VI, his next completed building, that is considered by many to be his most important and

96. Dining area with "stair transformation" above

most controversial work of the period. In historical perspective, House VI stands out in the series of Eisenman's projects as perhaps his most original and carefully executed house design.

House VI stands near the edge of a deep ravine on a partly wooded lot at the outskirts of the tiny rural town of Cornwall, Connecticut. The house is a small two-story structure of post and beam construction whose exterior is made up largely of glass, translucent panels, and plywood painted in various soft shades of grey and white. The surface is glossy and smooth to disguise individual textures and materials. The exterior of the building is perceived as a series of intersecting planes and volumes with a crossing of two large "fin walls" that anchor and divide the house. Each facade remains neutral with respect to traditional front-back and left-right relationships; only the placement of a large flat stone at each of two otherwise well-disguised doors indicates a place of entry. On entering the house, the sensation is one of spaciousness and light, despite its small overall dimensions (approximately forty feet by twenty feet). The front door opens into a small foyer, which gives into the dining and kitchen areas. There are no rooms in the conventional sense, but rather spaces that have been designated for a particular use by the clients' furnishings—a sofa, chairs,

dining table, and coffee table. Only the sink, cupboards, and spaces for the appliances were planned by the architect, and even some of those features were unusually proportioned.

Because of the lack of conventionally planned rooms, inconvenient or unsettling spaces sometimes result and, indeed, the building might seem to be a house only after the fact. The most obvious and therefore the most commonly cited "unconventional events" of the house include such features as two columns which stand in the dining area as part of the notational system of the house but which serve no structural purpose. Other columns hang suspended above the ground on the vertical edge of exterior walls. The kitchen cabinets are set higher than usual for formal reasons and are thus difficult to reach. A bright red staircase hangs upside-down from the ceiling of the two-story dining area in 45-degree juxtaposition to a conventional staircase painted in complementary green. This "stair transformation," as Eisenman calls it, signals the formal organization of the house about a 45-degree diagonal datum line. The composition of the house would, in effect, remain the same if turned upside-down.

Upstairs, one enters the bedroom area through a passageway that is actually a narrow slot in the wall made wider by the opening of a hinged piece of the wall itself—a concession to the owner who found the slot too narrow for comfort. A glazed slit through the depth of the second floor divides the bedroom in half, making the use of twin beds necessary to preserve the aesthetic integrity of the design. The dressing and bath areas are divided from the bedroom by another doorway that assumes the form of a piece of hinged wall. Each of these elements exists to preserve the integrity of the design, even at the cost of comfort and utility. This approach to architectural design and its manifestation in built form are, to say the least, controversial.[3]

House VI has engendered significant response from architectural critics and journalists, as well as from the interested public in general. It has been discussed from many points of view on a variety of levels, from purely intellectual discussions of a deep philosophical or theoretical nature to considerations of purely functional and practical matters. House VI has been called a "hermetically sealed architect's Chinese puzzle"[4] and a "full-scale house of cards."[5] It is an architecture that is "purely intellectual, coldly alienating, maddeningly non-functional, and as maddeningly impossible to ignore."[6] It has been derided as an "architectural example of black (or at least grey) humor,"[7] and a house that "walks in the shadow of the Valley of the Death of Architecture."[8] It has also been called "literally breathtaking—one of the superb visual experiences of modern design."[9]

The design of House VI was partly the result of Eisenman's attempt to reconcile linguistic theories with architectural design. His interest in the work of Noam Chomsky, especially his theories of syntax, led to the investigation of possible analogies between language and

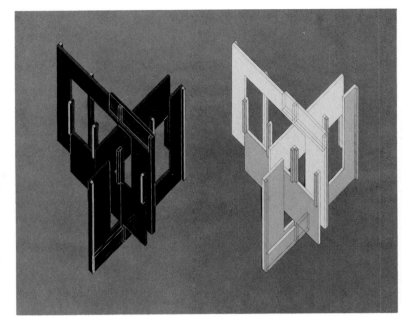

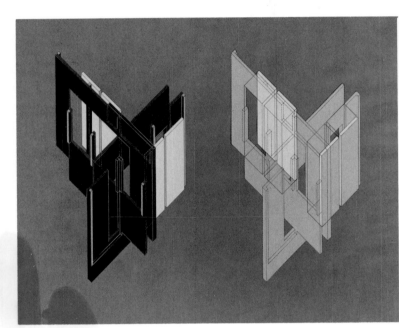

129

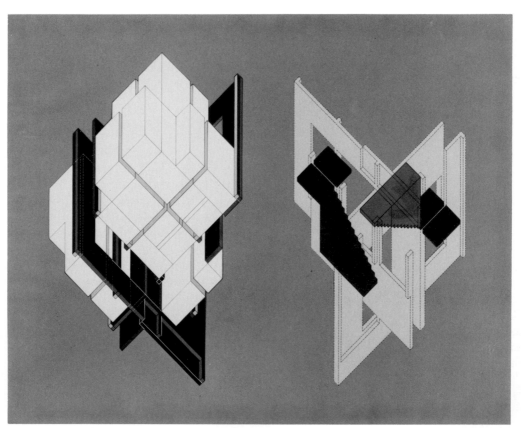

110-111. Transformational drawings 13 and 14

senman's ability to illustrate his concepts in the physical form of House VI. While an acknowledged relationship exists at some level between the house and the axonometric diagrams, it is assumed, at least by those critics writing on the subject, that the house should be made to stand critically on its own without reference to published explanation. With the publication of Eisenman's 1977 article on the house, however, this assumption could no longer be taken for granted. Eisenman wrote (in what seems to be a direct response to Pommer's observations) that the conceptual structure of House VI could not be understood through any physical or perceptual experience, but that it was revealed to the viewer only from a reference point outside the house.[17] This point of reference evidently required a study of the axonometric diagrams of the house, diagrams that, as Eisenman stated in 1977, were "symbiotic with its reality." The use of the term "symbiotic" would suggest that Eisenman intended the house and the diagrams to rely on one another to the extent that each would lack essential meaning without the other. Is it then valid to judge the success of the house alone on its ability to convey Eisenman's design concepts to the viewer? Despite Eisenman's attempts to the contrary, his work did continue to be judged in this manner. In the long review of *Five Architects* published in 1979, Rosemarie Haag Bletter pointed out that Eisenman's architectural proposals had a "curiously and specifically graphic dimension," and concluded that the built result lacked force: "we can follow his proposals in an axonometric projection, but the argument loses some of its force when transferred to a three-dimensional structure."[18]

One possible explanation for this apparent lack of clarity in the final form of House VI is that there are numerous discrepancies between the original design concept and the building as it stands. This fact is alluded to in discussions of the relationship of the drawings to the house, but it is rarely directly noted and never discussed at length.[19] Such a major feature as the division of the originally proposed two-story living area into separate floors to allow for more reasonable proportions in the second-story rooms necessarily meant a change in the perception of the entire structure. Martin Filler made a point of this issue and summed up by remarking upon "a certain poignance in Eisenman's inability to reconcile what he can imagine with what he can build."[20]

Another issue related to Eisenman's process of design is the exclusion of cultural references in architecture, which he conceived as an attempt to free the architecture from associative connotations. The theory, according to Eisenman, is that a structure void of any conventional signs and signals will allow the viewer to be more receptive to an untapped level of communication ideally latent in pure architectural form.[21] In this respect, Eisenman said, the pragmatic and functional aspects of architecture—doors, stairs, walls—must be placed in a position of secondary importance to a reading of their position within a conceptual structure.[22]

112. View from staircase toward second floor

This approach raises two important questions. First, as Paul Goldberger asked, is it really possible that all cultural references can be separated from "what is still, in the end, a house?"[23] And, second, can the resulting structure successfully fulfill its programmatic requirements?

In discussing the first point, Goldberger pointed out that our perception of every element of House VI, despite Eisenman's altered use of form, is partly a result of our own cultural experiences. Goldberger maintained that the forms of House VI are as suggestive of an association with modern architecture and its traditions as they are of any purely formal association Eisenman might propose. In this respect, House VI has frequently been compared to the architecture of the De Stijl group in early twentieth-century Holland. Eisenman had already disputed this comparison as inappropriate in the 1977 *Progressive Architecture* article where he stated that House VI was actually an "inversion of many De Stijl ideas."[24] Apparently, Eisenman's attempt to refute this association was unsuccessful, for in November 1980, Martin Filler again referred to an influence of De Stijl architecture on House VI.[25] Filler quoted John Hejduk's original reference to House VI as "the second canonical De Stijl house."[26] (It

113. House VI

was this reference, of course, that Eisenman had taken as the point of departure for the comment in his earlier article.)

There were some critics, on the other hand, who found Eisenman's attempt to remove all cultural references quite successful, undesirable, and even dangerous. Many viewed Eisenman's approach as irresponsible for a professional architect, while others saw his work as nothing less than a negation of life itself. One outraged commentator proclaimed that Eisenman had indeed "successfully eradicated . . . all allies and metaphors of habitation from House VI."[27] The same critic stated that "the stone step, placed by the clients at the front (?) door, is the only clue that life as we know it exists in House VI." This point of view induced some critics to label House VI as "nihilistic."[28] Charles Jencks stated that "House VI . . . conveys, if we can attach any meaning to it, a fundamental nihilism. It is of course a sensual and dignified cancellation of all positive belief."[29] For some critics then, Eisenman's success in removing cultural references spelled architectural failure on precisely this account.

If the labeling of House VI as "nihilistic" represents an extreme point of view, the pervading attitude toward Eisenman's approach, evidenced especially in comments from the general public, is that it represents irresponsible design.[30] At the same time, critics raised serious questions about the idea of "cultural negation" in a field that is usually considered a service profession. John Morris

Dixon, editor of *Progressive Architecture,* summarized the reservations expressed by many of these critics: "it is work of this kind that is often seen as dangerous by other professionals—as a flouting of functional obligations and practical constraints, as a possible exploitation of the client, as a threat to the credibility of architecture as a service profession."[31] A juror of the 1974 AIA Residential Design Awards, in which House VI received an honorable mention, expressed these feelings in his comment that the house "caused some of our jurors great pain. Eisenman does not start out by thinking that Mrs. Jones wants to stand in her kitchen and see her dining room. He does not permit that to be a determining factor. I like to know where Mrs. Jones wants to stand."[32] It is significant that, despite the reservations of the jury, House VI nevertheless received an award.

There were, naturally, some critics who attempted to understand more completely their discomfort with Eisenman's approach in light of similar researches in art. Of the modernist aesthetic in general, Robert Gutman asked, "Was the price for liberating the artist or the medium the suffering of the audience?"[33] Gutman maintained that while modernism in the arts sometimes required "hard work" on the part of the mind and sensibility, there was an end reward: "The pain associated with the labor of the intellect and the senses was transformed into a renewed sense of satisfaction, awareness, and delight." He concluded that "the new architecture does not seem to work this way. . . . The column that interrupts your dining room conversation is still there even after you become aware of what the column is intended to mean. . . . These design imperatives become more intrusive after they are understood: not less, but more insupportable." Perhaps the most eloquently argued justification of Eisenman's controversial design appeared in an essay by philosopher William Gass in *Progressive Architecture* for June 1977:

> Form, like justice, is blind to persons. Form answers only to itself, and when form contains surprises, the surprises are as eternal as the triangle; whereas we shall just get used to ducking while downing the stairs and no more notice the width of doors than we do the pattern on our china. The column that comes up incompetently short must not be simply saying to us: "You see, I do not reach, think again about support." It must also, and more essentially, say "I am where I am, and I fall short the way I do, because the maximum expression of the nature of this structure requires both—precisely by this much, right now, right here.[34]

Regarding issues of function, the remarks of the critics represent a seriously considered point of view. Nevertheless, comments by the owners of House VI would seem to support the view that the apparent lack of consideration for functional and practical matters is not as important as the overall intention of the architecture. Richard Frank is quoted as having said that "there are a lot of little things that make me curse every so often—I used to bang my head on the stairs a lot, for example, but now I've learned to bend down." "The point," he continued, "is that things like that are little—living here, you forget about them because it is a constant process of learning about form and space."[35] In reference to House VI, some commentators have asked whether it is "really the task of the architect to upset people's normal lives, interfere with their preferences, and reverse their values."[36] In light of remarks like Frank's, it has been argued that the architect was not reversing the values of the clients but rather illustrating them. During the annual *Progressive Architecture* awards in 1979, in reference to Eisenman's House XIa, but equally applicable to House VI, juror Werner Seligmann commented, "You have to be very careful about this one. . . .I can assure you that in this case the client went to the architect knowing full well that this was the kind of thing he was going to get."[37] "That a house like the Franks' is not for the typical client is obvious," said Paul Goldberger, "but there is no reason why the success of a piece of architecture must be measured in terms of its worth as a model for replication."[38]

It has been said that Eisenman "sought to rebuff potential house clients who might be unprepared for his rigorous exclusion of the conventional accommodations an architect is generally expected to make to the patrons of architecture."[39] The importance of this statement would transcend the issue regarding the role of the architect, for it points out that the houses were designed for very specific clients who were aware of and ready to accept Eisenman's terms. Unfortunately, the realities may have been otherwise: one author mentioned the case of a client who hated his house and lived in the basement before moving out.[40] Other clients were prepared for an aggressive and challenging design but unprepared for unscheduled construction costs, late completion dates, and continuous repairs—often due to the performance of the contractor, but no less exasperating for that.[41] Clearly the unconventional and exacting design of these houses required special care in budgeting, scheduling, and above all, contracting.

For the most part, clients who expressed reservations on certain points were quite pleased with other aspects and with the house designs in general. One client loved his house design even though a "transformation. . .drove a column smack through his marital bed"—an inaccurate but far from singular reference to House VI.[42] Richard Frank, owner of the house for ten years now, said only that if Peter Eisenman had been fifteen percent more pragmatic, House VI would be sensational.[43] Robert Miller expressed considerable anger and frustration over all of the unforseen problems in building and maintaining House III, only to say that he loved the house "warts and all—with a passion bordering on obsession."[44]

In addition to the issues raised by the design concept, articles on the house in more popularly oriented publications often focused on isolated aspects of the building, the sensational elements that make for enticing photographs and clever copy. Thus, comments on the building were often limited to a citation of unconventional elements, such as the upside-down staircase, the columns alongside the dining table, and always, the slot in the bedroom floor, which, "wreaking its ultimate havoc on domesticity. . .divides the marital bed in two."[45] With occasional slips in fact, a *Newsweek* article of October 4, 1976, stated that House VI "shakes the viewer at every turn: spectacular views of nature are blocked by concrete; columns with no structural function bisect the bedroom; the front door opens into the kitchen; stairways run into blank walls."[46] The article illustrated none of the aspects cited, and only a single photograph of the exterior of the house was presented. The column next to the dining room table induced some to say that "Eisenman wants to force people to see their new dinner partner—architecture."[47] Robert Gutman offered a more measured evaluation of this feature in observing that "easy conversation during mealtimes is hard to sustain because of the notational columns that for no structural reason descend into the only convenient space for a dining table."[48]

It had been noted that Eisenman had little to do with the choice and placement of the furnishings in House VI, a fact that led Filler to observe that Eisenman "has always preferred to think in terms of spaces rather than rooms, and the intrusion of furnishings into those spaces. . .is for him at best a necessary evil, one which a client might indulge in, but in which Eisenman will take no direct part."[49] One might maintain, as Gutman did, that Eisenman has created spaces which are awkward and difficult to furnish comfortably. Even so, a contrary point of view might be argued from the evidence of a five-page article in *House & Garden* for which Massimo Vignelli decorated the interiors of House VI.[50]

Vignelli was asked to furnish and decorate House VI specifically for a photo-layout of the house, and his furnishings were removed after the work was completed. In general, the furnishings he employed were colorful, simple in form, and flexible in their use and position within the spaces. For example, mattress-like sofas with pillows and bolsters, copies of Rietveld's "Z" chairs, and pedestals for floral arrangements filled the living area, while a simple but elegant table constructed of the same pedestals with a clear plastic slab and more "Z" chairs furnished the dining area. While the article dealt little with the architecture *per se,* it served to question the validity of the criticism that House VI must of necessity be uncomfortable and uninviting.

To be sure, buildings are not immutable objects. For practical reasons, the owners of House VI added a pitched roof to the original flat-roofed structure, and even this episode created a flurry of contention. According to Filler,

> this unfortunate intervention by the house's owners reminds us how the architectural artifact is routinely susceptible to destructive alteration. In due course, the addition of a pitched roof to House VI might well be seen either as an act of self-preservation or as an act of cultural vandalism—or perhaps as the first unwitting architectural landmark of the post-Post-Modernist Age.[51]

In 1982, the Franks replaced the pitched roof with one that is flat.[52]

From a review of the literature, it may be suggested that a significant quantity of the criticism of House VI may well have been generated by Eisenman's explanatory passages and diagrams that often accompanied its publication and served for some observers to all-but-completely obscure a clear perception of what was constructed. Nevertheless, though its level of practicality was less than acceptable to many, House VI was frequently acknowledged as an important exploration in modern architectural design. In August 1977, in an editorial in reply to the overwhelming reader response to the publication of House VI by *Progressive Architecture,* John Morris Dixon stated that "We know architecture is a service profession, but ultimately the only element that architects alone can contribute is design."[53] "If architectural design is not now serving the public to the fullest," he continued, "then *design* exploration is, in fact, very much in the public interest." Later, in December 1979, Dixon returned to this matter in an editorial entitled "Ethics VI — Looking Good," in which he remarked that

114. Staircase and "stair transformation"

115. House VI with interior design by Massimo Vignelli for *House & Garden* magazine

134

"The relationships between aesthetics and social responsibilities are highly complex, and are now undergoing thorough reexamination."[54] Dixon went on to say that "the profession has a very real obligation to test, in some way, the public reception of its aesthetic efforts. . . .And it has an equally serious obligation to increase the public understanding of design issues — through works that are visible design lessons, and through deliberate educational efforts." To illustrate this role of House VI and to explain its effect, Richard Frank was once quoted as having said of the dining space, "No one ever really complained about the column. . . Everyone notices it at first, and it makes them think about the house and how its structure works, but once you sit down and start to eat, even guests don't really think about it."[55]

Kathleen Enz Finken

Notes

1. C. Ray Smith, "Peter D. Eisenman," *Contemporary Architects*, ed. Muriel Emanuel, New York, 1980, 231.
2. *Five Architects—Eisenman, Graves, Gwathmey, Hejduk, Meier* (preface by Arthur Drexler, introduction by Colin Rowe, critique by Kenneth Frampton, postscript by Philip Johnson), New York, 1975. Originally published by Wittenborn and Company in 1972, this book drew considerable critical response. For the best known replies, see Robert Stern, Jacquelin Robertson, Charles Moore, Allan Greenberg, and Romaldo Giurgola in "Five on Five," *Architectural Forum*, 138, May 1973, 46–57. For a discussion of both *Five Architects* and "Five on Five," see Rosemarie Haag Bletter's review of *Five Architects* and "Five on Five" in the *Journal of the Society of Architectural Historians*, 38, May 1979, 205–207.
3. In "Book of Lists," *Progressive Architecture*, 60, December 1979, 56, Suzanne Stephens cited Peter Eisenman as the most controversial architect of the 1970s according to a reader response: "Peter Eisenman, who has been published only three times in the last 10 years, excluding the Design Awards program, . . . has a batting average of 1000 for making 'the most controversial list.'" The publications in *Progressive Architecture* include House VI (June 1977), House III (May 1979), and 'On Reading Architecture' (March 1972). House VI ranked third on *Progressive Architecture*'s list of most controversial buildings of the 70s. House III ranked eighth.
4. Kenneth M. Moffett, "Views: Letters from Readers," *Progressive Architecture*, 58, August 1977, 8.
5. David A. Greenspan, "Views: Letters from Readers," *Progressive Architecture*, 58, August 1977, 8.
6. Smith, "Peter D. Eisenman," 231.
7. Charles Jencks, *Late Modern Architecture and Other Essays*, New York, 1980, 177.
8. Greenspan, "Views: Letters from Readers," 8.
9. Robert Gutman, "House VI," *Progressive Architecture*, 58, June 1977, 65.
10. A lengthy discussion of Eisenman's researches into the application of linguistic models to architectural design, in particular to his own work, is found in Rosalind Krauss, "Death of a Hermeneutic Phantom: Materialization of the Sign in the Work of Peter Eisenman," *Archi-*

tecture and Urbanism (A + U), 112, 1980, 188–220. House VI is discussed in some detail on page 207. See also Mario Gandelsonas, "From Structure to Subject: The Formation of an Architectural Language," *Oppositions*, 17, Summer 1979, 11–29. For Eisenman's thoughts on the subject, see Eisenman, "From Object to Relationship II: Giuseppe Terragni: Casa Giuliani Frigerio," *Perspecta*, 13–14, 1971, 36–61. In this article Eisenman described his initial interest in these studies and their meanings and application in art and architecture in general and specifically in the work of Giuseppe Terragni (1904–1943), an Italian architect.
11. Charles Jencks, *The Language of Post-Modern Architecture*, New York, 1977, 73.
12. Peter D. Eisenman, "Notes on Conceptual Architecture: Towards a Definition," *Casabella*, 359, December 1971, 51. Mario Gandelsonas analyzed Eisenman's interpretation of Chomsky's theory in "On Reading Architecture. Peter Eisenman: The Syntactic Dimension," *Progressive Architecture*, 53, March 1972, 85. Others who referred to Eisenman's use of the term "deep structure" included Rosemarie Haag Bletter, *Five Architects* and "Five on Five," 205–207, and Robert Stern and Jaquelin Robertson in "Five on Five," 47, 50. Stern proclaimed himself a non-believer: "I do not believe that structure, no matter how "deep", is a particularly expressive tool in architecture."
13. Peter D. Eisenman, "House VI," *Progressive Architecture*, 58, June 1977, 59.
14. Richard Pommer, "The New Architectural Supremacists," *Artforum*, 15, October 1976, 38–43. The article is a review of the symposium entitled "Positions in Architecture" held at the Rhode Island School of Design in the spring of 1976, which involved the discussion of "Modernism" in architecture in the 1960s and 1970s. Among those who feature prominently in the article are Peter Eisenman and the critic Colin Rowe.
15. Pommer, "Architectural Supremacists," 39–40.
16. For example, see Gandelsonas, "On Reading Architecture," 82; Bletter, *Five Architects* and "Five on Five," 206; and Pommer, "Architectural Supremacists," 39–40. The current interest in Eisenman's diagrams and drawings as art objects should also be noted. In addition to the many photographs in art and architectural journals (e.g. "Transformations, Decompositions, and Critiques," *Artforum*, 19, March 1981, 48–51), examples of his work have been included in books on architectural drawings (e.g., David Gebhard and Deborah Nevins, *200 Years of American Architectural Drawings*, New York, 1977), as well as in exhibits (see Ada Louise Huxtable's review, "Poetic Visions of Design for the Future," *New York Times Magazine*, April 27, 1979, 32).
17. Eisenman, "House VI," 59.
18. Bletter, *Five Architects* and "Five on Five," 206.
19. Paul Goldberger mentioned some changes in the proposed kitchen arrangement and the adjustment of the upside-down staircase in "The House as Sculptural Object," *New York Times Magazine*, March 20, 1977, 74ff. The earliest published plans for the house appeared in *Casabella*, 386, 1974, 27. These differed markedly from those found in later publications as, for example, in *L'Architecture d'aujourd'hui*, 186, August/September 1976, 63. To our knowledge, there are no publications

that include plans of House VI exactly as it was built.

20. Martin Filler, "Peter Eisenman: Polemical Houses," *Art in America*, 68, November 1980, 129. Filler commented that, along with a written text on the formal development of his buildings, Eisenman's works are "accompanied by numerous drawings of the structures in their various stages leading to the realization of their final form. In doing so, Eisenman clearly hopes to make his design process appear rational and comprehensible at every step along the way. . . . Yet the disparities between what Eisenman says and how the architectural artifacts finally appear indicate that, as much as Eisenman would like to be seen as the successful fabricator of intriguingly visual and profoundly intellectual puzzles, not all the pieces always fit."

21. Peter D. Eisenman, "Conceptual Architecture," *Casabella*, 386, 1974, 25: "It is my belief that in every building we make as architects, no matter what meaning we may give to it—functional, social, or symbolic—there is a potential level of communication which may exist merely because of our capacity to understand that nature, because of the way we see and the way we think. My work is an attempt to raise our level of consciousness about this potential communication to the point, where as designers and users, our architecture may have a more precise mode of communication, and thus hopefully a more enriched meaning. My premise for undertaking this work is based on my belief that architectural form is not merely geometric abstraction or a repertory of conventional signs, but in essence, a set of archetypal relationships which affect our most basic sensibilities about our environment."

22. Eisenman, "Notes," 51: "To make something conceptual in architecture would require taking the pragmatic and functional aspects and placing them in a conceptual matrix, where their primary existence is no longer interpreted from the physical fact of being a bathroom or closet, but rather the functional aspect bathroom or closet becomes secondary to some primary reading as a notation in a conceptual context."

23. Goldberger, *"House as Sculptural Object,"* 84.

24. Eisenman, "House VI," 59: "John Hejduk has said that House VI is the 'second canonical De Stijl house,' but for me this perception tends to overlook or obscure the basic intentions of the house." Eisenman began his essay with this statement and went on to compare at some length both De Stijl architecture and the architecture of Le Corbusier to House VI on points of spatial disposition ("spatial strategies," as Eisenman called it) and the conception and perception of the architecture. He concluded on each point that House VI is actually very different from both the work of Le Corbusier and that of the De Stijl architects.

25. Filler, "Polemical Houses," 130.

26. Eisenman, "House VI," 57.

27. Greenspan, "Views: Letters from Readers," 8.

28. Greenspan, "Views: Letters from Readers," 8: "That Eisenman has succeeded in constructing a full-scale house of cards cannot be questioned or even approached. What can and must be questioned is why an architect as brilliant and erudite as Dr. Eisenman chooses to widen the credibility gap between architects and their clients, and, more fundamentally, why he is

so obsessed with the architecture of nihilism." In his 1971 article "Notes on Conceptual Architecture," Eisenman had discussed nihilism as one of "three basic attitudes in conceptual art with respect to the object" (Eisenman, "Notes," 48).

29. Jencks, *Late Modern Architecture*, 178. He further states that House VI "foreshadows Eisenman's explicit nihilism of 1977 and his House X."

30. For a sampling of such letters, see "Views: Letters from Readers," *Progressive Architecture*, 58, August 1977, 8. John Morris Dixon addressed this issue in his editorial "Socially Useful Architecture" in the same issue.

31. John Morris Dixon, "Editorial: Socially Useful Architecture," *Progressive Architecture*, 58, August 1977, 6.

32. Norma Skurka, "Housing Out of Tune With the Times," *New York Times Magazine*, February 24, 1974, 75.

33. Gutman, "House VI," 67.

34. William Gass, "House VI," *Progressive Architecture*, 58, June 1977, 64.

35. Quoted in Goldberger, "House as Sculptural Object," 74.

36. Gutman, "House VI," 66.

37. "Citation: Architectural Design—Peter Eisenman," *Progressive Architecture*, 60, January 1979, 84.

38. Goldberger, "House as Sculptural Object," 77

39. Filler, "Polemical Houses," 132.

40. Dennis Sharp, *The Rationalists: Theory and Design in the Modern Movement*, London, 1978, 219. The client is not named.

41. These facts were revealed in reference to House VI in a personal interview with Suzanne and Richard Frank, April 8, 1984. An especially interesting statement was given by Robert Miller, then owner of Eisenman's House III in Lakeville, Connecticut, in "I Guess You Win, Peter," *Progressive Architecture*, 55A, May 1974, 99–98.

42. Sharp, *The Rationalists*, 219.

43. Personal interview, April 8, 1984.

44. Miller, "I Guess You Win," 94.

45. Charles Jencks, "Post-Modern History," *Architectural Design*, 48, January 1978, 51.

46. Douglas Davis, "Real Dream Houses," *Newsweek*, October 4, 1976, 66. The author clearly did not visit the house. The dangers of not seeing the architecture before discussing it are obvious. In an otherwise insightful article in *The New York Times Magazine*, March 20, 1977, Paul Goldberger twice referred incorrectly to the "green" upside-down staircase, and to the conventional staircase as "red."

47. Smith, "Peter D. Eisenman," 231.

48. Gutman, "House VI," 66.

49. Filler, "Polemical Houses," 129. According to Suzanne Frank, the choice and placement of the furniture was not an issue that the architect was involved with (personal interview, February 28, 1984).

50. "Space Alive," *House and Garden*, January 1978, 70–75, 123.

51. Filler, "Polemical Houses," 132.

52. Personal interview, April 8, 1984.

53. John Morris Dixon, "Socially Useful Architecture," 6.

54. John Morris Dixon, "Ethics VI—Looking Good," *Progressive Architecture*, 60B, December 1979, 8.

55. Goldberger, "House as Sculptural Object," 77.

INDETERMINATE FACADE
Best Products Showroom

Houston, Texas

Architects: SITE, Inc.

116. Indeterminate Facade (color plate on page 40)

Founded in 1956 by Sydney and Frances Lewis, Best Products is a company that sells merchandise from catalog showrooms throughout the country. These retail outlets have generally been located in suburban shopping plazas and this is true for the Indeterminate Facade showroom, commissioned by Best Products in 1974 and unveiled on September 12, 1975 at the Almeda-Genoa Shopping Center in a suburb of Houston, Texas. The standardized design for Best showrooms has been a 65,000 square-foot, two-story brick structure with a pedestrian canopy, whose shape is hardly more distinguished than a rectangular box with the entrance indicated by a simple metal overhang. What makes the Houston showroom unique is the design of two sides of the exterior to resemble tall brick walls in a state of col-

lapse, with a massive pile of bricks heaped where they fell onto the protective canopy.

The Indeterminate Facade showroom is the work of a group known as SITE. The design group was organized formally in 1970 by Alison Sky, Michelle Stone, and James Wines, who is the leading spokesperson for the group. In the early 1970s, Best Products Company hired SITE to design an eye-catching showroom facade; the result, the Peeling Wall of 1972, was the first of what was to become a series of unusual facade designs. The Peeling Wall showroom in Richmond, Virginia was built of brick and epoxy-based mortar to look as though the front facade wall is peeling away from the rest of the building—a radical statement in the worlds of architecture and commerce. That the patrons were well pleased may be

117. View from adjacent residential area

judged by the subsequent commissions from Best Products Company, including the Indeterminate Facade in Houston. In addition to the Richmond and Houston projects, Best Products executed SITE's designs for the Notch showroom in Sacramento, California (1977) with its mobile, jagged, 14-foot corner entrance, and the Tilt showroom in Towson, Maryland (1978) with its precariously tilted facade wall. Other SITE designs commissioned by Best Products include two projects in Miami, Florida: the naturalistic Hialeah showroom and the surrealistic Cutler Ridge showroom were executed in 1978–1979.[1]

That these buildings do not appear to be examples of conventional architecture is perhaps a result of the varied interests of SITE's principals. Sky was trained in art and literature, Stone in photography and sociology, and Wines in sculpture.[2] When the group first began designing together, the results were hailed as thought-provoking by some commentators and ridiculed by others. The degree to which the firm has earned professional recognition may be measured in part by Wines's appointment as chairman of the environmental and interior design department at Parsons School of Design in New York City

in 1983.[3] This conspicuous appointment indicates the continuing importance of Wines's contribution to SITE, which remains an active and controversial design group.

The appearance of a modern building that seems to be in the process of deterioration is obviously shocking, but the effect is also just as obviously calculated. The white brick of the Indeterminate Facade rises above the height of the standard showroom. Missing sections and gaping holes appear in the false front and side wall, as if they were attacked or eroded by unseen forces. Directly above one of the three entrance doors appears a dramatic remnant of the implied destructive force — loose bricks have tumbled from a broad gap in the facade onto the metal canopy. In its new context the stability of the canopy looks seriously threatened by the weight of the brick rubble and the impending collapse of the entire wall. The sense of danger is heightened by the location of the crumbling mass directly over the shoppers' entrance.

The local reactions to the Houston showroom have been varied, and a number of amusing anecdotes have been recorded. One of the most popular tales recounts

138

118. Cascade of bricks

the visit of a city building inspector; according to published rumor, the inspector chose to note the effects of "hurricane damage" on his official forms rather than record what he saw as deliberate design.[4] Wines recalled that during the construction, a passerby commented, "That's just what I've always wanted to do. Kick the s--- out of one of those buildings." "I knew then," said Wines, "we were on the right track."[5] Another local tale involves two policemen summoned to the showroom by a passing motorist who had reported that the building was collapsing. While the policemen waited for the manager to arrive, each of them purchased a watch.[6] A resident, who claimed to be "the only person in Harris County who likes it," also said that the facade "does just exactly what it was meant to do—it attracts attention."[7] The fine arts editor of the *Houston Chronicle,* Ann Holmes, was reportedly "crazy about it" because "it shows that architecture doesn't have to be stuffy."[8] Other recorded reactions and incidents include that of a woman in Houston who stated that her nine- and ten-year-old children were afraid to enter the building. A man who drove to the store and saw the crumbled front drove elsewhere to shop, assuming "the thing had been burned out;" another man wondered if a plane had hit the store.[9]

In reality, the local reaction was probably less gullible than it has been portrayed, and the public adjusted to the novelty of the facade with a promptness that surprised even the merchandisers. Said one well-acclimated viewer, "If they ever fixed it, it wouldn't look normal." Even a consumer who was reputedly "appalled" by the Indeterminate Facade was undeterred by it: "I'd shop in a barn if they had the prices," she said.[10] In fact, while the price of the facade was said to be about five percent of the total construction costs, a Best Products spokesperson claimed that the Houston store has set sales records exceeding projected estimates by forty percent.[11]

In a broader forum the Indeterminate Facade has been discussed, criticized, and praised in national newspapers, in the foreign press, and in architectural journals. In business and professional magazines, its importance and its success have been frequently discussed. And although the Houston showroom has not met with anything like universal acceptance in architectural circles, the designs of SITE and the writings of James Wines have had considerable impact on the profession and have influenced the critical reputation of the group.

Wines has consistently described the concept of SITE's work with the word "de-architecture," a term that has appeared in countless articles since its publication in 1974 and that continues to be used by Wines in essays in the 1980s.[12] Wines most clearly defined his meaning for the term "de-architecture" and the way that it characterizes the work of SITE in a compendium of contemporary architects.[13] Here he described the work of SITE as "involved with subtractive, fragmented, and inversionist aspects of architecture." The results of such work are of-

ten hybrids "suspended between the definitions of art and architecture" and imbued with commentary about society, politics, and architecture.

> De-architecture is a general way of defining an attitude or means for changing standard reactions to the urban context by using inherent circumstances to alter and/or invert the original intentions of a particular situation. Whereas, for example, the commonly sanctioned view of architecture has been exemplified by a relationship between form and internal motives of function, the work of SITE deals with a relationship between content and the external influences of social and cultural context.[14]

Elsewhere, Wines made reference to the ideas of Marcel Duchamp, who "questioned every premise, every assumption, and who finally rejected historical precedent in order to establish an entirely new set of definitions." In this context, Wines remarked upon the commonly held notion that much of the art of the twentieth century has been about art, but he appended the concept that "de-architecturization is art about architecture."[15]

In an article published before the Indeterminate Facade was built, Wines discussed the intentions of the design as a "contrary reaction to the ongoing economic and construction boom within the state [of Texas]."[16] The concept was to depart sharply from the local emphasis on "glossy conformity" in favor of the potential fascination of unfinished imagery, fragmentation of whole elements, and missing parts. "In our age," wrote Wines, "when the monolithic institutions are crumbling under their own weight, it is really 'missing parts' and fragmentary pieces that represent the real vitality of urban life." Wines elucidated these concepts by providing analogies to ruins:

> The fascination with missing parts is universal. Witness the magnetism of demolition or construction sites and archaeological ruins. Their attraction is a visual dialogue requiring the spectator to reconcile the known and the void as interactive events, to accept a dialectic of entropy and equivocation as the fundamental bridge between architecture and environment.

Returning to the issue of the Indeterminate Facade, Wines stated that "It is intended that the project become a catalyst between constructive and reductive processes."[17]

Despite the earnest tone of these statements, there were many misgivings and much misunderstanding of the facade design among professionals. The most blatant example of incomprehension was the publication in the *Architectural Review* of a photograph of the Indeterminate Facade with a caption that began with these words: "Are

119. View from the store's parking lot

you finding it hard to design new buildings, to add some meaning to the language of modern architecture?"[18] The basic intent of the photograph and the caption was to treat the facade design as a joke: "dismissive" was the term that the *Architectural Review* used to describe its initial reaction to the "crumbling building" two-and-a-half years later when, in 1978, the magazine published a serious review of works by SITE.[19] In this review by Lance Wright, the works (including the Indeterminate Facade) were seen to be making two points about architecture: first, it is a medium that "has been unable to make the jump from 'formalism' to 'conceptualism', " as has painting or sculpture; second, because modern buildings serve to perpetuate this notion, SITE attempts "to reverse the time-honoured notion of the other arts as the accessories of architecture and to make architecture the accessory of the new, conceptual, Urban Art form."[20] For Wright, the art historical precedents of SITE's work are to be found in surrealism and eighteenth-century ruin architecture, but with an appeal that is "direct and universal."

Indeed, one of the stated reasons for the magazine's reconsideration of SITE was to recognize the rarity of "people who have the drive and conviction to be funny about their buildings," in addition to making general "amends." Ultimately, however, Wright found the ideas of SITE "doomed to fail because what people ask from art is communication . . . and this is just what 'conceptual art' cannot give."[21] And if the criticism of modern life is devastating, it is compromised (in Wright's view) by the fact that those doing the criticizing have accepted "the premises" of the society that is their target.

Wright's article had been designed to redress the dismissive tone of the caption for the Houston facade, and the *Architectural Review* gave Wines the opportunity to respond to the new assessment in a text that immediately followed Wright's appraisal. Wines's response began with the suggestion that the humor of the Indeterminate Facade was also "about certain issues—architectural, psychological, sociological—which cannot be simply dismissed as 'funny'. "[22] Wines also took issue with the

141

interpretation of the buildings as ruins; for him they were "more about the state of being 'unfinished'. " With regard to the matter of accepting the premises of the life and society that is being criticized, Wines maintained that the mere acceptance of a commission puts every artist in this category, which is itself unremarkable.[23] Concluding on a plaintive note, Wines recounted how initially no one thought such interesting ideas could be built, that once they were built by SITE they were not seen as real architecture, and that as soon as they became commercially viable SITE was perceived as too commercially oriented. "Obviously," wrote Wines, "one can't win."[24] The fact that SITE's buildings function well in all the traditional ways is interesting, claimed Wines, but finally less important than questioning whether the "formalist/functionalist modern legacy" ought to be "the only legitimate concerns of architecture."[25]

By the time that Wright's article and Wines's response had appeared in the *Architectural Review,* the Indeterminate Facade had already been frequently published, becoming a popular feature in the journalistic literature.[26] Writing in the *Architectual Record* in March 1977, Gerald Allen noted that few stores have ever been discussed as major works of architecture and that commercial buildings tend not to attract imaginative solutions.[27] For Allen, the Best showrooms by SITE are "good" because they combine the familiar and the unfamiliar in a shocking unity: the usual shop in the suburban shopping center turns out to be surprising, funny, attractive to the curious, and powerful, for "SITE's juxtaposition of the modestly familiar with the stunningly unfamiliar is like a bomb that arrives in a shoebox."[28] All "good" architecture, Allen argued, "is vividly like something we already know about and, with an equal vividness, unlike anything else in the world." Allen foresaw a problem in the architects' cleverness only in the potentially limited repertoire to which a standard commercial warehouse building could lend itself.[29] Some of these notions were incorporated in a review of the Best showrooms that appeared in the London *Times* in January 1978, while the reviewer for the *Washington Post* preferred to understand the showrooms as contemporary expressions of the follies that were built as artificial ruins in eighteenth-century parks.[30]

The question of the relationship of ruins to the Indeterminate Facade has been difficult for critics to sort out. Arthur Drexler pointed out that "collapse and decay as architectural motifs have ample precedent," but that the Houston showroom has an effect that is significantly different from Gothic or Roman ruins intended to evoke contemplation on the transience of earthly achievements.[31] "The Houston showroom's environment is not exactly pastoral," Drexler explained, "and the building's apparently ruinous state pertains not to a world long gone but to our own—giving a slightly different twist to the phrase 'business as usual'. "[32] Evidently, the notion of the facade as ruin was a concept that Wines could not defeat. This fact may in part be due to self-generated

publicity that more than once featured conspicuous photographs of ruins in juxtaposition with the SITE designs.[33] If the ruins were intended only to explicate the social commentary of the designs, the message was ambiguously related to the formal aspects of the designs as well.

The state of being "unfinished," the interpretation preferred by Wines, was articulated at length by Bruno Zevi in an essay included in a recent book devoted to SITE. In the essay, entitled "The Poetics of the Unfinished," Zevi viewed SITE's erosion of the box-like showroom form at Houston as an attempt to establish a visual dialogue between the building and its surroundings: the irregularity of the jagged top of the Indeterminate Facade and its perforated walls created a dynamic relationship to the sky.[34] Zevi contrasted the Houston showroom to the World Trade Center, whose towers formed a "double box" that precluded such dynamic relationships. By relating SITE's work to accepted monuments of architectural history, Zevi attempted to argue in favor of these unconventional designs; parallels were made to the manner in which Frederick Law Olmstead merged the built environment with the natural environment ("each complete in itself") and to the manner in which Frank Lloyd Wright destroyed the "building box by eliminating its frame."[35] Similarly, the concept of the "unfinished" was related to medieval and baroque town plans and to the architecture and sculpture of Michelangelo:

> The notion of the "unfinished" is very elementary. It was expressed in the Medieval and Baroque towns, where no building is complete in itself or isolated, but defines its own image through the integration of other elements. The concept of "finito" and "non-finito" was technically formulated by Michelangelo both in his architecture and in his late sculptures.[36]

By the time this essay appeared in print, however, the Indeterminate Facade and other designs by SITE needed no argument for acceptance among the journalists who, in Europe and the United States, responded positively to the challenge of the new concepts.

In Europe as early as 1976, Franco Raggi developed a detailed sequence of ideas that attempted to explain the showroom in more abstract terms than Zevi, but to much the same effect. For Raggi the effect of the "missing parts" is both formal and psychological.[37] The use of "missing parts is the positive interpretation of the negative, the search for less in a world of more," according to this view; at the same time, this quality of ambiguity is "the only quality which makes urban life tolerable."[38] As such, Raggi stated, "the building questions the 'form follows function' ethic of modern architecture." Francesco Torres, writing in 1977, considered the Indeterminate Facade as a socio-political statement directed at the quality of life in the United States, a premonition of the eventual destruction of American society.[39] Without much regard for the artistic implications of the design, he related it to

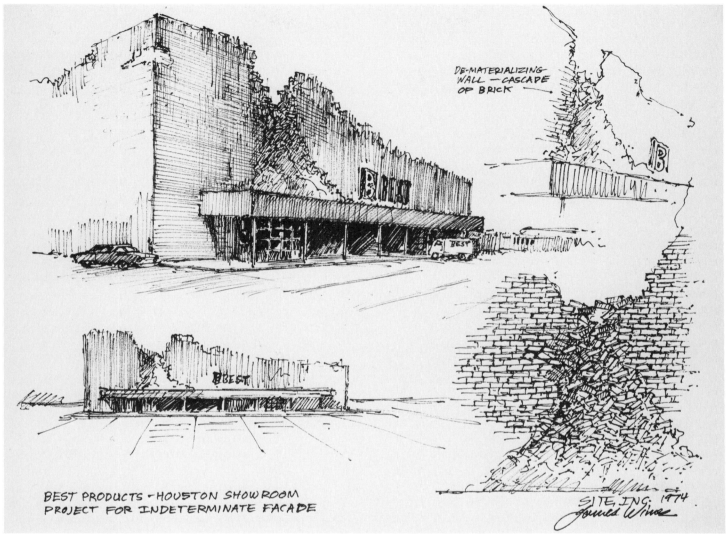

BEST PRODUCTS - HOUSTON SHOWROOM
PROJECT FOR INDETERMINATE FACADE

DE-MATERIALIZING
WALL — CASCADE
OF BRICK

SITE, INC. 1974

120. Drawing for design of the Indeterminate Facade by James Wines

the decadence illustrated by the ubiquity of television and electric appliances. By contrast, in 1979, Philip Jodidio dealt with the showroom in terms of philosophical and psychological content, drawing parallels to Werner Heisenberg's *Principle of Uncertainty (1927)*, a book whose thesis was that science and technology are not the answer to the complex problems of the modern world.[40] These were prevalent attitudes in the 1920s and 1930s, and Jodidio cited precedents in the surrealism of De Chirico and the art of Duchamp, as well as recent developments in pop art. Jodidio also quoted a passage from Samuel Beckett written in 1938, and often used by Wines: "The time is perhaps not altogether too green for the vile suggestion that art has nothing to do with clarity. does not dabble in the clear, and does not make clear."[41]

The American press has accepted the work of SITE and the Indeterminate Facade, but on grounds that are more closely related to social commentary and commentary on the state of the architectural profession than on philosophical bases. William Marlin's article published in

the *Christian Science Monitor* in 1977 treated the design in terms of estrangement, loneliness, and chaos in our society and environment.[42] Marlin described the Houston showroom as a "nonmonument to nonmaterialism" and sympathetically reviewed the work of SITE as serious artistic signals to an acquisitive, materialistic society."[43] In a debate where the topic was "Design-Architecture and New Directions," Leon Krier attacked precisely this notion and called the work of Wines and his partners "tragic" and a set-back for serious architecture.[44] And while American and European colleagues hastened to Wines's defense, there have been others who criticized SITE on this basis, or saw its work as illustrating a new ''pessimism'' in the United States.[45]

Perhaps John Dreyfuss was already a little behind the times in 1980 in arguing to his readers that there really was serious content in the SITE designs; when he stated that "almost no one viewed them as serious social commentary," he was slightly wide of the mark.[46] In retrospect, however, it is more interesting to note his

121. Aerial view

emphasis on aspects of social commentary. By contrast, Paul Goldberger had maintained that the key aspect of these designs was their concern for questioning the relationship between art and architecture.[47] In the final analysis, Goldberger praised the intention of jolting the tradition of "dreary" architecture on the American commercial strip in the suburbs, but he found a paradox in the fact that SITE did not deal with the interior of the showroom. Because the firm did not do so, the Houston building remains "ordinary" and, as such, the Indeterminate Facade becomes the sort of building that SITE was "polemicizing against."[48] In this early assessment Goldberger did not appear to take fully into account the nature of the commission, nor did he appear to be responsive to Wines's argument that "the building's impact . . . is based upon the fact that we changed the reality of the physical circumstances very little, but we changed it a great deal on the psychological level."[49]

Allan Temko sympathetically characterized the Houston showroom as "a horselaugh at the pomposity and ineptitude of the architectural profession whose lunkhead buildings everywhere deserve to fall apart, as some of them actually do."[50] But precisely this point has apparently offended some professional circles in the United States, as C. Ray Smith explained:

> One American architecture journal wrote that it would not now, or in the future, publish any of SITE's work. . . . It is not as though architects are so unaware or so humorless that they do not appreciate SITE's dead-serious belly laughs. But they take it as attacks on their profession for

anyone to make sculpture, art, or display out of the idea that, for instance, a roof leaks—as if that had only to do with the craft of building. . . .[51]

Smith's sympathies lay clearly in SITE's camp, but the issues he raised had broader currency than the literature would indicate.

Indeed, Smith touched on a recurring critical assessment when he discussed the apparently democraticizing imagery that can be understood on some level by nearly every observer:

> The idea that anything is understandable to all is the very antithesis of art. Adherents of the vanguard usually feel that touching a mass audience indicates middlebrow thinking. To them, art for art's sake and abstruse obscuration, which promise hidden and untouchable riches, are hallmarks of the highest art.[52]

Pilar Viladas suggested much the same point in a contemporaneous assessment: "A large cross-section of the American public can relate to them [the showrooms] without the aid of an architectural history book, precisely because the buildings speak to our subconscious, and not to a relatively alien cultural heritage, rooted in Europe, that is common to both Modernism and Post-Modernism alike."[53]

Such notions as these are, of course, closely related to pop art, and many of the critics have depended heavily on this relationship to understand the Indeterminate

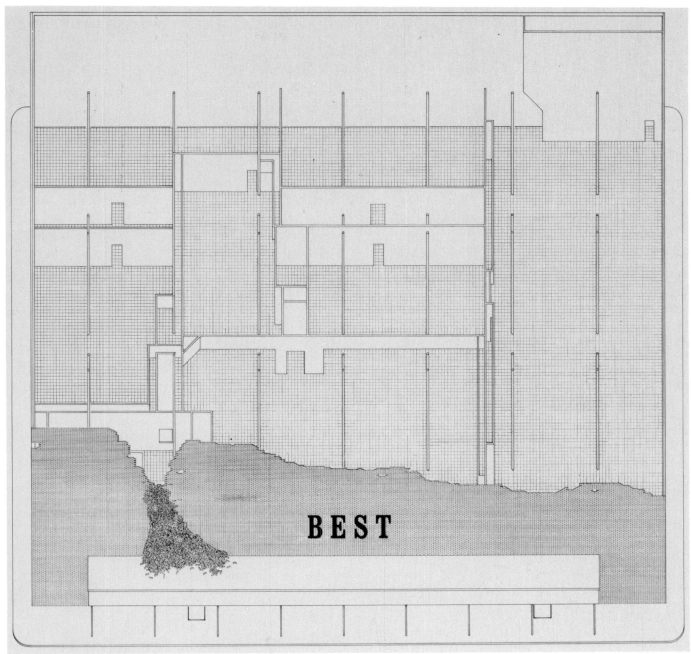

122. Cavalier oblique projection

Facade. In *Artforum,* Nancy Foote maintained that SITE "would probably never have found its way into architecture without Pop Art."[54] In this framework, the immediate precedents of the designs would be the architecture and theory of Robert Venturi, who accepted and legitimized the American vernacular, and Claes Oldenburg, whose sculpture relied for its effect on ordinary imagery and colossal scale. (Foote suggested that the success of the SITE buildings is due in part to the fact that "their actual-size scale avoids the disappointment one feels when Oldenburg's proposed colossal monuments shrink to real objects."[55]) In Richmond, Virginia, the hometown of Best Products, Robert Merritt compared SITE to the environmental artist Christo in the way that both "relish" the va-

riety of critical reactions to their work, and surely the comparison is even deeper than that.[56]

Curiously, it was precisely on this basis that Lebbeus Woods found the designs by SITE for the Best Products Company lacking in sustained interest. In a thoughtful review of schemes by SITE, Woods asserted that "the thoroughness with which they have been designed and anticipated, their very explicitness and lack of spontaneity in execution denies them the power to provoke the imagination into a spontaneity of its own, to lead it past the intended message to a variety of personal interpretations."[57] This point of view represents a careful statement of the notion that the designs constitute "one-liners" without sustaining power to continually provoke new

123. View from nearby highway, Indeterminate Facade on horizon

perceptions in viewers. As Woods suggested, "When the artist pounds his message home too blatantly he may create a strong impression, but not a work that lives and grows with individual experience of it."[58] He elaborated, bringing to bear precisely the kind of considerations from which other critics have come to different conclusions:

> If SITE were to approach its idea with gestures of ambiguous intent, for example, a few implications of decay that may or may not be "real", there would be no feeling of contrivance and theatricality to interfere with the free play of feelings in response. If these implications were expanded or somehow developed over a period of time, the implication of a living process of decay overlaying growth would involve people in a drama whose ending would be left entirely to their imaginations.[59]

For some observers, including Wines, this is precisely what the designs do accomplish.

What is certain from the extensive literature on SITE is that its works have become entrenched among the notable buildings of the 1970s. As Alastair Best noted, "Not many visiting architects can begin a lecture at the RIBA [Royal Institute of British Architects] by saying, without a trace of arrogance and with absolute accuracy, that 'by now everyone in this room must be over-familiar with our work', " as James Wines did in London in 1980.[60] The same critic characterized the Indeterminate Facade as "one of the best known monuments of the twentieth century, the built equivalent of Dali's soft watches."[61] By 1981, Douglas Davis claimed in *Art Express* that the controversy surrounding SITE's designs had subsided; as proof he quoted a resident who, when asked whether she wanted the company to correct and improve the walls of the Houston showroom, replied, "No, that wouldn't be normal."[62] For Davis,

> These works are so well known, so iconic, that they are now as American as Grant Wood or

Charlie Chaplin. SITE, the fierce enemy of institutional architecture, is now an institution. Their arcane view of the world—as the lady in Houston confirms—is reality.[63]

It would be tempting to write off this success to the attention of the media and to the skills of the firm as publicists, Davis suggested, but to his way of thinking "SITE has succeeded on the ground of content—that is, the substantive nature of their message, directly implied in all their images."[64] The message that the once-controversial firm conveyed was seen by Davis as the suggestion that the act of designing architecture is neither a science nor a profession but rather "an act of culture" that must be frankly confronted rather than avoided.[65]

It is perhaps true, as Davis argued, that SITE has fallen out of controversy. In 1978, Wines wrote that three years after construction, the Indeterminate Facade "attracts more controversy, more critical analysis, and more visitors than ever," having even been placed on a list of notable monuments to see when touring the United States.[66] By 1981, the showroom facade was included among the most significant buildings of the 1970s by one journal, and the work of SITE gained greater recognition as evidenced in awards for other projects and publications.[67] In 1981, *Progressive Architecture* awarded SITE a Design Citation for a South Dakota bank project, and in 1984 the *Architectural Record* published five new projects by the firm.[68] Whether buildings such as the Indeterminate Facade will fade from the lists of significant monuments of its decade is a matter that time will decide. A review of the literature suggests that there has been no critical consensus on an approach to the intentions and the meaning of the design, and as long as that remains the case, the Indeterminate Facade will also remain among the most problematic—hence ambitious—buildings of its time.

Michael J. Bzdak

Notes

1. For a brief survey of these buildings, see Arthur Drexler, *Buildings for Best Products*, Museum of Modern Art, New York, 1979, 8–12. There are useful photographs in Patricia Roberts, "SITE: For Sore Eyes," *Aloft* (National Airlines), March 1980, 14–15. For the patronage of the Lewis family, see Carleton Knight III, "Building Collections/Collecting Buildings," *Portfolio*, III, October 1980, 82–87.

2. There is more information on the members of SITE in the in-house pamphlet *Best Products Co. Houston Showroom by SITE, Inc.*, New York, 1975.

3. Wolf von Eckardt, "The Bricks Come Tumbling Down," *Time*, November 28, 1983, 81. For more detailed information on the career of James Wines, see Don Hibbard, "James Wines" in *Contemporary Architects*, ed. Muriel Emanuel, New York, 1980, 891–892. The Houston showroom had attracted national attention in the year of completion: Douglas Davis, "Houston Falling," *Newsweek*, December 22, 1975.

4. Roberts, "SITE: For Sore Eyes," 18–19.

5. *Ibid.*

6. Paul Slansky, "Apocalypse Now?," *New Times*, September 30, 1977, 43. Here the story of the passing Texan who wanted to kick the building is repeated with a statement that the man claimed, "I'd shop at a place like that."

7. Tom Curtis, "A Store Front That's Tough to Love," *Washington Post*, September 12, 1975, D, 7.

8. Quoted in Curtis, "A Store Front," D, 7. See also the review by Ann Holmes, "Best Products' Building Featured in Exhibition," *Houston Chronicle*, June 7, 1975, 6.

9. Cited in John Moore, "The Ruin, the Tilt and a Gaping Hole Are Luring Shoppers," *Wall Street Journal*, February 27, 1979, 1. See other reactions in Lew Sichelman, "The Humorous Side of Architecture," *Chicago Tribune*, February 2, 1977; and Roy Close, "De-architecture Builds Attention," *Minneapolis Star*, November 28, 1975, B, 4.

10. Quotations from Moore, "The Ruin, the Tilt," 1.

11. Moore, "The Ruin, the Tilt," 1, reported that the additional costs were between two and seven percent of the total expenses for the SITE showrooms which, according to Best president Andrew Lewis, are "repaid very quickly." Best spokesperson Edwin Slipek, Jr., told Moore that the Houston showroom is one of several designed by SITE that boast of sales regularly surpassing predictions. In an article by Slipek, "How Best Products Profits from SITE, Inc.'s Designs," *Architectural Record*, 161, March 1977, 129–130, Lewis was quoted as having said that "in Houston, sales exceeded our budgeted sales estimate by 40 percent." Lynn Bershad, "Your Store's Collapsing," *Chain Store Age Executive*, January 1977, 38–39, reported that Houston showroom sales climbed forty to fifty percent higher than projections for the first year and did thirty percent better on sales than any other Best showroom. According to Bershad, "Sales for fiscal 1976 (ended June 26, 1976) were $295 million; earnings per share jumped to $1.71 from 35¢ in fiscal '75." It is difficult to gauge the role of the SITE designs in this remarkable gain, as numerous other factors must have been involved. For a more recent assessment of Best Products, see "Onto the Right Side of the Tracks," *Financial World*, June 1, 1980, 44–46.

12. Wines's early articles on "de-architecture" were published in "De-architecturization," *Architecture and Urbanism* (A+U), June 1974, and July 1975; "Ent-Architekturierung," *Kunstforum International*, October 1974; "De-architecturization: the Iconography of Disaster," *Architectural Design*, 45, July 1975, 426–428; "De-architecture," *L'Architettura*, 263, July 1975; "De-architecturization," *Arts in Society*, Fall-Winter 1975; "Il linguaggio eretico della disarchitettura," *Modo*, November 1977; "L'Architecture du Risque," *Architecture Intérieure Crée*, 165, April-May 1978, 43–48; "Notes on De-architecture," *L'Architettura*, 725, December 1980, 725 f.

13. See the statement by Wines in *Contemporary Architects*, ed. Muriel Emanuel, New York, 1980, 892.

14. *Ibid.*

15. See the article by Wines republished in *Esthetics Contemporary*, ed. Richard Kostelanetz, Buffalo, 1978, 266 f. (especially page 279). For a sample of the extent to which the theories of Wines have been used to explain the work of SITE, see "Pre-distrutto nel Texas," *Domus*, 551, October 1975, 32; Peter Papademetriou, "The Joke Is Out of SITE," *Progressive Architecture*, 57, January 1976, 29; Max Blagg, "SITE," *Art Direction*, February 1976, 48–49; Slansky, "Apocalypse Now?," 43; Charles Jencks, *Bizarre Architecture*, New York, 1979, 32; "Off-the-Wall Architecture," *Life*, April 1980, 117.

16. Wines, "The Iconography of Disaster," 428.

17. *Ibid.*

18. *Architectural Review*, 158, October 1975, 192. The full caption reads as follows: "Are you finding it hard to design new buildings, to add some meaning to the language of modern architecture? This showroom in Houston, Texas, has the answer. Described, with all seriousness, as an 'indeterminate facade project' it incorporates a cascade of loose bricks flowing down the facade over the canopy. The 'artist' involved, James Wines, seeks to create an 'iconography of indeterminacy' and in this showroom he sees his work as 'a dialogue between constructive and reductive processes' and a 'tentative and precarious imagery' . . . precarious is the word."

19. See Lance Wright, "Through the Looking Glass," *Architectural Review*, 163, March 1978, 132–135. For a more recent article in the same journal, see Deyan Sudjic, "Latest Best," *Architectural Review*, 167, April 1980, 221–225.

20. Wright, "Through the Looking Glass," 132.

21. Wright, "Through the Looking Glass," 134.

22. Wines in Wright, "Through the Looking Glass," 135.

23. *Ibid.*

24. *Ibid.*

25. *Ibid.*

26. Papademetriou, "The Joke Is Out of SITE," 29; Gerald Allen, "Bringing in the Business," *Architectural Record*, 161, March 1977, 115–117; Wolf von Eckardt, "Business among the Ruins," *Washington Post*, January 14, 1978, E, 1; Tony Rocca, "The Man Who Put the

Bomb under American Architecture," *Times* (London), January 15, 1978.

27. Allen, "Bringing in the Business," 115.

28. Allen, "Bringing in the Business," 117.

29. *Ibid.*

30. Rocca, "The Man Who Put the Bomb," and von Eckardt, "Business among the Ruins," E, 2. According to von Eckardt, the irony of ruins in the shopping center "may be more expressive of our time than the humorless glass towers downtown."

31. Drexler, *Buildings for Best Products,* 10.

32. *Ibid.*

33. For prominent examples, see the in-house pamphlet *Best Products Co. Houston Showroom by SITE, Inc.;* and the still photograph from the motion picture "Earthquake" that was published in Wines, "De-architecturization: the Iconography of Disaster," 426.

34. Bruno Zevi, "The Poetics of the Unfinished," in *SITE: Architecture as Art,* New York, 1980, 9–11.

35. *Ibid.*

36. *Ibid.*

37. Franco Raggi, "SITE Indeterminate Facade," *Casabella,* March 1976, 42–43.

38. Raggi, "SITE Indeterminate Facade," 42–43: "Since every detail of contemporary life is defined by industrial and financial autocracy, it has become redundant in the extreme for corporate facades to persist as a constant reminder of this oppression. . . ." Raggi noted that ambiguity is usually considered an anathema to formalist architecture and that the vocabulary of missing parts suggested that humanizing questions may be more interesting than "autocratic answers".

39. Francesco Torres, "SITE Empresa Deconstructora," *Artes plasticas* (Spain), March/April 1977, 49–50.

40. Philip Jodidio, "Une Esthetique de l'Incertitude," *Connaissance des Arts,* 330, August 1979, 34–37.

41. Quoted by Wines in the pamphlet *Best Products Co. Houston Showroom by SITE, Inc.;* and in Wright, "Through the Looking Glass," 135.

42. William Marlin, "Halfway between Building Design and Modern Art," *Christian Science Monitor,* March 11, 1977.

43. *Ibid.*

44. Jo Werne, "Architects Clash on 'Morality' of U.S. Designs," *Miami Herald,* October 28, 1979, H, 20, reported on the tenth annual urban workshop, which was sponsored by the Florida South Chapter of the American Institute of Architects. Other participants included Frank O. Gehry, Robert Krier, and Massimo Scolari.

45. See Pierre Schneider, quoted in Wines, "L'Architecture du Risque," 45.

46. John Dreyfuss, "Firm Designs Serious Funny Buildings," *Los Angeles Times,* March 9, 1980. The newspaper had published an earlier article by David Kinchen,

"Architectural Firm's Reputation in Ruins," *Los Angeles Times,* May 9, 1976.

47. Paul Goldberger, "Architect's Unstable Designs Relieve Monotony," *New York Times,* June 27, 1977.

48. *Ibid.*

49. Wines, quoted in Marlin, "Halfway between Building Design and Modern Art."

50. Allan Temko, "The Wild and Crazy Catalog Showrooms," *San Francisco Chronicle,* January 28, 1980. See also the comments by Walter Herdeg, *Archigraphia,* Bern, 1981, 192–195.

51. C. Ray Smith, *SITE: Buildings and Spaces,* Virginia Museum, Richmond, 1980, 6–7.

52. *Ibid.*

53. Pilar Viladas, "Insights on SITE," *Interiors,* August 1980, 79–80.

54. Nancy Foote, review of *Buildings for Best Products* (Museum of Modern Art) and *SITE—Ten Years: Drawings and Models of Completed and Proposed Projects* (Ronald Feldman Fine Arts), *Artforum,* 18, March 1980, 70.

55. *Ibid.*

56. Robert Merritt, "Marriage from Fairyland But Is SITE Show Art?," *Richmond Times-Dispatch,* June 15, 1980.

57. Lebbeus Woods, "Buildings for Best Products," *Skyline,* February 1980, 12–13.

58. Woods, "Buildings for Best Products," 12–13. Martin Filler raised unresolved questions on this issue in "Harbingers: Ten Architects," *Art in America,* Summer 1981, 121.

59. Woods, "Buildings for Best Products," 12–13.

60. Alastair Best, "Vintage Wines," *Architects Journal,* 172, October 29, 1980, 834–835.

61. *Ibid.*

62. Douglas Davis, "SITE to Post SITE," *Art Express,* September-October 1981, 19–20, related the same story cited in note 10 above.

63. *Ibid.*

64. *Ibid.*

65. *Ibid.*

66. Wines, in Wright, "Through the Looking Glass," 135.

67. See "La Facade Indéterminée, Magasin Best," *L'Architecture d'aujourd'hui,* 213, February 1981, 38. On SITE and post-modernism, see Babs Shapiro, "Architectural References: The Consequences of the Post-Modern in Contemporary Art and Architecture," *Vanguard,* May 1980, 6–13.

68. For the award, see *Progressive Architecture,* 62, January, 1981, 126–127. The award is mentioned by Carter Wiseman, "The New York Debut of 'De-Architecture,' " *New York,* June 29, 1981, 45; and the new projects by SITE are presented in Douglas Brenner, "Between Utopia and Apocalypse: Five Projects by SITE," *Architectural Record,* 176, March 1984, 134–145.

PIAZZA D'ITALIA

New Orleans, Louisiana

Architects: Perez Associates
and
Charles Moore, Urban Innovations Group

124. Piazza d'Italia (color plate on page 41)

The Piazza d'Italia in New Orleans is an ambitious urban scheme consisting of specialty shops, offices, restaurants, and a piazza with a fountain to serve as a focus of the city's Italo-American community. The complex was intended to be realized in five phases. At present only the first phase including the piazza and the fountain has been constructed, yet the project has drawn voluminous criticism and praise. The vehement position of some of its detractors is demonstrated in the titles of articles that refer to the fountain as an ugly swan,[1] New Orleans' Coney Island,[2] and an architectural joke.[3] Even before the design for the monument was begun, the proposed demolition of existing buildings was debated; when

that issue was resolved, the selection procedure for the architect became a source of contention. In retrospect, it is hardly surprising that evaluations of the completed Piazza range from "monstrosity" to "masterpiece."[4] In fact, it has been described as one of the most controversial projects published by *Progressive Architecture* in the 1970s.[5]

In March of 1973 the mayor of New Orleans, Moon Landrieu, announced the formation of an Italian-American Citizens' Executive Committee to examine the feasibility of creating an Italian piazza.[6] This public space was to be constructed as a symbol of friendship between the citizens of New Orleans and Italy. Equally important,

125. Lykes
Building, with
Piazza d'Italia at
its base

it was to be built to honor the achievements of the Italian community which composed nearly 15 percent of the New Orleans population. Dedicated on March 19, 1978, the Piazza d'Italia was conceived to give identity to Italian descendants in a city traditionally dominated by other ethnic groups and was to be similar in concept to other public memorials located in the city. Under a previous mayor, New Orleans had begun monuments called the Plaza de España, which Landrieu saw to completion, and the Place de France to commemorate those national groups.[7] In time there would also be a British Place and a Martin Luther King Memorial to honor other components of the diverse racial and ethnic heritage of the city.

Located in the midst of the business district on the edge of the historic core of New Orleans, the Piazza d'Italia occupies the block bounded by Poydras, Tchoupitoulas, Lafayette, and Saint Peters Streets.[8] This lot proved to be a difficult one to work with because of the diversity of the architecture already established there. Tchoupitoulas was encumbered with nineteenth-century commercial buildings, while the corner of Poydras and Saint Peters Streets was dominated by the Lykes Building, a modern structure completed in 1968. Despite this obstacle, by November 1973 the landscape architects, Cashio-Cochran Incorporated, submitted a preliminary design for the Piazza d'Italia. This included an open public space with a large fountain surrounded by shops and restaurants. The scheme drew much opposition from architectural preservationists, journalists, and the City Hall planners who objected to the demolition of warehouses

126. Aerial view of Piazza d'Italia and surrounding buildings

necessary to prepare for the proposed fountain.[9] The impasse was resolved when mayor Landrieu noted that the structures represented an American "Italianate" style and deserved to be preserved.[10]

Once it was decided that the nineteenth-century commercial exteriors would be saved, a revised scheme was needed which would include the pre-existing buildings. Thus, on July 23, 1974, a plan for the selection of architects was recommended by the Piazza d'Italia Committee.[11] Architects interested in the project were invited to submit their qualifications to members of the mayor's staff and the Piazza d'Italia Committee who would then select six semi-finalists to compete for the commission. The six firms would each be paid $1,000 to design a concept for the Piazza d'Italia. The mayor's staff would recommend the best three plans, and the mayor would make the final selection.[12] In other words, the competition would be judged by the patrons of the project.

Interestingly enough, this procedure did not conform to the rules established by the American Institute of Architects. The New Orleans chapter of the AIA even warned its members that participation in the competition would be considered unethical, and that those who did enter would be subject to public censure unless the selection process was revised.[13] At this point Dr. Nick Accardo, president of the Piazza d'Italia Committee, explained that the system of selection was devised to encourage an imaginative solution for the development of the Piazza.[14] Evidently the argument was persuasive, for shortly thereafter the AIA notified the Piazza d'Italia Committee that their selection procedure had been approved. Architects were free to compete without reprimand,[15] and by November 19, 1974, six contributors were selected from a field of forty-six participants.[16] On January 26, 1975, the winner of the competition was announced: August Perez and Associates of New Orleans was selected, and Charles W. Moore of the Urban Innovations Group based in Los Angeles was the runner-up.[17]

The Perez scheme, designed by R. Allen Eskew and Malcolm Heard, and the scheme of Moore's group included many strikingly similar design concepts. Both included a public space at the nucleus of which was a fountain, and both contained a campanile in their preliminary schemes. There were some differences, how-

151

127. The pergola beside the Lykes Building, and the campanile

ever. Eskew and Heard emphasized the importance of the Italian community, designing their plaza with many specific Italian references. In addition, their plan outlined provisions for the conservation of the facades. Moore's proposal concentrated on an elaborate fountain to be situated within a public space of superimposed concentric ellipses. Centrally located within the area, the fountain would consist of a campanile behind a cascade of water.[18]

Moore's plan was well received by the selection committee and, at its suggestion, Eskew and Heard contracted Charles Moore and his colleague, Ronald Filson, to act as consultants for the fountain. Thus the two schemes were integrated to produce the design which was awarded a citation for superior urban design and planning by *Progressive Architecture* in January of 1976.[19]

Although both the Urban Innovations Group and August Perez and Associates proposed a campanile in their preliminary schemes, Moore initially presented it in the center of the Piazza. The execution of the structure, however, followed the plan of Eskew and Heard who positioned it at the main entrance on Poydras Street. The campanile is constructed with a veneer of stucco applied over a steel frame. Thin layers, punctured with geometric openings reminiscent of fenestration,[20] are juxtaposed above a triangular base of spidery legs which seem to provide inadequate support for the spire above. The exterior of the structure was originally painted a misty blue-gray and pale orange while the interior was rendered in darker hues.[21] Such a color combination created a hollowed effect emphasizing the thinness of the steel planes. The tall, geometric shape of the campanile coalesces well with the urban surroundings, and the height recon-

128. View within the Piazza, Corinthian wall at center

ciles the difference between the towering Lykes Building
and the lower Piazza beyond.

When it was finally executed, the public space of the
Piazza d'Italia followed the circular area proposed by
Eskew and Heard, rather than the elliptical one designed
by Moore. Moore's idea of concentric arcs, however,
was retained. These are composed of pale granite and
dark slate arranged in alternating bands around the center of the space creating a target-like effect. The broad
arcs extend in ever greater radii from the focal point at
the center of the space, across sidewalks to the avenues
surrounding the Piazza. Because it is tucked behind the
nineteenth-century warehouses and the twenty-two story
Lykes Building, the Piazza cannot be easily seen from
the streets; thus, the black and white pattern of the arcs
serves to capture the visitor's attention at the edge of the
scheme and leads to the concealed Piazza beyond. The
contrasting pattern is also similar to the alternating black
and white vertical design of the Lykes Building, formally
relating the Piazza to the surrounding urban district.

Although Eskew, Heard, and Moore each proposed a
fountain for the center of the Piazza, it became the vehicle through which Eskew's and Heard's Italian theme
was transmitted. Aware of the local customs of the Italian
community, the Perez architects suggested that the foun-

tain be dedicated to Saint Joseph, patron of family life,
and that it be designed to function as an altar on the
saint's feast day, a gala event in New Orleans. Along its
perimeters, the fountain is composed of a series of five
concentric hemicyclical colonnaded sections painted
brilliantly in rusts, yellows, and orange. (These were
originally designed as parallel structures, but the rigidity
of this format was inconsistent with the curved arcs on
the ground.) Connected by buttressing elements composed of wide arches, each colonnade represents one of
the five Roman architectural orders: Tuscan, Ionic, Corinthian, Composite, and Doric. The playful, historicizing
aspect of this classical assemblage was emphasized by
the presence of a sixth order, the "Delicatessen Order,"
invented to frame a proposed but unexecuted restaurant.[22]

With the aid of hydraulic engineers, the architects devised methods by which various streams of water could
be manipulated to recreate classical architectural elements: columns from the Tuscan wall, egg-and-dart
moldings which decorate the Ionic wall, acanthus leaf
capitals from the Corinthian wall, and the capitals and
bases from the Composite wall are all simulated by patterns produced with water. On the Doric wall, water
falls from a stainless steel abacus to create a fluid, Doric

shaft, and it acts as a liquid counterpart to sculpted metopes which Moore refers to as "wetopes."[23]

Neon lights update the classical motifs by outlining the architectural forms which are composed of richly veined Italian marble and modern materials such as stainless steel and concrete. Flanking the arch of the Doric wall are roundels which contain a portrait of Charles Moore, who spits water as he smiles, a surprise homage by his colleagues. All of this highly innovative decoration is topped by an entablature on the Corinthian wall which proudly hails, "This fountain was given by the citizens as a gift to all people," in Latin, using Trajanic majuscules.[24]

Recessed within the center of the hemicyclical colonnades, a shrine-like space, which functions as the altar on Saint Joseph's Day, has been erected. The structure consists of two superimposed arches; the outermost is supported by Corinthian columns, the recessed arch by Ionic. From this hollow stretches an eighty-foot long replica of a map of Italy, constructed of slate, marble, cobblestones, and mirrored tiles arranged at varying levels to suggest the topography of the actual Italian peninsula. Sicily, the island from which most of New Orleans Italian citizens are descended, was placed at the geometric center of the space as a commemorative gesture.[25] Water is disseminated throughout the miniature Italy in three currents representing the Arno, Po, and Tiber rivers. These cascade into two receptacles representative of the Tyrrhenian and Adriatic seas.

During design sessions, the architects created two additional structures, a pergola and an archway, to enhance the Italian theme. The pergola is a skeletal fabrication made of poured concrete and standard plumbing pipe. It is strongly reminiscent of a tempietto with columns, pediments, and a pitched roof.[26] Constructed near the campanile, it marks the main entrance from Poydras Street. The base of the pergola is trapezoidal, diminish-

ing in shape between the greater width of Poydras Street and the narrower width of the forecourt beyond,[27] guiding the visitor from one space to the other.

The Lafayette Archway, located opposite the Poydras Street entrance, also augments the classical Italian theme of the Piazza. It demarcates the entrance to the proposed Lafayette Mall. When viewed from within the Piazza, the arch is simply adorned with a clock with Roman numerals. The exterior of the Lafayette Archway, however, assumes the form of a triumphal arch. Bold colors of red, white, and green symbolize the Italian flag. Black and gray graphic designs conform with the urban environment; decorative patterns imitate voussoirs and a giant keystone.

Upon the completion of the Piazza d'Italia, members of the Italian-American community enthusiastically heralded the monument which would serve as a focal point for community activities.[28] The excitement that anticipated the dedication ceremonies on March 19, 1978, was succeeded by equally positive reviews in the Italo-American press: Tommy Griffin, for example, described the fountain's beauty as "eye-popping;"[29] Louise S. Glickman noted how the Piazza d'Italia ". . . touched the souls of . . . many," characterizing it as a place to enjoy a bag lunch or a quiet conservation.[30] Gayle Gagli-

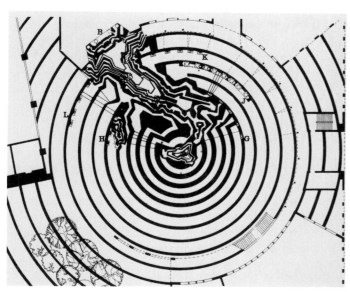

129. Plan for replica of map of Italy

130. Lafayette Archway

ano praised the lively combination of Italian traditions with modern American design, observing that the range of colors is suggestive of what is seen in Italy; that stainless steel is a material whose use was pioneered by Italian and American artists; and that the neon lights are commonly seen in Italian piazzas at night, as well as in the works of contemporary sculptors.[31]

Even before construction of the Piazza d'Italia had begun, however, the members of the jury who awarded the prestigious *Progressive Architecture* citation in January 1976, verbalized some of the issues that became increasingly controversial. Raquel Ramati, for example, commented on the ambiguous relationship between old and new elements,[32] and Cesar Pelli questioned whether the Piazza design would suit its location. Despite these reservations, Donald S. Appleyard and Ramati agreed that the scheme was imaginative and innovative.[33]

The enthusiasm of the *Progressive Architecture* jurors was matched two years later by that of the architecture critic Martin Filler. His article "The Magic Fountain," which appeared in *Progressive Architecture* in November 1978, was the first professional appraisal of the completed monument. The article began:

> Great architecture tends to inspire admiration, reverence, humility, awe, and other such solemn emotions, but rarely does it fill its beholders with feelings of happiness, romance, warmth, joy, and love. The new Piazza d'Italia is one of those rare exceptions.[34]

The article thoroughly reported the history of the Piazza and gave a vivid description of it.

More importantly, Filler addressed the issues raised by the jury that awarded the *Progressive Architecture* citation. Like Ramati, Filler noted an uneasy marriage of historicizing and modern elements. In his opinion, the Piazza d'Italia represented ". . . the richest expression yet of the historicist revival in contemporary architecture. . ." and employed classical architectural vocabulary with deep feeling.[35] Yet, he also observed that some members of the Italian community disliked the use of the modern neon lighting. On this basis, Filler concluded that such vernacular motifs could not be understood or enjoyed outside of their original context—that the use of popular images or objects would necessarily be associated with popular meaning.[36] Filler, like Pelli, also considered the contextural environment and questioned whether the Piazza would survive near the heart of the commercial district of New Orleans. Since Pelli could only base his opinion upon a model of the monument, he was unable to explore the full implications of the issue; Filler also reserved judgment, believing that the integration of the Piazza into the life of the city would be successfully attained in the future.[37] Filler addressed a third concept that would be discussed by numerous critics thereafter: the appeal of the architecture to a multitude of tastes and interests. He noted that the histor-

ically-minded observer would find the Piazza an engaging recollection of the ancient marine theater and the Canopus at Hadrian's Villa at Tivoli, while the general public could enjoy its colorful playfulness as a kind of movie palace or a stage set reminiscent of a Cecil B. DeMille epic.[38]

In addition to professional scrutiny, the Piazza d'Italia also received national recognition. Like Filler, Douglas Davis, the staff critic for *Newsweek,* trumpeted the monument as a revolt against the International Style and, thus, a revolt against the clean, rational, efficient buildings which embody the utopian tenets of modernism. Rather than an architectural Prometheus or prophet of social change, Davis perceived the role of the architects of the Piazza as the one played by the frolicsome Pan, eager to please themselves and their public.[39] However, not all of the reactions were as amiable, particularly in the New Orleans press. In December of 1978 Pie Dufour adamantly rejected Davis's opinion as nonsense. Dufour used adjectives such as monstrous, ugly, sterile, and vulgar to describe the Piazza, equating its boldness with the daring of the Emperor's "New Clothes."[40]

By early 1979, a "Back-Splash," as *Progressive Architecture* termed it, spilled into the heretofore predominantly positive literature.[41] In January 1979, *Progressive Architecture* published a collection of negative views concerning the Piazza d'Italia with contributions from practitioners rather than critics. Architect-planner, David P-C Chang declared the Piazza d'Italia the ultimate horror,[42] and John Steinichen claimed that he and fellow-planners at a New Orleans meeting reacted with laughter to the Piazza.[43] One of the most determined rejoinders was written by Lebbeus Woods who addressed the issue of historicism. According to Woods, the Piazza damaged rather than encouraged the emerging concepts of historical allusion, architectural symbol, and metaphor. The decoration of the architecture with color and light was reduced, in his opinion, to cheap effects.[44] Woods stated:

> The jocular triteness and flamboyant emptiness of these effects seems quite intentional, as though Moore meant to parody not only the Disneyland mentality of Americans but also the seriousness of architecture and of art itself. The fountain is a sequence of one-line jokes adding up to nothing more than a burlesque of Post-Modernism. With it, Moore can lay claim to being the P. T. Barnum of contemporary architecture, or its most prominent comedian.[45]

In the same collection of reader responses, architect Jan Reiner declared that "no amount of pseudo-classical vocabulary, neon décor, magic fountains, etc., can turn 'eclectic appreciation' into a creative act."[46] Reiner argued that the architectural elements of the Piazza d'Italia are superficial surface treatments. Questioning the function of the architect within a society, Reiner apparently preferred Prometheus to Pan, suggesting that the role of the architect is to promote an architecture and urbanism of serious social concern rather than to transform "inner city blocks into Magic-kingdom fantasies."[47] In agreement with Davis, who saw contemporary architecture as a vehicle for delight, the editors of *Progressive Architecture* found Reiner's notion that social responsibility precludes fantasy a disturbing one. They suggested the possibility of meeting social ends by accommodating the public's desire for fantasy in both its private and commercial settings rather than relying on "the regimented concrete stairs and planters that now represent social commitment in cities all over America."[48]

By March of 1979, a second wave of "back-splash" penetrated the editorial pages of *Progressive Architecture*; now practitioners responded to the hostile criticisms of their colleagues.[49] The interior designer, Walter L. Goodwin, for example, saw the humor of the Piazza d'Italia as a reflection of human values and experiences. He understood the work as the manifestation of happiness rather than of utopianism, believing that architecture is more than a social responsibility.[50]

Architect Nicholas Pyle commented on Woods's objection that the jocularity of the Piazza damages the emerging concepts of historical allusion. Pyle questioned the validity of such a notion by comparing the Piazza with the plays of Molière which, he contended, are not serious in tone but are serious in their content.[51]

The early literature in professional journals dealt with questions regarding the context of the Piazza d'Italia and the legitimacy of its style, in addition to its reception among the citizens of New Orleans and the architectural community. The controversy expanded to embrace questions of terminology for a monument which is arguably "pop," "modern," and "post-modern," depending on how it and the terms themselves were understood. In the *Architectural Review* of May 1979 for example, Lake Douglas acknowledged the popular appeal of the Piazza in its use of contemporary vernacular elements such as neon lights and splashing water. He questioned whether the term "pop architecture" was appropriate for the monument recognizing that its academic references may be too obscure for the general public. Douglas interpreted the Piazza as an architectural joke, but one that cannot be appreciated unless "one has a sense of humour to match the architects', one understands the elements of classical architecture and the confused state of contemporary architecture, and one is privy to the customs of New Orleans. . . ."[52]

The issue of how the Piazza d'Italia should be understood was discussed by Paul Goldberger in the *New York Times* in February of 1979. Goldberger considered the monument one of the most significant urban spaces constructed in recent American architectural history. He wrote that although a visitor may initially perceive the playful embellishments of the Piazza d'Italia as a vulgar reproach to classicism, the visitor must later realize that the architects are not mocking the antique references.

Rather they are joyously embracing the classical tradition by exploring the meanings of its parts. In this way, the visitor is encouraged to think about the components of a classical column and how they function.[53] As such, the Piazza d'Italia itself functions in an educational capacity from which a student may learn the lessons of contemporary and historical architecture.[54]

Not all critics agreed that the multiple levels of appeal are successful. George Baird, for example, felt that the paradoxical elements of the Piazza d'Italia do not relate to any one group in any specific manner. He contended that the materials of the classical Roman components emphasize their fakeness, destroying the illusions they actually try to create. Furthermore, Baird argued that the playful iconography of Disneyland is not clearly simulated in the Piazza. Thus, the meaning for the casual visitor is lost.[55]

Although the dichotomous nature of the Piazza d'Italia created by its appeal to both popular taste and classical erudition may be an issue for dispute, for Charles Jencks it represents one of the essential characteristics of post-modern architecture.[56] According to Jencks, the Piazza d'Italia succeeds as a post-modern structure in several ways. Like Douglas, Jencks observed that the monument cannot be appreciated unless it is understood on various levels. Because of this, it is, to use Jencks's term, double coded, including elements that are modern in addition to those that are revivalist, local, commercial, metaphorical or contextual.[57] Thus, a variety of people can enjoy and understand the monument for different reasons. According to Jencks, architectural historians can appreciate the Piazza because it recalls the ancient marine theater of Hadrian and the nineteenth-century triumphal gateways of Karl Friedrich Schinkel. They can understand the precise proportions of the columns based on the principles established by the Renaissance architect Vignola and the individual elements, such as capitals formed to recall the classical orders. Italians and Italo-Americans can enjoy the Piazza because of its references to piazzas and fountains in Italy, such as the Trevi fountain in Rome, because of the inclusion of a Latin inscription, and because of the prominent map that replicates the contours of Italy.[58] The monument appeals to modernists in its use of current technologies and modern materials as well as in its acknowledgment of the surrounding urban environment. Because of the sensuousness of the materials, such as polished stainless steel and rich Italian marble, the architecture has a direct appeal.[59]

Another characteristic of post-modernism embodied in the Piazza d'Italia, according to Jencks, is radical eclecticism, that is, a given style or mixture of styles based on three determinants: attention to a variety of cultures and tastes, contextual setting, and multiplicity of functions.[60] The first determinant, attention to a variety of cultures and tastes, is actually the concept of double coding which, according to Jencks, is manifested in the monument on several levels.[61]

contextual setting. For the Piazza, the architects created an open public space which coherently merges with nineteenth-century warehouses, the modern Lykes Building, and other contemporary structures. Certain elements of the Piazza consciously contrast with the regularized urban surrounding; the brilliant colors of orange, yellow, and rust do not conform with the greyness of the preexisting environment, isolating the Piazza and creating an air of prominence which seems overly rhetorical. When viewed from the street, however, the colors are restricted to gradations of greys which conform to the urban district. In addition, the black and white pattern of the paved concentric arcs echoes the vertical tones of the Lykes Building. Furthermore, the geometric shape of the campanile blends with the angularity of the contemporary structures. Although the brilliant colors were meant to isolate the actual public area, the architects were careful to incorporate a variety of elements which would harmonize with the urban environment.

The primary purpose of the monument is to commemorate the achievements of the Italian-American community. On this level the Piazza, apparently, can be judged a success by the pride that the community takes in the project. The Piazza was also intended to function as a place for Italians to assemble and hold festivities; here, too, the Piazza succeeds. Year after year the Italian community gathers at the Piazza to enjoy the celebrations of Saint Joseph's Day and the Festa d'Italia. This variety of functions characterizes Jencks's third determinant.

Jencks believed that the Piazza succeeds as a postmodern structure in at least one other way — in its concept of space. Post-modernist space, he contends, is historically specific and rooted in conventions while it is simultaneously limited or ambiguous; the boundaries are often left unclear and the relationship between the parts and the whole is frequently irrational.[62] The Piazza d'Italia has no boundaries. The concentric colonnades are freely arranged in an open space and do not create any interior rooms. The ambiguity is created by the overlapping walls placed at varying heights. Not a single border is defined by the architecture.

Jencks interpreted the ambiguous, unlimited space of the Piazza d'Italia as a characteristic of post-modernism; yet Christian Norberg-Schulz believed that it is specifically this quality which defines the monument as modern. He argued that the space of the Piazza is based on the fundamental modernist principles of free plan and open form.[63] He defined free plan as a simultaneity of places:

> Physically we are, of course, in one place at a time, but existentially we may be in several places simultaneously. The free plan makes this experience possible through a "virtual openness," that is, a spatial organization that implies interaction rather than self-sufficiency.[64]

According to Norberg-Schulz, this notion was achieved in the Piazza d'Italia by the asymmetrical and discontinuous arrangement of its hemicyclical colonnades placed at varying heights and levels, producing an open continuum rather than static rooms. In addition, a closed effect is counteracted by overlapping the various parts and by creating illusionistic transparency with water and open colonnades. Overlapping and transparency are, according to Norberg-Schulz, modernist principles.[65] The historicism of the Piazza simply aids in the existential transport of the visitor to another place and time. The modernist concept of open form as defined by Norberg-Schulz also achieves simultaneity of places by juxtaposing diverse elements in a collage-like fashion. This quality is achieved by overlapping and transparency, creating an ambiguity of place. Thus for Norberg-Schulz, if modern architecture is capable of embodying a complex and contradictory world, the Piazza d'Italia must be characterized as modern.[66]

Two final issues must be examined in order to give a full account of the controversies associated with the Piazza: its success as a public space and its physical deterioration. To be sure, few citizens of New Orleans visit the Piazza. Furthermore its success as a public space is difficult to determine because the buildings which were intended to surround it and give it life have never been constructed. Pelli wrote that the project cannot be judged until after its completion, and then," . . . if people use it, it's good, if they don't, forget it."[67] At present

131. "Festa d'Italia" poster, depicting Piazza d'Italia

132. View within the Piazza

the Piazza has been only partially finished, yet David Littlejohn felt that it does, in fact, succeed as a public space *in potentia* and that it will succeed even more fully when it is complete.[68] Architectural critics have observed certain basic problems that hinder the success of the Piazza as a public space. Although the Lafayette Archway contains facilities such as storage areas and restrooms to accommodate the visitor's comfort, Goldberger noted the lack of seating, observing that only a few benches are scattered at the periphery, far from the fountain.[69] Despite this situation, the Italian community fills the Piazza whenever it celebrates a feast day, using the elevated topography of the replica of Italy as a resting place.

The issue regarding the dilapidated condition of the Piazza d'Italia has recently been discussed by Robert Guenther, who noted that since its dedication in March of 1978, the monument has been left to deteriorate to the point of ruin.[70] He observed that the neon does not light, the marble bases of the columns are cracked and chipped, the water in the fountain is not turned on, and the receptacles for the liquid are filled with trash. The mirrored surfaces of the tiles have worn away, and minerals from the polluted Mississippi River, the source for the water, have stained the polished surfaces of the fountain. As early as January of 1979, Mimi Crossley noted the poor condition of the Piazza, mentioning that the neon piping had to be replaced often and that paint on

the columns had begun to peel. She also observed that maintenance on the complicated fountain plumbing was proving to be difficult.[71] Goldberger, too, noticed that neon lights were out and that water jets malfunctioned.[72]

These problems exist because the maintenance of the Piazza was intended to be left to the responsibility of private developers who were to renovate the warehouses and construct new restaurants, offices, and shops. When plans for a retail shopping center failed, Lincoln Property Company of Dallas, Texas, proposed to erect a new hotel. This proposal failed when difficulties were encountered in pouring footings at the foundations of the nineteenth-century warehouse facades. Lincoln then deferred to a Denver developer who had more experience with older buildings, and city officials now insist that construction is imminent.[73] Because its maintenance expenses are so high (it is estimated that annual operating costs run from $100,000 to $150,000), the city has discontinued operating the fountain. In addition, $150,000 would have to be spent for repairs in order to restore the monument to its original state.

Despite these administrative and practical difficulties, Guenther questioned whether the architects Eskew, Heard, Moore, and Filson can be faulted for a design which is unsuitably delicate and too expensive to maintain. According to Guenther, the fountain nozzles are so fine that they are quickly clogged by mineral deposits.

The neon lighting is also a problem because transformers frequently overheat and mist from the fountain shorts out the lights.[74] Even architectural students from Tulane University expressed their concern regarding the fountain's durability.[75] Although Moore admitted that some of the problems associated with the maintenance are inherent in the design of the Piazza, he also defended it, stating:

> If I had to do it over again, I'd put in fewer, bigger nozzles and try not to be so fine-grained with the water effects. On the marble, I wouldn't have exposed the edges. . . . We just didn't count on it being exposed and unattended. The design was appropriate for what we were led to believe was going to occur. . . . To an extraordinary extent, the work was done right.[76]

The controversial nature of the Piazza d'Italia is manifested in the written word, without which the monument may very well have fallen into the depths of obscurity, tucked away and hidden from view. Indeed, now that a decade has passed since its conception, critics and scholars are still publishing their reactions to the work.[77] In fact, it is precisely by these written responses that Charles Moore has judged the Piazza d'Italia a success. In his most recent comment regarding the monument, the architect stated:

> . . . my pride in the project was amplified by the vigor of the responses. I had noticed long before that what I regarded as the best work I was involved in has drawn the heaviest fire; that makes the Piazza our best effort. . .[78]
>
> Jennifer C. Toher

Notes

1. Errol Laborde, "The Piazza d'Italia: N.O.'s Ugly Swan," *Gris Gris* (New Orleans), January 29–February 4, 1979, 22.
2. Augusto Miceli, "Piazza d'Italia: It's Coney Island," *States-Item* (New Orleans), March 24, 1979, 6.
3. Robert Guenther, "No Light in the Piazza: An Architectural Joke," *Wall Street Journal*, February 24, 1984, 30.
4. Pie Dufour referred to the Piazza as a monstrosity in "Piazza d'Italia," *States-Item*, December 28, 1978, 17; Martin Filler referred to it as a masterpiece in "The Magic Fountain," *Progressive Architecture*, 59, November 1978, 81–87.
5. Suzanne Stephens, "Playing with a Full Decade," *Progressive Architecture*, 60, December 1979, 53.
6. Several articles had been written in local newspapers regarding the announcement. See "New Italian Plaza Gets Official Push," *States-Item* March 19, 1973, 44; "Italian Plaza Group Formed," *Times-Picayune* (New Orleans), March 19, 1973, I, 21; James H. Gillis, "Italian Plaza for N.O. Is Aim," *Times-Picayune*, March 22, 1973, I, 1; "Let's Hear It for the Piazza d'Italia," *Times-Picayune*, March 23, 1973, I, 10; "City of N.O. Will Fund Italian Plaza," *States-Item*, March 23, 1973, 2.
7. "New Italian Plaza Gets Official Push," 44.
8. This lot was made available for the construction of the Piazza through a land exchange approved on November 29, 1973, between the city of New Orleans and real estate developer Joseph Canizaro. Canizaro obtained 3.7 acres of land from the city in order to erect a multi-building complex, and in return the city received approximately 1.7 acres of more highly valued land for the Piazza. The exchange was complicated by Councilman Peter H. Beer who questioned the evaluations of the property owned by the city on the basis of reductions made for servitude encumbrances (the property was reserved for railroad tracks and utilities rights-of-way). Despite such contentions, the trade was considered a secure investment, and on April 1, 1974, the properties were finally exchanged. For all of these events, see Jack Davis, "Warehouse Area Revival to Feature Italian Piazza," *States-Item*, November 28, 1973; Ed Lepoma, "Beer Still Shows Doubt Over Piazza Land Swap," *States-Item*, January 11, 1974, 9; Jack Davis, "New Orleans Italian Piazza," *Italian-American Digest*, October 14, 1974, 3.
9. The importance of these commercial edifices could be seen in their identical facades which were made to appear as one continuous structure, nearly a block long. Impressive cast-iron columns adorned the ground floor, and graceful rows of arched windows were employed as decoration above. As Jack Davis noted, "To tear down three of these. . . would be to pass up an increasingly rare chance to save a matched set of such commercial buildings." See Jack Davis, "Fountain Flaws Promising 'Piazza d'Italia'," *States-Item*, December 4, 1973, 10.
10. Davis, "Fountain," 10.
11. The date for the recommendation of the selection procedure was noted in Davis, "New Orleans Italian Piazza," 3.
12. Davis, "New Orleans Italian Piazza," 3.
13. The AIA requires winners of architectural competitions to be selected by a jury including professional peers to ensure that judgments are based solely on the merits of the scheme designed. See "AIA Members Are Warned of Part in Piazza Project," *Times-Picayune*, October 22, 1974, I, 11.
14. "Piazza Architect Selection Plan Is Approved," *Times-Picayune*, November 13, 1975, I, 22.
15. "Piazza Architect Selection Plan," 22.
16. These included Caldwell and Turchi; Cashio-Cochran, Incorporated with Stewart Farnet; Charles Colbert with Jack Cosner; the Italiano Art and Landscape Foundation; Charles W. Moore; and August Perez and Associates. See "Six to Submit Piazza Plans," *Times-Picayune*, November 19, 1974, II, 5.
17. "Perez Winner of Piazza Job," *Times-Picayune*, January 26, 1975, I, 36. See also "Competition Held for New Orleans Restoration," *AIA Journal*, 63, May 1975, 12 and 14.
18. Ronald Filson, "La fuente mágica de la Piazza d'Italia," *Arquitectura*, 215, November–December 1978, 61.
19. Ronald P. Bowie, "The Twenty-third Awards Program:

August Perez and Associates," *Progressive Architecture,* 57, January 1976, 82–83.

20. The punctured walls of the campanile are reminiscent of the "cut-out-cardboard-model" quality of the buildings created by Moore for the Kresge College in 1974 at the University of California in Santa Cruz. See Sally Woodbridge, "How to Make a Place," *Progressive Architecture,* 55, May 1974, 76–83.

21. Filler, "The Magic Fountain," 86.

22. Filler, "The Magic Fountain," 86–87.

23. Filler, "The Magic Fountain," 87.

24. Translation by Filler, "The Magic Fountain," 84.

25. Moore and Filson suggested that Rome, the capital of Italy, be placed at the center of the Piazza. However, when reminded by Eskew and Heard that many of New Orleans' Italian citizens are descendants of Sicily, a replica of that island was used as the center instead.

26. Such a skeletal structure is reminiscent of Robert Venturi's Franklin Court in Philadelphia, as suggested by Filler, "The Magic Fountain," 86. Designed in 1976, the outline of Benjamin Franklin's home was constructed by the architect in steel tubing. See "Franklin Court," *Progressive Architecture,* 57, April 1976, 69–70. Thus, the employment of modern materials to recall older architectural forms is repeated in the tempietto.

27. Filler, "The Magic Fountain," 86.

28. See "Piazza Design Wins Award," *Italian-American Digest,* March, 1976, 3; and "Piazza d'Italia Salutes St. Joseph's Day Tradition," *Italian-American Digest,* March 1977, 24. Reproduced in *Avviso Piazza d'Italia Newsletter,* Spring 1977.

29. Tommy Griffin, "Interfest Sparkles at Piazza d'Italia and Edelweiss," *Figaro* (New Orleans), August 2, 1978, 21.

30. Louise S. Glickman, "Piazza d'Italia: A Little Italy in Downtown New Orleans," *Italian-American Digest,* Autumn 1978, 3.

31. Gayle Gagliano, "A New Glow for New Orleans," *Italian-American Digest,* Autumn 1978, 19. According to R. Allen Eskew, the colors chosen by consultant Tina Beebe were also intended to recall those seen on the architecture in the historical section of New Orleans, thus combining in color scheme the new Piazza and the old Vieux Carré. Information obtained by the author in an interview with R. Allen Eskew in New Orleans, April 1984.

32. It is unclear whether Ramati was referring to the new Piazza in the older site or, as I suspect, historicizing and modern elements of the Piazza itself. See Bowie, "Twenty-Third Awards Program," 82.

33. Bowie, "Twenty-Third Awards Program," 82.

34. Filler, "The Magic Fountain," 81.

35. Filler, "The Magic Fountain," 87.

36. To quote Filler, "The Magic Fountain," 87: "With one detail of the design are some members of the Italian community less than pleased: the neon lighting that outlines the arches and columns at night, which to them speaks of sleazy barrooms and cheap hotels, an indecorous addition to an otherwise nice place to take the family. This is further proof of the impossibility of reassigning meanings to popular images, a problem faced by architects who wish to use vernacular motifs outside of an authentically vernacular context."

37. Filler, "The Magic Fountain," 87.

38. *Ibid.*

39. Douglas Davis, "Designs for Living," *Newsweek,* November 6, 1978, 91. Not long afterwards, *Time* published a short comment regarding the Piazza d'Italia in Robert Hughes, "Doing Their Own Thing," *Time,* January 8, 1979, 58.

40. Pie Dufour, "Piazza d'Italia," *States-Item,* December 28, 1978, A, 17.

41. "Views—Magic Fountain: Back-Splash," *Progressive Architecture,* 60, January 1979, 8.

42. Letter to the editor by David P-C Chang, "Back-Splash," 8.

43. Letter to the editor by John Steinichen, "Back-Splash," 8. Ted Wu, architect and industrial designer, also regarded the Piazza d'Italia as a mockery and a joke; see his letter to the editor in "Views—Piazza: Mixed Reaction," *Progressive Architecture,* 60, February 1979, 8.

44. Letter to the editor by Lebbeus Woods, "Back-Splash," 8.

45. *Ibid.*

46. Letter to the editor by Jan Reiner, "Back-Splash," 8.

47. By "Magic-Kingdom fantasies," Reiner must be alluding to Filler's perception of the Piazza d'Italia as a "Magic-Fountain." Although Filler used the term in a positive manner, Reiner's usage is derogatory.

48. Editors' comment in "Back-Splash," 8.

49. For another critic who viewed the Piazza d'Italia in a positive light, see Mimi Crossley, "Bit of Italian Fantasy Down in New Orleans," *Houston Post,* January 28, 1979, AA, 3.

50. Letter to the editor by Walter L. Goodwin, "Views—Piazza Defended," *Progressive Architecture,* 60, March 1979, 14. Russell C. Jordan enjoyed the humor of the Piazza d'Italia, ". . . I find it refreshing that a work of architecture can instill joviality in a public space. . . ." See his letter to the editor in "Views—Battle of New Orleans Continued," *Progressive Architecture,* 60, April 1979, 6.

51. Letter to the editor by Nicolas Pyle, "Battle of New Orleans," 6.

52. Lake Douglas, "Piazza d'Italia," *Architectural Review,* 165, May 1979, 256.

53. Paul Goldberger, "New Plaza in Downtown New Orleans in a Wild and Mad Vision," *New York Times,* February 9, 1979, B, 8. This article was reproduced in "Piazza d'Italia," *States-Item,* March 6, 1979, 81.

54. Errol Barron from Tulane University stated that the Piazza heightens the sense of what is possible in architecture and that the lessons to be learned from it are many. Among others, these include how to find the appropriate architectural response for a given situation; the importance of scholarship, erudition, and wit as creative sources for inspiration; and the necessities of

proportion and color used in an innovative manner. See letter to the editor by Errol Barron, "Mixed Reaction," 8.

55. George Baird, "Problems of Representation," *Places*, 1, Winter 1984, 12.
56. Charles Jencks has written two important books discussing the issue of post-modernism. The Piazza d'Italia is included in both. See Charles Jencks, *The Language of Post-Modern Architecture*, New York, 1977, and *Architecture Today*, New York, 1982.
57. Jencks, *The Language of Post-Modern Architecture*, 6. According to Jencks, double coded architecture is partly modern and partly vernacular, revivalist, local, commercial, metaphorical, or contextual. See Jencks, *Architecture Today*, 117.
58. Jencks, *Architecture Today*, 118. David Littlejohn agreed that the Piazza d'Italia suited Jencks's definition of double coding. See Littlejohn, *Architect: The Life and Work of Charles W. Moore*, New York, 1984, 259. (The chapter on the Piazza d'Italia was also presented in Littlejohn, "Waiting for the Water," *Places*, 1, Winter 1984, 8–10.)
59. Jencks, *Architecture Today*, 117.
60. *Ibid.*
61. For the concept of double coding and its relationship to the Piazza d'Italia, see discussion above.
62. Jencks, *The Language of Post-Modern Architecture*, 118.
63. Christian Norberg-Schulz, "Free Plan and Open Form," *Places*, 1, Winter 1984, 15.
64. Norberg-Schulz, "Free Plan," 15.
65. *Ibid.*
66. *Ibid.*
67. Bowie, "Twenty-Third Awards Program," 82.
68. Littlejohn, *Architect: The Life and Work*, 260.
69. Goldberger, "New Plaza in Downtown New Orleans," 8.
70. Robert Guenther, "No Light in the Piazza," 30.
71. Crossley, "Bit of Italian Fantasy," 3.
72. Goldberger, "New Plaza in Downtown New Orleans," 8.
73. Guenther, "No Light in the Piazza," 30.
74. *Ibid.*
75. Letter to the editor by Errol Barron, "Mixed Reaction," 8.
76. Guenther, "No Light in the Piazza," 30.
77. The most recent opinions and information on the Piazza d'Italia can be found in "Place Debate: Piazza d'Italia," *Places*, 1, Winter 1984, 7–31. The contributions include David Littlejohn, "Waiting for the Water," 8–10; George Baird, "Problems of Representation," 11–12; Robert S. Harris, "Inquiry, Essence, Awkwardness," 13–14; Christian Norberg-Schulz, "Free Plan and Open Form," 15; Jay Claiborn and Tom Aidala, "Ethnic Design or Ethnic Slur," 18–19; Ron Filson, "Remembrances and a Look at Ethnicity," 20–22; Allen Eskew, "A World's Fair," 24–26; Donlyn Lyndon, "Being There," 26–27; Charles W. Moore, "Ten Years Later," 28–30; and Ron Filson, "A Youthful Tribute," 31.
78. Moore, "Ten Years Later," 28–29.

133. The Portland Building, Fifth Street facade at left, Madison Street facade at right (color plate on page 42)

THE PORTLAND BUILDING

Portland, Oregon

Architect: Michael Graves

The architectural office of Michael Graves designed the Portland Building in 1979-80, the scheme was officially commissioned in February 1980 after a hotly contested competition, and the official dedication took place on October 2, 1982.[1] As early as April 1981, Paul Gapp had called the Portland Building "one of the most unusual, controversial, and important buildings of the last 30 years."[2] Paul Goldberger hailed it one week after its dedication as the most significant American building of the decade.[3] Not surprisingly, most of the citizens of Portland and nearly every critic in the country had something to say about the quality of the architecture.

The design competition was held in late 1979 by the Portland Public Buildings Corporation for a structure with 362,000 square-feet of floor area to occupy a 200 square-foot block in downtown Portland. The block is bordered by Fifth Avenue, Fourth Avenue, Madison Street, and Main Street. The site is surrounded by preexisting structures including a shopping plaza along the Fifth Avenue side, a landscaped park along the Fourth Avenue side, and two classical revival buildings—the City Hall and the Courthouse—along the Madison Street and Main Street sides respectively. The Portland Building was to house city services and, on the first two floors, publicly accessible functions including retail spaces, an auditorium, a restaurant, meeting rooms, and space for an art gallery. The budget was strictly set at $51 per square foot, and the total allowance was to be approximately $22.4 million.

The competition committee was composed of local politicians and business people, as well as the architect Philip Johnson as a professional consultant. The three finalists selected in February 1980 included Michael Graves, Arthur Erickson, and the firm of Mitchell-Giurgola. Graves's design offered the most economical solution; it was the only design to fall within the specified budget; and with Johnson's endorsement it was awarded the commission. Nevertheless, Graves's shockingly innovative design for the building provoked opposition among City Council members and, as a result, a second competition between Graves and Erickson, the first runner-up, was held. In this competition, both architects submitted design schemes with revisions that were in-

tended to strip the Graves design of its decoration in order to compare the essential components of the designs. In April 1980, as a result of this second competition, Graves was awarded the final commission.[4] The basis of the decision was a post-modern design that was more economical to build and more energy-efficient than its competitor.[5]

The Portland Building, as completed in October 1982, is tripartite in composition, consisting of a green base which rises in three steps, a mostly cream-colored box-like middle section, and an aqua-colored, square penthouse level crowned with a smaller rectangular structure. The base is covered with colored tile, while elastomeric paint has been used on the remaining wall surfaces and decorative elements. Included within the tiled base is an open arcade that extends across the entire Fifth Avenue facade, and continues along the Madison Street and Main Street facades. Two sets of stairs on the Main Street side and one set on the Madison Street side permit access to the arcade from the sidewalks, which vary with the level of the terrain. The base is also articulated with square windows that are especially numerous on the Fourth Avenue side of the building where there is a square two-story entrance to the parking garage centered in the facade. Centered above the automobile entrance is a larger square window which reiterates Graves's emphasis on the square as a compositional element. A wide rectangular opening centered in the arcade along Fifth Avenue permits access to the arcade and the main entrance doors of the building.

The elevation of the box-like middle section of the building is identical on the Fourth Avenue and Fifth Avenue sides; and the Madison Street and Main Street sides have another, different scheme. The Fourth and Fifth Avenue sides feature a large square area of reflective glazing seven stories high in the middle of the facade. This area contains two narrow strips of masonry that divide the glazing into four huge squares of equal size. Running up six of seven stories of glass are twelve concrete strips painted dark red and topped with projecting "capitals," one capital for each set of six pilasters. Above the capitals is a gigantic reddish keystone shape painted on the wall surface, which is penetrated with the recurring

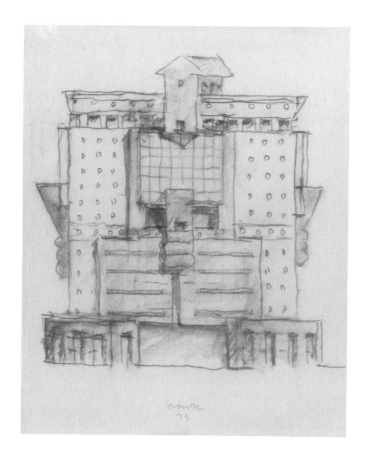

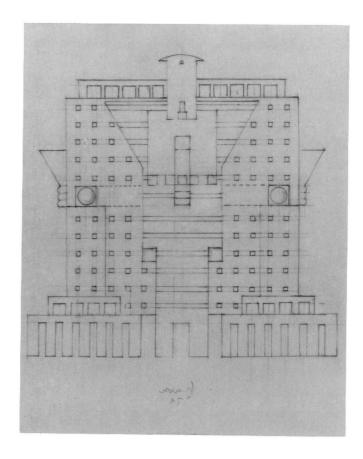

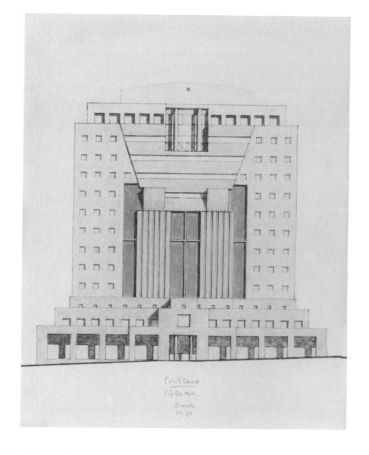

134. Four drawings by Michael Graves for the design of the Portland Building. The drawing at the lower right, with minimal decoration, was produced for a second, final competition review

square windows. Notched into the upper portion of the keystone element is a trabeated look-out, a belvedere. The remaining area of the cream-colored wall is punctured by 4 × 4-foot square windows. The Madison Street and Main Street facades feature wider areas of reflective glass that leave only one vertical row of windows at the corners on each side of the glazed area. Here, there are four sets of five dark red "pilasters" over each area of reflective glass, and these are topped with decorative garlands that were restored to the design by a special appropriation of funds.[6] The remaining portion of the wall is penetrated with the 4 × 4-foot windows. The uppermost two or three feet of all four sides of the middle section of the building are penetrated by small square cross-shaped openings which correspond to the shape of the arcade detailing.

The penthouse floor is a crowning device, square and set slightly back from the plane of the rest of the building. It is a simple trabeated structure, interrupted by the two belvederes on the Fourth Avenue and Fifth Avenue sides of the building. Resting on the penthouse level is another simple post and lintel structure containing the mechanical devices of the building. This small, narrow, rectangular element is two stories in height and is situated in the center of the roof, its length extending across the Fourth and Fifth Avenue facades.

The state of controversy surrounding the Portland Building is a result of its flamboyant style and its function as a public monument constructed at the taxpayers' expense; but the fact that the building was the first large-scale project by Michael Graves, and that his design intentions were extensive and debatable added to the energetic outpouring of opinions from journalists, professional critics, politicians, and the public.[7] Although his design offered the most space and the highest energy efficiency for the least amount of money, some commentators felt that since most of Graves's designs for large-scale projects had remained on paper, Graves must be an academician whose building experience did not warrant such a conspicuous commission. A portion of the early criticism seems to center on Graves instead of on his design, and although his inexperience was certainly the impetus for some of these comments, the additional fact of his blossoming celebrity status was another contributing factor. As Martin Filler later pointed out, "It's a rare thing for a young architect to be featured in the pages of *People*, to be mobbed by autograph seekers at the dedication of a building he designed, and to be interviewed on the *NBC Nightly News*."[8] Graves's widest recognition had come in part as a result of exhibits of his architectural drawings, and this led to charges that "Graves is more an artist than an architect; his real media are the maquette and the sketch pad rather than the full-size edifice."[9] Thus, the building was subjected to more than its share of coverage in the popular press, and nothing short of an architectural biopsy was performed on it by critics and those in the profession.

The first to be concerned about the design were, of

135. Fourth Street facade

course, the people of Portland, who expressed their opinions in letters to the editor.[10] Some citizens thought that the building was unflattering and that they were the objects of a monumental joke. "We may have a paragraph in *Time* but we're going to also get three pages in *National Lampoon*," said one resident. Another maintained that neighborhood associations should have the right of approval for such a building and that, if they did, it would not have been commissioned. Other citizens responded negatively to the specific imagery of the building, suggesting that it represented a fortress mentality that excludes pedestrians, ignores the park, and focuses on itself to the exclusion of its downtown neighbors. The building conveyed for some observers the message that "government is monolithic, imposing and remote." "Our public officials are not gods," wrote an indignant citizen, "Why build them a temple?"

Other commentators were less hostile, although they were at first in the minority. These people praised the work of a "serious and talented architect" and his "distinguished" designs. One thoughtful resident suggested that the architect "may have a vision that we do not possess at this time"—a statement that, in light of later opinion, may seem to be prophetic. Mainly, however, there was just plain disagreement. Where a senior citizen could claim that Graves simply did not know Portland, another of unspecified age claimed that "one thing is clear": Graves had studied the city and the context of the building carefully.[11] For the latter writer the proof of the archi-

136. View down Fourth Street showing City Hall, the Portland Building, the Courthouse

tect's sensitivity to the location was incorporated in the use of rustication, cornices, porches, escutcheons and garlands, a colonnade mid-height, and a roof pavilion— all features that are part of the City Hall and the Courthouse buildings that flank the new monument.

Another notable aspect of the early criticism is the degree of vehemence with which the local architects opposed the scheme. "This is a dog building, a turkey," said the noted architect John Storrs, "I regret that we always have to face east for 'the word.' "[12] Another Portland architect, A.D. Benkendorf said, "I hope that others concerned about the future of downtown will join with me in urging the City Council to send 'Graves' Temple' back to the East Coast."[13] Pietro Belluschi, the one architect of international stature among these professionals, was hardly kinder. In a letter addressed to the City Council on behalf of the Portland Chapter of the AIA, Belluschi termed the Graves design an "enlarged juke box or the oversized beribboned Christmas package."[14] He urged that Graves build the building somewhere else, such as Atlantic City or Las Vegas, "Or better yet he should live a little while among us and absorb the genius of our city, and then begin anew." It was a statement

that Belluschi would later regret. In general, however, the opposition was resigned. Said one respondent: "Psychiatry and architecture have always competed in the definition of mental disorders. This rivalry becomes visible in public buildings as megalomaniacal masonry, and I personally fail to see why our City Council should be hindered in its faithful adherence to tradition."[15]

Graves did offer explanations of the symbolism he intended in the design of the Portland Building. Anthropomorphism would be represented in the building's division into "head", "body", and "foot". The paired pilasters would express the internal core of the building, and they would only extend to the highest floor occupied by the city offices, therefore "supporting" the final four floors that were to be leased to commercial tenants. The masonry garlands were to be interpreted as ancient symbols of welcome, and the statue "Portlandia" would represent the city's culture and industry. The green color of the base was meant to represent foliage, the terra-cotta and cream-colored middle section was to be suggestive of the earth, while the aqua-colored roof would be analogous to the sky.[16]

Incorporating the overall elevation, color and orna-

166

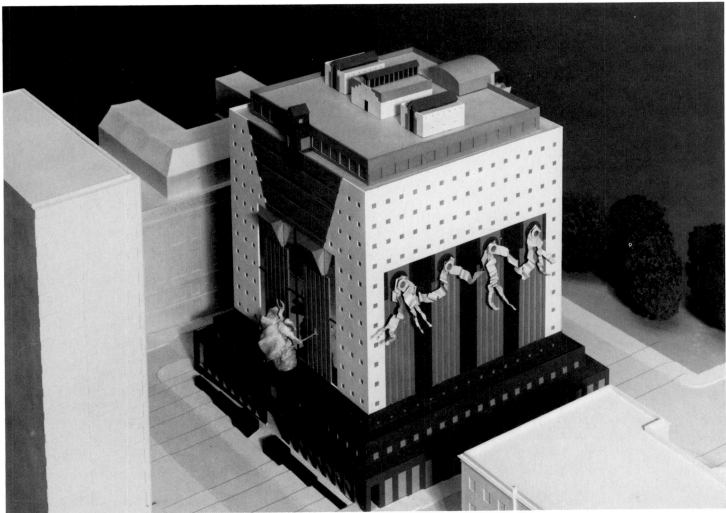

137. Competition model for the Portland Building, with "village" on roof, "Portlandia" sculpture on Fifth Street facade (left), garlands on Madison Street facade (right)

ment of the design, the apparent symbolism of the building has been a source of critical concern and even misunderstanding. It was certainly Graves's intention to include symbolic references in his scheme for the Portland Building, but some writers have read symbolism where none was intended or even possible. One example concerns the small group of structures that were to constitute a "village" resting on the roof of the building. This design detail in the original drawing and model was removed as part of the well publicized submission of a second design solution meant to satisfy opponents of the original proposal. Five months after the building had officially opened, however, an interviewer for *Progressive Architecture* asked Graves, "The Portland Building, when first designed, was an acropolis with a small group of buildings on its head. What was the symbolic implication of removing them?"[17] This was a curious question, for although the structure had intentional symbolic meaning, the decision to remove the crowning buildings was a pragmatic one. Graves answered, "I thought it quite reasonable to describe with those buildings the paradigm of the city organization. But it didn't seem reasonable to the

majority of the local fellows of the A.I.A. who were opposed to the building. So, now, in fact, the new symbol becomes the *removal* of that group of buildings."[18] It is interesting that this line of questioning was followed since this particular design change had been repeatedly discussed in print during the two and one-half years prior to this interview.

Eleni Constantine, writing for the *Architectural Record* in August 1980, was one of the early converts to the symbolic aspects of the Portland Building on many different levels.[19] She noted the relationships of the various functions on different floors to external articulation, and she was particularly enthusiastic about the classical references of the "symbolic temple." For Constantine, the classical style was an enduring "symbol for representative, participatory democracy" that had come down to us through a vocabulary of forms developed in classical Greece, medieval Bologna, republican Rome, and in the United States during its early history. Constantine also maintained, as did later critics, that the Portland Building was "contextual" in its deference to the street pattern of the city, but that other buildings such as the Guggenheim

Museum in New York City by Frank Lloyd Wright, and the Metropolitan Museum facade by McKim, Mead, and White were criticized for not being contextual in their day.

In the *Architectural Record* two and a half years later, Douglas Brenner disputed the accessibility of the intended symbolism:

> There is an implicit anthropomorphism of 'foot', 'body', and 'head' in Graves' tripartite composition, but the sum of these parts bears so slight a resemblance to any familiar proportional canon—anatomical or architectural—that the uninitiated observer is not likely to grasp such analogies. One would have to read the architect's scholarly gloss to discover, for example, that the swollen keystone denotes rental floors, supported figuratively as well as literally by the municipal offices below.[20]

Additionally, of course, symbolism as expressed through the various specific uses of the interior spaces could be rendered meaningless with any changes in the city's need for space.[21]

Graves did express interest in the ". . . idea that people can identify with this building. . . ," however, he has maintained that "architecture must communicate not just on a populist level, but on an educated level as well."[22] As Graves said elsewhere, "I am interested in seeing how the work can be made accessible on the one hand to those who are not interested or not aware of not participating in literate levels of meaning, but feel things in their senses. At the same time I would not be doing my job if I didn't also attract the sternest critic to the work."[23]

To be sure, there were many who could not respond to the symbolism of the building and who remained disturbed by the use of unusually scaled classical forms. Martin Filler disliked the mixing of scales, such as the use of a small order and tiny windows on the huge bulk of the building as though they were fragments "from some Brobdingnagian salvage sale, at once suggesting an overgrown Vienna Secession power station, and a footstool of the gods."[24] But the fact that Filler was discussing the form of the building as well as its meaning was a significant departure. Ada Louise Huxtable stated this attitude more directly in an article in which she called the Portland Building the "post-modern building of the year."[25] As she put it, "Graves's insistence on an almost Druid-like significance for every element of the design has obscured the fact that this is a thoughtfully and economically planned structure that beat out its competitors easily. If it promises a surfeit of symbolism, it also proposes some efficient and interesting spaces."

As the building began to take shape in Portland, residents began to reappraise it, no doubt in part because of the positive comments that had come from the professional critics. Interestingly, it was particularly in Seattle that the Portland Building enjoyed a good press. Seattle design critic Roger Downey praised its integrity and its relationships to the surrounding buildings and concluded that "planning, politics, and chance conspired for once to push innovation forward."[26] Norman Johnston, who was then president of the Seattle chapter of the AIA, wrote a calm and reasoned plea for a building as good as Graves's for the city of Seattle.[27] Ed Weiner's enthusiasm set off a rash of controversy of its own in the form of letters to the *Seattle Times*.[28] Two months previously, Jack Sidener, writing in the same newspaper, proposed that Portland had a higher level of design because of its openness to outsiders, such as Belluschi from Italy, Halprin from San Francisco, and Skidmore, Owings and Merrill from New York.[29] Even in the Portland *Oregonian*, the critical consensus shifted slightly. An editorial claimed that the building might even become "a great credit to the human spirit and mind in an age that scarcely knew what it was seeing when it looked."[30] Another slightly later editorial lambasted the "unfair attacks, launched sometimes by an establishment that has trouble defending its lockstep style that wiped out many of the 19th century's exciting buildings in the name of progress and modernity."[31] The opinions of the citizens can best be summarized by the title of an article in the *Oregonian* that appeared late in 1981: "Architect Holds Steady View . . . While Critics Slowly Alter Theirs."[32] Comments in the article echoed the tenor of those who claimed that the Portland Building was not so bad after all, that it was "growing" on people who became fonder of it as construction progressed.

The change in local attitudes is certainly striking to anyone who reviews the material; given the vehemence of early opposition the shift in opinion among architects, critics, and the citizenry may even be unprecedented. To be sure, there were still those who continued to decry the huge scale of the mass, the ostentatious decoration, and the small windows; but local sentiment had moved in the other direction.[33] The architect John Storrs (the originator of the "turkey" appellation) praised Graves for the loggia that would offer a covered walkway to retail customers on the ground floor.[34] Even Belluschi could admit apologetically, "I'm getting used to it. I've seen it from a distance and it has its own character. Frankly, I'm sorry I made any adverse comment at all."[35]

Just when local opinion was drifting in a distinctly positive direction, however, the critic of *Time* magazine, Wolf von Eckardt, paid a visit to Portland. He was reported in the local press to have said that he hoped the Graves approach "doesn't catch on."[36] The reason, he explained, was that "it's wonderful for Portland to have a little fun with architecture, but it's also dangerous." "It is," said von Eckardt, "poisoning the minds of the kids in architecture." He criticized the design as "capricious" and suggested that contrary to the designer's intentions, "It doesn't help the relationship of the government to the people." In another article, von Eckardt was quoted as having claimed that the Portland Building "forgets the re-

138. Detail showing geometricized garland decoration and square windows

sponsibility of architecture—it threatens the extinction of the architectural profession as a force shaping the built environment."[37] To his interviewer he tried nevertheless to be consoling: "Don't make such a big fuss about this building. This is a big city. It can take it."[38] These notions and others of a similarly negative sort characterized the review that appeared in *Time* magazine several months later. Von Eckardt classified the style of the Portland Building as "Pop surrealism that uses classic design elements the way Walt Disney cartoons used the physiognomy of a rodent to create Mickey Mouse."[39] Again, he maintained that the building was "dangerous," and he was not referring to its structure but rather to its style. "Modern architecture is ripe for a radical change," von Eckardt maintained, "but Graves would replace Satan with Beelzebub."

In retrospect, the interesting fact of this adamant point of view, which was carried in a national newsmagazine, is the degree to which it seems not to have influenced the opinions of people in Portland or the readership of *Time*. We have given fair account of the local sentiment. Of the four letters to the editor of *Time*, three defended the building, and one suggested that the supporters of the design "should be boiled in treacle for permitting defacement of their revitalized city by Graves' marzipan monstrosity."[40] Those readers who supported the building doubted that it was dangerous and praised its human scale and refreshing style.

Generalizations about the critical reception of the Portland Building after its dedication are hard to make in part because of the diversity of opinions. On the issue of color, Pastier wrote that the finished design contained far too much contrast; in execution, the colored surfaces de-

stroyed "what once was a balanced dialogue between solid mass and surface pattern."[41] For Robert Campbell, "The mastery of color and of a rich variety of surface effects would alone make this a remarkable building. . . . The colors resonate."[42] Patricia Failing evidently agreed with Pastier that the colors were much brighter than the drawings suggested, and she termed the building a "histrionic masquerade."[43] Brenner judged the colors duller than those in the drawings and concluded that "For all the messages it was meant to convey, the Portland Building remains eerily mute."[44] Filler believed that the range of colors "adds needed brightness to a city whose skies are overcast for most of the year."[45]

On the matter of the size of the windows there has been perhaps greater agreement, for most critics found them too small. Originally, they were to be nine square feet rather than sixteen square feet as executed. Graves claimed that their size was determined in relation to the individual desk size, and the fact that they are small was also due to energy considerations. More than likely, however, the size of the windows has to do with the architect's aversion to the "window wall" of modernist buildings. "We as a culture have always regarded the wall as a solid, the window as a void," said Graves, "to have a 'window wall' devalues the primary attributes of both."[46] Elsewhere, the architect has indicated that he suffers from vertigo if he stands next to a window with wall to wall glass; besides, he maintained, "It's just madness to give the base of a table a view!"[47] On the other hand the critics have reported that occupants of the new office building must "crane for a tantalizing view" of the landscape, and workers in some offices have gone as far as to tape cardboard "bars" over their windows.[48]

139. Main lobby

Other complaints reported in the press include doors that open awkwardly, inadequate soundproofing, lack of light, poor ventilation, low ceilings, and a low level of lighting that makes reading difficult in the office spaces. The auditorium has sight lines that are blocked from some seats. The guard station in the lobby is not well positioned to watch the lobby doors or the elevators. There is a problem with a sloping floor.[49] Some of these difficulties are considered the fault of the architect, some of the interior designer. Many of the problems could have been overcome with a more generous budget. But the critical literature does not deal with these matters at length. Those issues that are addressed have apparently generated no sustained discussion of the functioning building, the critical reputation of which seems to rest exclusively on responses to matters of style.

The lobby serves as an example of differing opinions on features of the design. One enters the main lobby by passing through the glass doors recessed and centered in the arcade along the Fifth Avenue side of the building. On the left of the two-story lobby is a security counter, on the right an information counter. The lobby is embellished with tile, semi-circular "chair rail" moldings made out of sheet metal, painted walls, and terrazzo floors. For Filler, all of this works well together: "Glossy black terrazzo flooring, fat bolection moldings painted a shiny green, and dadoes tiled in blue-green work well with walls painted in muted, fleshy pastels."[50] For Neil Levine, the foyer was "beautiful," but he felt that more money should have been spent on it; this is a notion that would surface in other reviews.[51] Filler also found that "The central two-story atrium is a magnificent composition, big enough to seem appropriately monumental, but not so large as to diminish the visitor's sense of his own individuality."[52] For Pastier the two-story lobby was "poorly proportioned and self-consciously embellished."[53] Forster wrote of the lobby surrounded by a mezzanine gallery "of very crammed porportions."[54]

From these statements we learn nothing of the building, but a good deal about how little agreement there is on matters of decoration and judgments of space. In general, the opinions of the critics about the lobby simply reflected their response to the whole building. Levine, for example, was enthusiastic about the "lively and dignified" building, although his response was tempered by some disappointment in the heaviness of the base, the loss of the roof details, and the flatness of the mass because of the loss of the original garlands to budgetary concerns.[55] Similarly, Forster was equally unenthusiastic about the "tenuous fashion" by which the exterior details of the elevation suggest classical columns, capitals, and keystones.[56] Here, as in other instances, Forster determined that the classical references do not work well: he recognized in the scheme of the lobby a "unilinear" organization with respect to the rest of the public spaces on the lower floors; and this scheme "betrays at once its origin in the configuration of the ancient Roman house."[57] For Forster, this configuration does not do jus-

tice to the free-standing aspect of the building or to its context.

On the issue of context, there has been significant disagreement. Before it was built, Jencks characterized the design, stripped of its ornaments "as an ultimate 'skylump', that epitome of real estate forces . . ., but made interesting, humanly scaled and responsive to the context."[58] For Alan Hayakawa, a critic for the Oregonian writing after the dedication ceremonies, the Portland Building "looks out of place" with reference to its size, its style, and its materials—painted surfaces rather than the stone and brick of older buildings.[59] Goldberger found the issue less a matter of correspondence than of harmony: "If it does not blend easily with its neighbors, in no way does it fight them. It is as though a handsomely painted car has pulled up into a line of limosines, not to show them up but simply to take its place among them."[60] Vincent Scully has been the most consistently outspoken advocate of the contextualism of the Portland Building. In form, the mass is "exactly in accord with that of the buildings beside it," according to Scully.[61] He perceived the colors as the "equivalents" of the older buildings under restoration in the central downtown area, and the "piers and tondi find their echoes in adjacent buildings."

At a conference on the building held at the Institute for Architecture and Urban Studies, the discussion about the issue of contextualism proved the extent to which observers could hold diametrically opposed views.[62] Scully maintained his thesis, adding that the little temples on the Portland Building would have created a visual effect similar to the cluster of little houses on the hills around Portland; "this," he said, "is real contextualism." Philip Johnson reportedly asserted that "There is no 'contextualism' really possible here." John Burgee maintained that it was contextual "in that it is a civic building among other civic buildings: it doesn't imitate the other buildings, but it does indicate that it is part of the group." Perhaps the dilemma posed by these divergent opinions could be resolved if the term itself were better defined.

The most widely acceptable judgment on the Portland Building was the comment that it "has had its flaws examined all out of proportion to the possibilities inherent in an inexpensive building by an architect inexperienced in large-scale work."[63] Pastier suggested that the building failed "not through timidity, but through its very boldness."[64] Gapp thought it failed as a "leaden, gloomy bore."[65] "It is particularly vulnerable," wrote Gapp, "because it lacks the panache of impudence that might have blunted some of the fresh opprobrium now being heaped on it." This assessment was similar to that of Buchanan, who called the style of the building "Deco-Classicism," the oddly scaled features of which do not raise the result above the level of "banal."[66] Philip Johnson, who played a major role in the commission of the building, claimed finally to have been disappointed with the outcome, which was only as good as the funds available could obtain.[67] Johnson missed the sculpture, liked the layering

140. View through second floor elevator corridor, with small "Portlandia" sculpture at far end

effect of the elevation scheme, and concluded that Graves had "decorated the undecorated box." For Scully, "By any reasonable definition of the term, it is an entirely modern building, finding 'new objective correlatives' for every one of the great, traditional shapes which it employs, and reproducing none of them. Because of them it should be taken as a major and highly creative step toward the salvation of our cities from the mindless junk with which they have recently been strewn. It enhances the meaning and enlarges the emotional scope of the office building program . . . ."[68]

From this review of the literature, it appears that more than just the shape and style of a building was at issue in these commentaries. Exactly what factors conspired to make the Portland Building one of the most debated works of architecture in history will long remain a matter of discussion. It is clear that this building is not just good or bad, boring or fascinating, beautiful or ugly. In debate, Scully asserted that the only architects in his experience who had been criticized "in quite the same defensive way" were Robert Venturi, Le Corbusier, and Frank Lloyd Wright.[69] At the AIA convention in New Orleans, Michael Graves stepped into an elevator full of conventioneers wearing buttons. On some the Portland Building was depicted with a red slash through it, while others displayed the words "We Don't Dig Graves."[70] The architect was only slightly shaken; he was on his way to accept a national AIA Honor Award for his Portland Building.[71]

David L. Gilbert

Notes

1. Previously known as the Public Service Building and the Portland Public Office Building, the official name became the Portland Building in 1981. See Jo Dana, "City Can't Pirate Name of Old Portland Building," Oregonian (Portland), October 27, 1981.
2. Paul Gapp, "Controversy Is Building Over Portland Edifice," Chicago Tribune, April 29, 1981, 1.
3. Paul Goldberger, "Architecture of a Different Color," New York Times Magazine, October 10, 1982, 43. Later, Goldberger called the completion of the Portland Building the most compelling event of the year in architecture because it heralded the influence of postmodernism on the cityscape. See Paul Goldberger, "The Modern Cityscape Now Finds Room for the Picturesque," New York Times, December 26, 1982, 27.
4. With questions of design, there were also political considerations. Frank Ivancie, then City Council member responsible for Public Works and a supporter of Graves, was running for mayor; his campaign on both fronts proved successful. For details of the selection process, see Steve Jenning, "Designers Present Three Building Plans to Jury of Citizens," Oregonian, February 16, 1980; Jenning, " 'Temple' Gaining Ground in Council," Oregonian, March 5, 1980; Jenning, "Design for Public Service Building: Chaotic or Poetic?" Oregonian, March 16, 1980; Jenning, "Temple Design Wins Tentative Approval," Oregonian, April 3, 1980; Dan Hortsch, "Smaller Temple Model Solves Design Anxiety," Oregonian, April 16, 1980 (substitution of model without garlands, roof buildings, Portlandia sculpture); Cynthia

Saltzman, "Architect Michael Graves: Changing the Horizon," *Wall Street Journal,* May 1, 1981; J.M. Dixon, "Portland Competition a Very Public Issue," *Progressive Architecture,* 61, May 1980, 25; John Pastier, "First Monument of a Loosely Defined Style," *AIA Journal,* 72, May 1983, 234–235.

5. See "Energy Analysis: Portland Public Office Building," *Progressive Architecture,* 62, October 1981, 108–109, for some of the impressive examples of energy saving concepts incorporated into the building. On questions of engineering, see "Sensible Framing Saves Face," *Engineering News Record,* October 9, 1980, 16.

6. Alan Ota, "$275,000 Voted to Add Garlands on New Building," *Oregonian,* December 24, 1981.

7. Relatively little attention has been paid in the critical literature to the process by which the Portland Building was commissioned, designed, and executed. The City Council wanted guarantees against cost overruns and construction delays and wanted a distinguished, avant-garde design. The solution was an international competition with Philip Johnson as advisor that would require a design produced by a "team" rather than an architect. The team consisted of architect, contractor, engineer, and consultants, who guaranteed the completion of the work on time and according to budget. Cost overruns would be absorbed by the team, and $9000 would be assessed for each day of construction over the scheduled completion date. The Graves team included Emery Roth and Sons (production architects), DeSimone and Chaplin Associates (structural engineers), Thomas A. Polise, Jr. (mechanical and electrical engineers), Cerami and Associates (acoustical engineers), Pavarini Construction Company and Hoffman Construction Company—A Joint Venture (contractors). Generally, the design architect works for the client, but in this case Graves would have to be responsible to his contractors who were making a substantial commitment by guaranteeing price and schedule. For this reason the client (the city of Portland) hired a project manager (Morse/Diesel Incorporated) to represent its interests, as well as an architectural advisor (Edward C. Wundram). For more on the design-build process, see Gordon Wright, "Controversial Option for Public Projects," *Building Design and Construction,* November 1981, 82–88. For a useful descripion of the case at the Portland Building, see the account by the project manager from the Graves office, Lisa Fleming Lee, "Building *the* Building," *Leading Edge,* October 1982, 65–72.

8. Martin Filler, "The Gallant Gamble of Michael Graves," *House and Garden,* January 1983, 168.

9. Pastier, "First Monument," 236.

10. We have taken the information for this paragraph directly from photocopies of undated letters to the editor of the *Oregonian* that were provided to us by the office of Michael Graves.

11. See Margaret Cabell, "Artificial Light" (letter to the editor), *Oregonian,* April 18, 1980; and Philip Thompson, "In Proper Context" (letter to the editor), *Oregonian,* December 8, 1981.

12. Spencer Heinz, "Proposed City Office Building Design Called 'A Dog'," *Oregon Journal,* n.d. (photocopy kindly provided to us by the office of Michael Graves).

13. Jenning, "Chaotic or Poetic?."

14. Belluschi's letter and others from the local press have been published by Charles Jencks, "Post-Modern Classicism, the New Synthesis," *Architectural Design,* 50, 1980, 133–142.

15. Lamar Tooze, "Keep Tradition" (letter to the editor), *Oregonian,* April 16, 1980.

16. See Steve Jenning, "Graves Aims at Building of Human Scale," *Oregonian,* March 16, 1980; Ian Blair, "Michael Graves" (interview), *Revue,* Summer 1980, 25–29; Abraham Rogatnick, "An Interview with Michael Graves," *Forum* (Canada), September 1980, 4–5, 27–30; Joanna Cenci Rodriguez, "Interview with Michael Graves," *Florida Architect,* Fall 1981; Michael McTwigan, "What Is the Focus of Post-Modern Architecture? An Interview with Michael Graves," *American Artist,* 45, December 1981. Lisa Fellows Andrus, "Taking Its Place on the Portland Skyline," *Northwest Magazine,* February 14, 1982, 6–8.

17. "Conversation with Graves" (roundtable discussion with Susan Doubilet, Thomas Fisher, David Morton, James Murphy), *Progressive Architecture,* 64, February 1983, 108–115, especially 114.

18. Doubilet *et al.,* "Conversation with Graves," 114. Of a different order is the symbolism that the building will project to the future as fantasized in Helene Melyan, "Temple of the Ancients, an Architectural Enigma," *Oregonian,* March 14, 1980, in which the author prophesied an archaeological symposium in the year 2980 devoted to "The Portland Dig."

19. Eleni Constantine, "The Case for Michael Graves's Design for Portland," *Architectural Record,* 168, August 1980, 96–101.

20. Douglas Brenner, "Portland," *Architectural Record,* 170, November 1982, 92.

21. Lance Knobel, "Graves' Deco," *Architectural Review,* 172, November 1982, 60–64.

22. Doubilet *et al.,* "Conversation with Graves," 114.

23. Rogatnick, "Interview with Graves," 27.

24. Martin Filler, "Michael Graves: Before and After," *Art in America,* 68, September 1980, 99–105.

25. Ada Louise Huxtable, "The Boom in Bigness Goes On," *New York Times,* December 12, 1980, 25–26.

26. Roger Downey, "Post-Modernism Comes to Portland," *Seattle Weekly,* June 10, 1981.

27. Norman Johnston, "Modern Architecture: Alive and Well in Portland," *Seattle Times,* October 18, 1981.

28. Ed Weiner, "The Most Famous Building in Seattle Is in Portland," *Seattle Times,* October 18, 1981. The title surely played a part in the subsequent fury recorded in "Letters" (letters to the editor), *Seattle Times,* November 1, 1981.

29. Jack Sidener, "Can 'Home-Grown' Become 'Ingrown'," *Seattle Times,* August 9, 1981. Belluschi had built the Equitable Life Building, Lawrence Halprin the Forecourt Fountain, and Skidmore, Owings and Merrill the Transit Mall in Portland.

30. "Portland Anchor of Postmodernism" (editorial), *Oregonian,* August 29, 1982. The editorial was a response to the article by John Russell, "Modernism to Postmodernism: A New World Once Again," *New York Times,* August 22, 1982, II, 1. Earlier in the month the architect had again put forward his view of the Portland Building; see Charlotte Graydon, "Architect Defends Build-

ing as Escape from Blandness," *Oregonian*, August 11, 1982.

31. "Architectural Revolt Long Overdue" (editorial), *Oregonian*, November 6, 1981, C, 10.
32. Richard Reed and Steve Erickson, "Architect Holds Steady View . . . While Critics Slowly Alter Theirs," *Oregonian*, December 20, 1981.
33. Grant Hildebrand, "Portland Building Raises Questions," *Seattle Times*, December 6, 1981; and the unsympathetic review of Alan Hayakawa, "Building's a Bane to City," *Oregonian*, October 10, 1982, C, 6. The latter article was written after the public dedication of the building.
34. Douglas Gantenbein, "Portland's Erupting Skyline," *Oregon Magazine*, July 1982, 24–29, 66–69.
35. Quoted in Kathie Durbin, "The Shape of Things to Come," *Portland*, September 1982, 17.
36. Charlotte Graydon, "Time Mag Critic Hits Portland Building," *Oregonian*, June 2, 1982, B, 8. Von Eckardt quoted Winston Churchill on the importance of the effect of architecture on a people's outlook.
37. Quoted in Douglas Gantenbein, "Portland's Outrage, Portland's Pride," *Pacific Northwest*, October 1982, 32–35.
38. Evidently, von Eckardt was correct about the ability of Portland to harbor architectural diversity, particularly in the building boom then under way; see Gantenbein, "Portland's Erupting Skyline," 24–29, 66–69.
39. Wolf von Eckardt, "A Pied Piper of Hobbit Land," *Time*, August 23, 1982. 62–63. The author claimed that the metallic festoons were not executed partly because they were considered too inviting for pigeons. We have found no reference to this in the rest of the literature.
40. See "Letters" (letters to the editor), *Time*, September 13, 1982, 5.
41. Pastier, "First Monument," 236, was comparing the building to the preliminary drawings for it.
42. Robert Campbell, "Graves Has the Courage," *Boston Globe*, April 12, 1983.
43. Patricia Failing, "If Gloria Swanson Were a Building," *Art News*, September 1982, 111–114. The author likened the building to the actress decked out for her comeback in *Sunset Boulevard*. Failing also referred to the "overbaked semiotics" on the exterior.
44. Brenner, "Portland," 92
45. Filler, "Gallant Gamble," 215.

46. "Guest Speaker: Michael Graves on the Language of Architecture," *Architectural Digest*, 40, April 1983, 30.
47. Doubilet *et al.*, "Conversation with Graves," 111.
48. Brenner, "Portland," 92.
49. Ginny Butterfield, "Inside Out," *Oregon*, October 1982, 72–73; "Portland Cries Tilt," *Metropolis*, March 1983; Spencer Heinz, "Dust Hasn't Settled at Year Old Portland Building," *Oregonian*, September 18, 1983, C, 1.
50. Filler, "Gallant Gamble," 215.
51. Andy Rocchia, "Art Historian Finds Graves' Plans Compromised" (interview with Neil Levine), *Oregon Journal*, July 29, 1982, 3. See also Doubilet *et al.*, "Conversation with Graves," 112.
52. Filler, "Gallant Gamble," 215
53. Pastier, "First Monument," 236.
54. Kurt Forster, "Portland: the Building," *Skyline*, January 1983, 18.
55. Levine in Rocchia, "Art Historian," 3.
56. Forster, "Portland," 18.
57. *Ibid.*
58. Charles Jencks, "Post-Modern Classicism," 142.
59. Hayakawa, "Building's a Bane," C, 6.
60. Goldberger, "Architecture of a Different Color," 48.
61. Vincent Scully, Jr. in *Michael Graves Buildings and Projects*, eds. K. Wheeler, P. Arnell, T. Bickford, New York, 1981, 297–298.
62. See "Portland: the Building," *Skyline*, January 1983, 16–21.
63. Doubilet *et al.*, "Conversation with Graves," 108.
64. Pastier, "First Monument," 236.
65. Gapp, "A Bore," claimed that the building induces "more yawns than lifted eyebrows." At most, he maintained, "it makes a clumsy attempt at mooning."
66. Peter Buchanan, "Graven Image," *Architect's Journal*, 176, November 17, 1982, 40.
67. Johnson in "Portland: the Building," 19.
68. Scully in *Michael Graves Buildings and Projects*, 298.
69. Scully in "Portland: the Building," 19.
70. Robert Guenther, "In Architects' Circles, Post-Modernist Design Is a Bone of Contention," *Wall Street Journal*, August 1, 1983, 1.
71. The news of the award was announced to the professional community in Portland in "Portland Building Wins National AIA Honor Award," *Architalk* (Portland, Chapter AIA), May 1983, 4.

RENAISSANCE CENTER
Detroit, Michigan

Architects: John Portman and Associates

141. Renaissance Center (color plate on page 43)

Renaissance Center in Detroit was an urban project promoted by Henry Ford II, Chairman of Ford Motor Company, with the assistance of fifty-one corporations that formed the Renaissance Center Partnership.[1] As its name implies, the Renaissance Center was a symbol of rebirth. It was hoped the Center would spearhead a revitalization of the downtown area, which had been devastated by the riots of 1967. Raised on a connecting podium four stories above street level and towering above the rest of Detroit, the Renaissance Center was, in its scope and its scale, a new concept in urban development. The ambitions of the Renaissance Center Partnership were to provide a visually attractive and exciting setting for a convention-size hotel, business offices, and for leisure activities, which together would serve as a reviving "catalyst" to a decaying central business district. This ambitious program naturally had its critics as well as its proponents, and both parties took their case to the local and national press, attracting the attention of a broad public and the architectural profession. As the controversies developed, they concerned the Center's isolation, its contextual relationship with the rest of Detroit, and its viability as a catalyst for revitalization.

The Renaissance Center, designed by John Portman and Associates, is located seven blocks from the center of Detroit on 32 acres of riverfront at the edge of the business district. It is separated from the rest of the city on the north by large concrete berms and the ten-laned Jefferson Avenue. On the west is an access road, Renaissance Drive, and the entrance to the tunnel to Canada. St. Antoine Street borders the east, and the Detroit River delimits the south of RenCen, as the Center is popularly known. The complex incorporates a hotel, offices, shops, restaurants, and entertainment and convention facilities.[2] The first phase of the project included a 73-story hotel, reportedly the tallest in the world; surrounding its soar-

ing, cylindrical shape are four 39-story octagonal office towers. Started in 1973, the first phase of construction was completed in 1977. Since then, two office towers to the east were added in 1981, but the intervening recession prevented the construction of additional office towers originally planned on both east and west and of condominiums along the riverfront.

RenCen was the brainchild of Henry Ford II. It was he who announced the plan for the riverfront project to mayor Roman S. Gribbs (1970–1973) and to the Detroit city council on November 24, 1971.[3] Ford also announced the choice of architect John Portman, a choice that was influenced by Portman's earlier designs in downtown locations, such as the Peachtree Center in Atlanta, Georgia.[4] Peachtree Center, which covers three city blocks, includes a 70-story, glazed, cylindrical hotel tower, and embraces some of the most lucrative commercial spaces in Atlanta. Similarly, the RenCen in Detroit was intended from the first as a profitable investment. "We're also in this to make money," Ford said, and he must have been serious.[5] The partnership for financing the operation "represented the greatest assemblage of business and industrial firms ever formed for a project of this nature," according to Wayne S. Doran, President of Ford Motor Land Development Corporation.[6] Apparently, not everyone involved agreed about the wisdom of the riverfront investment.[7]

There were, however, no major roadblocks to begin the project. The 32-acre site included warehouses and other structures, some of which had fallen into disuse. Furthermore, there was no housing and no need to relocate residents.[8] Thus, the rezoning of the area from mixed residential and industrial to multiple uses for planned development drew little opposition. On April 25, 1972, the Detroit City Plan Commission unanimously approved the rezoning, although the *Detroit News* noted

142. Site of Renaissance Center before construction

143. Model of master plan for Renaissance Center complex including additional lower office buildings (center) and condominiums (upper right)

177

that a few of the members had argued against the high-rise concept.[9] With little discussion the City Council enthusiastically approved the rezoning of the riverfront on May 3, 1972.[10] Editorials such as "Ford Epitomizes Detroit Spirit," "Expansion Applauded," and "Renaissance Center's Promise" typified the enthusiasm of the local press at this time, but the naysayers were soon to be heard.[11] The only indication of advice against the project appeared in Ford's announcement of the proposed Center in 1972, in which he referred to a feasibility study questioning aspects of the proposed plan.[12] Interestingly, there is no further discussion in the press of this feasibility study.

One early and serious criticism of the Renaissance Center questioned its viability as an urban project and its economic soundness. The developers Jerome Minskoff, partner of Sam Minskoff & Sons, and Vincent J. Peters, senior vice-president of Cushman and Wakefield, Inc., suggested that Ford was "making a grave mistake if he thought his development would revitalize downtown Detroit. . . . It will do just the opposite. . . . It will destroy it," they said.[13] In fact, Ford had never proclaimed that the Center would revitalize the city: "We see this project only as a beginning, a catalyst," he said. "Total revival and revitalization of Detroit is far too hard for any single company to attempt."[14] Minskoff and Peters contended that the new office buildings would drain tenants from other office buildings, including their own, and play havoc with their marketability.[15]

Apart from this early episode, the developers of RenCen pressed on through remarkably little opposition. At the opening of the hotel in 1977, a cautionary note was sounded in an issue of the *Detroit News,* but the writer was also quick to enumerate the benefits of the Center.[16] The grand opening, which took place on March 15, 1977, elicited much praise on the part of the local and national press. Articles such as "Downtown Detroit:

They're Saying Good Things" and "RenCen Makes a Difference" in the *Detroit News,* and "Revitalizing Effect of Renaissance Center Is Upgrading Detroiters' View of Their City" in the *New York Times,* typified the enthusiastic response to the Center.[17] But the opening also provided the opportunity for critics to begin to question the Center's plan, its location, and its contextual relation to its neighbors. Among the first to raise these issues was Paul Goldberger in his article, "A Modern Center in Detroit Sets Itself Apart From City," which appeared in March 1977, in the *New York Times.*[18] "Renaissance Center sets itself apart from Detroit, so dramatically that one almost feels compelled to question the developer's assertion that the project represents a 'vote of confidence' in the city . . . it fails to do the crucial things that all good urban buildings do — relate carefully to what is around them," Goldberger wrote.[19] Towering some 746 feet high, the hotel soars over every other building in an essentially low-built area.[20]

The Center's reflective, cylindrical forms, described as futuristic by Goldberger, set it apart from its surroundings.[21] The sense of physical isolation was increased, according to Goldberger and later critics, by the large berms that house the Center's heating system and other utilities and stand two stories high on either side of the entrance to the Center. Goldberger wrote that these "huge concrete structures . . . serve as further barrier between Renaissance Center and 'Old' Detroit."[22] Conceptually, too, Goldberger thought the RenCen was isolated. He saw it as a "suburban development . . . tall instead of short . . . dropped within the city limits instead of outside them. . . . To many tenants, the chance to hop from car to elevator and never set foot on a city sidewalk is ideal."[23]

Goldberger's article was followed by others in national and foreign architectural journals and periodicals and newspapers, the majority of which appeared in 1977

144. Concrete utility berm

and 1978.[24] It is interesting that a large portion of these contributions take up the same issues. The fortress-like character of the barriers and sense of isolation was the focus of much future criticism.[25] "Megaform Comes to Motown," by Bruce N. Wright, an article in the February 1978 issue of *Progressive Architecture,* was the first to deal with the Center's isolation in an architectural journal.[26] Wright reiterated Goldberger's criticisms, saying that "it (the Center) does not create a link with the existing city or relate to it in any way. Nor does it succeed as a 'thing apart,' standing alone as an example of formalistic architecture." Wright also noted that the Center was isolated from the rest of the downtown area, "located six to seven blocks away from the heart of Detroit and separated from it by ten-lane Jefferson Avenue and finally by large concrete berms. . . ."[27]

Reiterating Goldberger's criticism of lack of contextual relationship, Wright suggested that the glass exterior which is meant "to quietly link the complex with other city facades . . . neither blends in with the older brick and stone structures nor differs greatly in outside appearance from the newer glass and steel suburban Detroit office towers it challenges."[28] The notion of isolation was mentioned in *Newsweek* for March 28, 1977, which referred to the Center as a "self-contained white island," and much the same criticism appeared later in *Time* (April 18, 1977).[29] Wright likened this aspect of the building to a "snobby, rich kid shying away from low-class neighbors."[30]

According to one critic, a former associate of Portman, William Conway, the effect of stratification was even more serious. In "The Case Against Urban Dino-

145. View from Jefferson Avenue

saurs" (*Saturday Review,* May 14, 1977), Conway condemned megastructures such as the Renaissance Center for isolating "city dweller from commuter," for separating "classes of people within a city," for creating "barriers to pedestrian flow and interaction," and for "failing to relate to their environments."[31]

Some urban planners contended that the city would have been better off developing a smaller scale, friendly environment similar to developments such as Baltimore's Harbor Place or Boston's Quincy Market which would have better related to Detroit's history.[32]

In defense of the Center, Ford did not want a series of smaller, unassuming projects, but a project "with a certain catalytic effect" that he felt "any number of routine buildings would not produce."[33] Robert McCabe, President of Detroit Renaissance, a Detroit civic group, reinforced Ford's thoughts. "We wanted to build something with the kind of critical mass that would make people say something's really happening in Detroit," he said.[34]

Portman's solution was to create a building completely different from its surroundings, something spectacular which would lure people downtown. Portman saw his task as "one which would draw people back downtown not with pleas or threats, but by creating 'circumstances, where people want to return'."[35] In a recent interview in *Goodlife* (May 1984), Portman said:

> I've been criticized for turning my back on the city and building these great interior spaces, or building a plastic environment so that people don't have to go out on the streets. That criticism is beyond belief. It's like saying you shouldn't build these great spaces in a city even if the people enjoy it . . . a city is a great and glorious thing. A city can stand great interior spaces as well as great exterior spaces; it's an orchestration of all kinds of environments that adds variety and interest and excitement to a city.[36]

"What I wanted to do as an architect," Portman explained, "was to create buildings and environments that really are for people, not a particular class of people, but all people."[37] Portman indicated that the design of the building was intended to offer those inside a sense of security and to attract the middle and upper classes back to downtown Detroit. "I'm glad the Center offers a sense of security," he said in an interview, "Let's face it, cities and certainly Detroit have at least [the reputation] of being unsafe places. To reverse that, we have to make people city environments where they feel safe."[38]

Despite the reassurances of architect, patrons, and supportive critics, the city fathers responded to the criticisms of Renaissance Center's fortress-like isolation. In 1978 Coleman A. Young, mayor of Detroit and the city's Downtown Development Authority invited a team of architects from the American Institute of Architects (AIA) to

(AIA) to visit Detroit to study the problem.[39] The eight-member team consisted of architects, sociologists, and urban planners, a group chaired by Thomas Ventulett of the architectural firm Thompson, Ventulett, Stainback and Associates.[40] The report of this team suggested several ways of linking the Renaissance Center with the retail core of the city.[41] It suggested a clearly defined link through the use of graphics between the Center and Greektown, a picturesque, ethnic neighborhood several blocks from the Center. Also recommended was the construction of an archway over the berms in order more clearly to define the entrance and relate it to its immediate surroundings. In addition, the report proposed a pedestrian walkway over Jefferson Avenue to link the Renaissance Center and the new Millender Center, which is presently under development north of RenCen on Jefferson Avenue.[42] (Of these recommendations the link between the Renaissance Center and the Millender Center is being currently addressed, and a "people mover," a monorail to connect the Center with the rest of the business district and with the cultural center, is also under construction. It is envisioned as a positive step in linking the Renaissance Center with the rest of the downtown area.)[43] The AIA study of 1978 also criticized the city's reticence to prevent construction from blocking the disappearing public view of the river and found the city lacked overall planning.[44]

If the isolation and the contextual issue served as a focus for early and unfriendly opinions, the aesthetic evaluation of Portman's "futuristic" architectural imagery has been less consistent. Although critical of the concept of the building, for example, Goldberger admired its "sleek, fresh forms," the theatrical quality of the atrium and the good taste and honest design of the interior decoration and found much that was "visually attractive about the project."[45] And while Charles Jencks considered "the overwhelming massiveness of the cylinders, the squatness of the proportions, the awkward juxtaposition and inelegant volumes . . . not particularly proper for hotel rooms or urban space . . .," he also admitted that "perhaps if these monoliths were surrounded in the future by a sensitive urban infill, rather than parking lots or wide highways, their monumentality might become more acceptable."[46]

Ada Louise Huxtable much admired Portman's flamboyant interior spaces. In *Kicked a Building Lately?* (1976) she described his style as a combination of "a kind of Buck Rogers flash with an extremely astute and experienced sense of urban design."[47] Huxtable continued:

> When one is tempted to call these designs the stuff of which adolescent architectural fancies are made, one is drawn up short by their expertise as well as their showmanship. Their effects are shrewdly calculated in both architectural and functional terms. The efficiencies of prefabrication and other technology, the skillful dramatization of space, the knowing manipulation of

146. View from adjacent neighborhood

both structure and the street, the way they are joined together in a pattern of bridges, plazas, promenades, and shopping connectors on several levels with water, plants, trees, cafes, stores and (unfortunately) a little too much dubious art — all serve to create unusually good relationships of use and amenity.[48]

Of the interiors, Roger M. Williams, a free-lance writer with special interest in urban affairs, described the "cylindrical space broken up by myriad shapes and interesting angles at once stimulating and restful."[49] Another admirer of this interior space, Arthur Drexler of the Museum of Modern Art, claimed that, "no museum or concert hall rivals their lavish architectural incident."[50] Not all visitors were equally impressed. The American Institute of Architects team that visited the Center in 1978 contended that "the circular public spaces have acres of undifferentiated, exposed concrete, endless ribbons of escalators, ramps and spiral staircases leading the visitor round and round in baffling confusion."[51] In an extensive newspaper article in 1983, "What's Wrong With RenCen?" (Detroit News, January 11, 1983), Robert Benson, associate professor of architecture at Lawrence Institute of Technology, also contended that the interior spaces of the atrium were confusing.[52] He further criticized Portman for not creating any grand entrances to welcome the visitor.[53]

Controversy in the form of critics' disagreements even extended to the historical nature of the interior space. In obvious disagreement with Huxtable, Olga Gueft found "its grandeur and centrifugal movement closer to the Vatican than Buck Rogers," and praised Portman's use of industrial materials to achieve a Renaissance-Baroque space.[54] For other commentators, the interior space conjured up images of Piranesi's fantastic drawings, Boullée's grand projects, the interior of St. Peter's in Rome, the grand lobby of the 19th-century urban hotel, or Charles Garnier's Paris Opera.[55]

Whatever the sources or historical association, Portman's urban architecture has been remarkably consistent. He has employed the tall shimmering towers, the multistoried atriums with cantilevered balconies and walkways, the lakes, the hanging oval pods and glass-enclosed elevators in the Bonaventura Hotel in Los Angeles, the Embarcadero in San Francisco, and the Peachtree Center Plaza Hotel in Atlanta. And, as one might predict, even Portman's consistency of style has drawn critical censure. "He has set formulas that he drops in city after city," Cathy Stanton wrote, quoting one critic of the Center, in the AIA Journal of 1975.[56] Wright concurred, saying that Portman's "architectural tricks have become too facile and though RenCen is new, it has a strong sense of déjà vu."[57] The same phrase, "sense of déjà vu," was employed in a review of The Architect as Developer (co-authored by Portman and Jonathan Barnett, New York, 1977) by Morris Lapidus in the Journal of the Society of Architectural Historians in

December 1978.[58] Elsewhere in the review Lapidus finds nothing wrong with Portman's reuse of similar formulae in different buildings. "For me," Lapidus said, "it is not a criticism. Great architects throughout the ages are recognized by their own specific vocabulary and Portman, the super architect, is hardly an exception to this notion."[59]

Portman's structures have also been described as kitsch. Huxtable observed, "his big buildings are sometimes more readable as objects, or things (Zippo lighters and gift-wrapped cylinders not too far from the Pop vision of Claes Oldenburg) than as structures of human purpose."[60] This element of Portman's architecture is still unresolved for Huxtable. Jencks, on the other hand, views the Portman buildings as symbols of capitalistic wealth.[61]

Several of Portman's critics concede that people enjoy the grandiose, theatrical quality of the Renaissance Center. "People get a tremendous kick out of being there," noted Colden Florance in the AIA Journal of September 1977.[62] Another critic wrote, in Progressive Architecture of February 1978, that "the essence of Portman's architecture is found in the eyes of the people who visit his buildings."[63] Perhaps Philip Johnson, dean of American architects, came closest to the heart of the issue when he suggested that architects are envious of Portman. "His analysis of what people want and his ability to get it done are second to none," Johnson said.[64]

Portman's philosophy of architecture clarifies much of the controversy over his buildings. In answer to the criticism that RenCen was too large and "a dinosaur of energy inefficiency," Portman has replied that the atrium space was built to create spaces to "lift the human spirit . . . an atrium is an example of where the positive effect on people would outweigh strict and limited devotion to energy conservation."[65] Portman's goal was to design dramatic, open, interior spaces with natural elements to attract and please people.[66] "A hotel in the middle of a congested city needs open space," Portman said, "not just park space but space within the structure."[67] To acknowledge his architectural contributions, Portman was awarded an American Institute of Architects medal for innovations in hotel design in 1978.[68]

Many goals were ascribed to the Renaissance Center at its outset. It was seen as a "launching pad for the revitalization of Detroit," by Wayne S. Doran, spokesman for the Ford Motor Land Development Corporation.[69] Whether Renaissance Center has helped revitalize the city economically and spiritually is difficult to evaluate. One of the main controversies was whether or not the Center had attracted businesses from the suburbs. Critics claimed that the businesses and firms that moved into the office space at the Center did not move from the suburbs but were already located in the city.[70] Doran's answer: if these businesses had not relocated at the Center, they would have left the city altogether and moved to the suburbs.[71] In 1978 Stuart Matlin Associates, a New York-based management consulting firm, was hired by the Detroit Renaissance group to determine the impact of the

147. Hotel atrium

Center on the city of Detroit. The report concluded that the Center did "not appear to have affected downtown office vacancy rates in any significant way since those rates appear to have remained stable since 1976."[72] Furthermore, it reported that 30 percent of the businesses who responded to a survey of Renaissance Center tenants were from outside the city of Detroit, and the majority of these businesses would not have established themselves in Detroit if the Center had not been built.[73] Many other benefits were also cited.[74] "When you find the optimism in so many different places," Matlin said, "you have to conclude that it exists. It is a remarkable story of the rebirth of a city. . . ."[75]

Not all reports have been so favorable. According to a study (unpublished as of January 1984) by the Downtown Development Authority in July 1983, the 38 percent vacancy rate of the Renaissance Center's World of Shops was "high for a new highly visible retail office complex."[76] The study also stated that "the Center's World of Shops had been unable to position itself as regional shopping center or to capture a significant share of local residential market."[77] The report also points to a steady decline in retail business in the downtown area since 1967.[78] Of course, the degree to which the RenCen alone is responsible for these developments can never be determined with certainty. Wayne State University economist, Dr. John H. Mattula, had predicted that Downtown Detroit would fade as a retail center and bloom as a financial, legal, and business services area, and this may be largely true.[79] Indications are that while the retail center is only 60 percent leased, the office buildings are doing well and are 95 percent leased.[80]

Has the Center succeeded in attracting people back from the suburbs to live there? According to statistics compiled in 1982 by the City of Detroit, the population of the central business district was down 37 percent as compared with 1970.[81] This problem of dwindling population has been exacerbated by the lack of housing. Portman's original plan for the Center included condominium units to be built along the riverfront for middle to upper income housing. This housing was designed to attract occupants from middle to upper income groups, but the business recession prevented the development of the housing project, and there are no immediate plans to build it.[82]

The financial problems which plagued the country as a result of the recession have also plagued the Renaissance Center. The Center's financial problems have been widely publicized in the local and national press from 1980 to the present.[83] The January 12, 1983 issue of the Detroit News reported that the Center was in default on its mortgage payments for the second time in two years.[84] On January 13, 1983, the New York Times reported that the Renaissance Center had lost $140 million since it

had opened in 1977. According to the article, experts who assess the future of the Center attribute the Center's difficulties not only to the area's depressed economy, but also to longer-term local trends.[85] In the end, five first-mortgage holders — four insurance companies and a Ford Motor Company subsidiary — formed a new partnership, Renaissance Center Venture, and were granted 53 percent ownership in the Center.[86] The newly reorganized partnership is optimistic about the future, and points to increased occupancy rate of the hotel largely due to a lively convention trade and the fact that the four executive towers have a more than 90 percent occupancy rate.[87]

Will the prediction of William Conway, urban affairs consultant, about the fate of megastructures such as Renaissance Center become a reality? In his article, "Case Against Urban Dinosaurs," in the May 14, 1977 issue of Saturday Review, Conway wrote that "the megastructure guarantees neither investment of its owners nor the future of the city. Far from lending strength to downtown areas, these complexes create little more than a suburban island in mid-city. . . . Building them stimulates inflation, agitates the deterioration of the central city, which further divides the poor from the middle and upper classes."[88]

A companion article, "Saving Our Cities," by Roger M. Williams, took a more optimistic viewpoint.[89] "Without question the Center has transformed a substantial section of the riverfront and raised hopes for the rest of it," he said.[90] In a later article in 1978 in Horizon, Williams elaborated on the "spin-off" effect of the Center on the adjoining area.[91] He noted several new restaurants, the "return of suburbanites who had shunned Detroit for at least a decade," the building of a new sports arena, and the completion of the Senator Philip A. Hart Memorial Plaza, a theatre and recreational facility directly to the east of the Center along the waterfront.[92] "The arena location and perhaps its very existence, are directly attributable to the presence of the Renaissance," and "planning for the Memorial Plaza was speeded up dramatically when it became certain that Renaissance would appear to 'anchor' the area."[93] Projects also seen directly connected with Renaissance Center included a tenant-owned townhouse project, the restoration of two blocks of housing along Woodward Avenue, and the "people mover."[94]

Perhaps the bottom line at the moment may appropriately be suggested by a survey of attitudes about Detroit conducted by the market opinion Research Corporation for New Detroit (1978), which found that the city residents had greater faith in the city's future than they did in 1975 and 1977.[95] Without the image of the Renaissance Center it is doubtful whether these transformations would have occurred.[96]

Rachel B. Mullen

Notes

1. "Trois espaces marchandise," *L'Architecture d'aujourd'hui*, 189–194, October 1977, 54; Roger W. Williams, "Saving Our Cities: Facelift for Detroit," *Saturday Review*, May 14, 1977, 7–8.

2. Robert A. Popa, "Ford Riverfront Project Stepped Up," *Detroit News*, April 20, 1972, B,8. Popa notes that the original 500-million dollar plan for the riverfront project, intended to be built over ten years, was to include a hotel surrounded by four office buildings, office towers to the east and west, and condominiums along the waterfront. See also John Portman and Jonathan Barnett, *The Architect as Developer*, New York, 1977, 138–141, for drawings of original plans. Because of the recession only the first phase, a 375.5-million dollar project, was begun in 1973.

3. Robert A. Popa, "$500 Million Detroit Riverfront Plan Is Unveiled by Henry Ford," *Detroit News*, November 24, 1971, A,1.

4. Al Stark, "The Atlanta of John Portman," *Detroit News*, January 9, 1972, 18. Stark notes that Ford visited Atlanta's Peachtree Center in September 1971. After his visit, Ford wrote to Portman saying, "'I can't wait to see what you come up with for Detroit.'"

5. Popa, "Riverfront Plan," A,1. See also Al Stark, "The Challenge and the Reality," *Detroit News*, June 24, 1973, 30.

6. Robert A. Popa, "Ford Project Aide Rips Prophets of Gloom," *Detroit News*, January 23, 1973, A,15. Furthermore, the $200,000,000 loan obtained from four insurance companies and the Ford Motor Credit Company was "believed to be the largest permanent first-mortgage ever committed for a single real estate project," according to Robert M. Surdam, Chairman of the National Bank of Detroit. Surdam, "History of the Development of the Renaissance Center," speech given at the National Conference on Urban Economic Development, May 1977, 7–8.

7. Stark, "The Challenge and the Reality," 30. Stark found that "not everyone involved in debates within investor-companies, agrees about the wisdom of the riverfront investment."

8. Robert A. Popa, "70-Story Hotel is Center for Ford Riverfront Project," *Detroit News*, May 22, 1972, A, 21.

9. Robert I. Wells, "Rezoning Gets Initial O.K. for Ford Riverfront Project," *Detroit News*, April 26, 1972, B,12.

10. "Rezoning of Riverfront Site for Ford Complex Approved," *Detroit News*, May 3, 1972, B, 2.

11. "Ford Epitomizes Detroit Spirit" (editorial), *Detroit News*, November 25, 1971, B,18; "Expansion Applauded" (editorial), *Detroit News*, March 16, 1973, B,16; "Renaissance Center's Promise" (editorial), *Detroit News*, May 23, 1973, B, 18.

12. Popa, "70-Story Hotel," A,1. Ford is quoted as saying that without the encouragement from others . . . he might have accepted the study's findings and dropped the idea for the Center. "Instead his reaction was 'don't tell me why we can't do it, just tell me how and where we should do it.'"

13. Don Tschirhart, "Two Developers Attack Ford's Riverfront Plan," *Detroit News*, July 23, 1972, B, 14.

14. Popa, "70-Story Hotel," A, 1.

15. Tschirhart, "Two Developers," B, 14.

16. Peter R. Lochbiler, "Renaissance Center: It Is Offering Hopes but Few Guarantees," *Detroit News*, March 13, 1977, A,3 and A,18. The positive effects of the Center enumerated by Lochbiler include: the drop in crime rate; plans for further downtown improvements and development; plans for a "people mover," a monorail train to transport people around the downtown area, increased hotel business, and the attraction of more people downtown from the suburbs.

17. Norman Sinclair, "Downtown Detroit: They're Saying Good Things," *Detroit News*, June 28, 1977, A,1; Hugh McCann, "RenCen Makes a Difference," *Detroit News*, December 11, 1977, A,1; William K. Stevens, "Revitalizing Effect of Renaissance Center Is Upgrading Detroiters' View of Their City," *New York Times*, August 28, 1977, 26.

18. Paul Goldberger, "A Modern Center in Detroit Sets Itself Apart From City," *New York Times*, March 15, 1977, 16.

19. Goldberger, "Modern Center in Detroit," 16.

20. Popa, "70-Story Hotel," A,1. Surrounding RenCen are a variety of different buildings of different styles and periods, including brick buildings in the old section of Bricktown, classicizing buildings such as the County Court House, and old contemporary buildings in the international style.

21. Goldberger, 16.

22. *Ibid.*

23. *Ibid.*

24. For the architectural and design journals, see Colden Florance, "MXD: Detroit's Renaissance Center," *AIA Journal*, 66, September 1977, 28–31; "Trois espaces marchandise," *L'Architecture d'aujourd'hui*, 189–194, October 1977, 50–61; Olga Gueft, "Detroit Plaza Hotel," *Contract Interiors*, 137, December 1977, 66–75; "Selearchitettura," *Architettura*, 167, January 1978, 522; Bruce N. Wright, "Megaform Comes to Motown," *Progressive Architecture*, 59, February 1978, 57–61. For notices in books, newspapers, and general interest periodicals see, William G. Conway, "The Case Against Urban Dinosaurs," *Saturday Review*, May 14, 1977, 12–14; Roger M. Williams, "Saving Our Cities: Facelift for Detroit," *Saturday Review*, May 14, 1977, 6–11; "Detroit's Palazzo," *Horizon*, 19, July 1977, 48–49; Roger M. Williams, "Renaissance Plus One," *Horizon*, 21, April 1978, 14–21; August Gribbin, "Architects Take Swipe at RenCen," *Detroit News*, July 16, 1978, A,1 and A,10; Charles Jencks, *Architecture Today*, London, 1982, 60; Robert Benson, "What's Wrong With RenCen?," *Detroit News*, January 11, 1983, C,1–2.

25. Susan Dentzer and Richard Manning, "Hard Times for the 'RenCen'" *Newsweek*, January 24, 1983, 58, describe "massive steam-belching berms" which surround the Center's base and have "all the come-hither look of medieval ramparts." Other articles critical of these features include: Williams, "Saving Our Cities," 9; Gueft, "Detroit Plaza Hotel," 67; Florance, "MXD," 31; Wright, "Megaform Comes to Motown," 60, 61; Benson,

"What's Wrong with RenCen?," C,1; Wolf von Eckardt, "RenCen Follies: The Hard Lessons of Detroit's Renaissance," *Washington Post*, April 29, 1978, B, 2.

26. Wright, "Megaform Comes to Motown," 57–61.
27. Wright, "Megaform Comes to Motown," 51. Wright placed the blame for the Center's isolation on city planners and developers who failed to provide links between the Renaissance Center and the rest of the city. "RenCen is an isolated place, and it is as much the lack of strong city planning guidance as the architect's conscious provision of concrete buffers . . . that makes it so."
28. Wright, "Megaform Comes to Motown," 59.
29. Tom Nicholson and James C. Jones, "Detroit's New Towers of Hope," *Newsweek*, March 28, 1977, 60; "Motown Meets Renaissance," *Time*, April 18, 1977, 64.
30. Wright, "Megaform Comes to Motown," 58.
31. "RenCen: Bonanza or Useless Pyramid," *Detroit News*, May 15, 1977, B, 3. The article reports on Conway, "The Case Against Urban Dinosaurs," 12–14.
32. "Owners of Detroit Center Form a New Partnership," *New York Times*, November 6, 1983, 33.
33. Williams, "Saving Our Cities," 9.
34. Williams, "Saving Our Cities," 9. McCabe is quoted as saying, "We wanted a brick-and-mortar operation that would start important *physical* things happening."
35. William Dunn, "Success of RenCen Seen up to Public," *Detroit News*, October 28, 1976, A, 2.
36. Gene Griessman, "Portman on Portman" (interview), *Goodlife*, May 1984, 65.
37. Griessman, "Portman on Portman," 65.
38. Williams, "Saving Our Cities," 9.
39. Christopher Willcox, "Linking RenCen to Downtown," *Detroit News*, May 17, 1978, B, 2.
40. Willcox, "Linking RenCen," B, 2.
41. Christopher Willcox, "High-Rise Project Chills Architects," *Detroit News*, June 6, 1978, B, 1.
42. Ground breaking for the Millender Center took place in January 1984. This center, which will include apartments, a hotel, and retail space, will be connected to the Renaissance Center by a walkway, and is expected to become a major link between the Renaissance Center and the central business district.
43. City of Detroit, *Downtown Development Authority Retail Study* (unpublished preliminary copy of executive summary), July 1983, 6.
44. Gribbin, "Architects Take Swipe," A, 10. The Detroit City Planning Director, Anthony DeVito, answered the charges of lack of city planning: he said there was a plan, but not a written one, because the details of the mass transit system had not yet been formulated.
45. Goldberger, "Modern Center in Detroit," 16.
46. Jencks, *Architecture Today*, 61 and 63.
47. Ada Louise Huxtable, *Kicked a Building Lately?*, New York, 1976, 164.
48. Huxtable, *Kicked a Building*, 164, 165.

49. Williams, "Renaissance Plus One," 16.
50. Arthur Drexler, *Transformations in Modern Architecture*, The Museum of Modern Art, New York, 1979, 90.
51. Gribbin, "Architects Take Swipe," A, 10.
52. Benson, "What's Wrong with RenCen?," C,1. Benson writes, "The enticing atrium can be seen but not entered from the point of initial encounter. The search for access to it is disorienting. You move about its perimeter absorbed in the fantasy. The atrium cannot be perceived in its totality. It is experienced as a series of partial glimpses, momentary vistas and fragmentary views, which are at first enchanting and exhilarating, but cumulatively bewildering."
53. Benson, "What's Wrong with RenCen?," C, 1. Earlier critics had remarked on the lack of a suitable entrance: Willcox, "High Rise Project Chills Architects," B,1; and Dentzer and Manning, "Hard Times for the 'RenCen'," 58.
54. Gueft, "Detroit Plaza Hotel," 68.
55. Marco Dezzi de Bardeschi, "The Big Void," *Domus*, 606, 1980, 16; Jencks, *Architecture Today*, 25; Wright, "Megaform Comes to Motown," 58, compared Portman's interior spaces to Piranesi. Bardeschi included Boullée in his comparison. Bernard Leitner, "John Portman: Architecture Is Not a Building," *Art in America*, 61, March–April 1973, 80; and Olga Gueft, "Detroit Plaza Hotel," 68, compared the interior to that of St. Peter's in Rome. Suzanne Stephens, "Leaving the Natural Behind," *Progressive Architecture*, 39, February 1978, 45, compared the interior to the grand lobby of the 19th-century urban hotel. Drexler, *Transformations*, 90, compared it to Garnier's Paris Opera House.
56. Cathy Stanton, "Portrait: John Portman Architect Plus," *AIA Journal*, 63, April 1975, 61.
57. Wright, "Megaform Comes to Motown," 59.
58. Morris Lapidus, review of *The Architect as Developer* by John Portman and Jonathan Barnett in *Journal of Society of Architectural Historians*, 37, December 1978, 304.
59. Lapidus, review of *Architect as Developer*, 304 and 305.
60. Huxtable, *Kicked a Building*, 165. Charles Jencks, *Late-Modern Architecture and Other Essays*, New York, 1980, 164–165, and Marco Dezzi de Bardeschi, "The Big Void," 16, also described Portman's architecture as "kitsch."
61. Jencks, *Architecture Today*, 25. Jencks referred to Portman's style of "Geometric Expressionism," the leading style for public buildings of the seventies. "It is the ultimate Late-Modern exaggeration of program, geometry, interior space, slick-tech and cost. Dark glass towers house a massive concentration of power, the bastion of Henry Ford's financial monopoly. . . ."
62. Florance, "MXD," 31.
63. Ross, "A Star for Tinseltown," *Progressive Architecture*, 59, February 1978, 55. "The essence of (his) architecture is not found in the analysis of his aesthetic sys-

tems. . .but in the exhilaration (people) experience."

64. Stanton, "Portrait," 61. Stanton may have followed up similar quotes from Johnson cited in earlier publications: "Portman: A New Force for Rebuilding the Cities," *Business Week,* February 17, 1973, 60; and "The Portman Style," *Newsweek,* July 23, 1973, 53.

65. Douglas Ilka, in "Energy Code Still a Flop in Detroit Area," *Detroit News,* May 3, 1978, B, 1, refers to the Center as a "dinosaur of energy inefficiency." Portman's reply to such criticism appears in Stanton, "Portrait," 61.

66. "Portman: A New Force for Rebuilding the Cities," 62.

67. "Architect/Developer, John Portman" (interview), *RIBA Journal,* 84, December 1977, 509.

68. "National Trust, Portman and Gutheim to be Cited," *AIA Journal,* 67, February 1978, 12.

69. Popa, "Ford Riverfront Project Plans Stepped Up," B, 8.

70. Articles critical of RenCen's ability to attract businesses from the suburbs include: Goldberger, "Modern Center in Detroit," 16; Florence, "MXD," 30; "Motown Meets the Renaissance," *Time,* April 18, 1977, 61; William K. Stevens, "Revitalizing Effect of Renaissance Center Is Upgrading Detroiters' View of Their City," *New York Times,* August 28, 1977, 26; "Detroit's Downtown Gets a Tonic," *Business Week,* August 7, 1976, 52.

71. Florance, "MXD," 30.

72. Stuart Matlin's Associates, Inc., *A Survey of the Impact of Renaissance Center on the City of Detroit,* New York, 1978, 2.

73. Matlin's Associates, *Impact of Renaissance Center,* 1.

74. Matlin's Associates, *Impact of Renaissance Center,* 1–2.

75. Stephen Cain, "RenCen Aids Detroit's Boom" (editorial), *Detroit News,* November 3, 1978, B, 2–1.

76. City of Detroit, *Downtown Development Authority's Retail Study* (unpublished preliminary copy of executive summary), July 1983, 3.

77. *Downtown Development Authority's Retail Study,* 3.

78. *Downtown Development Authority's Retail Study,* 1. In 1967, 675 retail/service establishments were operating in the Central Business District, whereas in 1982, the number of businesses had declined to 367.

79. Lochbiler, "Renaissance Center," A, 18.

80. *Downtown Development Authority's Retail Study,* 9. The Downtown Development Authority's study suggested several improvements to aid the Renaissance Center's retail sales: the addition of quality merchandise stores, improvement of access to the Center, and better internal circulation and directional signals. Rick Ratliff and Betsy Hansell, in "Signs and Color Graphics to guide RenCen Visitors," *Detroit Free Press,* February 22, 1984, A, 1 and A, 5, found that several of the suggestions are in the process of being implemented and that the improvement of directional signs in the Center's retail area is expected to improve the retail trade in the Center.

81. City of Detroit, *Planning Report—Introduction and Syn-*

opsis (unpublished preliminary draft), November 1982, revised March 1983, 80.

82. City of Detroit, *Downtown Development Authority's Retail Study,* 6. The report predicted that: "the completion of several downtown residential developments including the Riverfront West and Millender Center projects" would bring "new residents into the downtown and support the concept of downtown as a place to work, live and shop."

83. The following articles in newspapers and journals reported on the financial problems of the Center: Bob Tamarkin, "RenCen Still for Rent," *Forbes,* April–June 1980, 49; Bob Luke, "RenCen: Downtown Paradox," *Detroit News,* October 17, 1980, E, 3; Trish Myers, "Dream Come True—Gave Hope to City," *Detroit News,* April 29, 1982, A, 14; David McNaughton, "Renaissance Center in Default on Mortgage," *Detroit News,* January 12, 1983, A, 10; Joshua Holusha, "Default of Renaissance Center Brings More Gloom to Detroit," *New York Times,* January 13, 1983, A, 18; Bruce Knecht, "Renaissance Center: Ford's Costly and Faulting Bid to Revive Detroit," *New York Times,* July 3, 1983, 4; Dentzer and Manning, "Hard Times for RenCen," 58; "Towering Debts," *Time,* January 24, 1983, 63.

84. McNaughton, "Renaissance Center," A, 10.

85. Holusha, "Default of Renaissance Center," A, 18. Dentzer and Manning in "Hard Times for RenCen," 58, find that "Critics of the Center have long warned that it suffers from fundamental flaws (its isolation, and the difficult approach for pedestrian traffic) that make it unlikely to thrive in the best of times."

86. "Owners Form a New Partnership," *New York Times* November 6, 1983, 33. In return for taking over the company, the five first-mortgage holders agreed to lower the interest rate of the existing mortgage and defer principal payments on the mortgage.

87. "Owners Form New Partnership," 33.

88. Conway, "The Case Against Urban Dinosaurs," 12.

89. Williams, "Saving Our Cities," 6–11.

90. Williams, "Saving Our Cities," 8.

91. Williams, "Renaissance Plus One," 17–19.

92. *Ibid.*

93. Williams, "Renaissance Plus One," 19.

94. Williams, "Renaissance Plus One," 18 and 19.

95. R. Stewart, "Building Plans for Detroit Raising Hope for Future," *New York Times,* November 8, 1978, 18. Only forty-seven percent of those polled in 1975 felt optimistic about the city, according to the survey. In 1978 the percentage had risen to seventy-one percent.

96. Williams, "Renaissance Plus One," 19. Corrine Gilb, the city planning director, quoted by Bruce Knecht in "Renaissance Center: Ford's Costly and Failing Bid to Revive Detroit," 5, found "The RenCen gave the city a symbol to rally around when it was at an absolute low point."

148. Vietnam Veterans Memorial, detail of vertex (color plate on page 44)

VIETNAM VETERANS MEMORIAL

Washington, D.C.

Designer: Maya Ying Lin
Architects of record: The Cooper-Lecky Partnership

The national Vietnam Veterans Memorial may well have generated more controversy than any work of architecture in recent memory. The issues surrounding the Memorial have ranged from aesthetics to patronage to politics, engaging veterans, veterans' organizations, architects, critics, the media, the legislative and executive branches of the federal government, and concerned private citizens in fiery emotional debates. The story of the memorial's development is a fascinating record of architectural design and imputed meanings, of pure form and political associations, of political meddling and compromise, and of accusation and recrimination on the part of involved interest groups. The unlikely result is a public monument that has become the most heavily visited site in Washington, D.C. since its unveiling in 1982. By all measurable accounts, it has also become a triumphant architectural success.

On April 27, 1979, Jan Scruggs, a Vietnam combat veteran and veterans' advocate, formed the Vietnam Veterans Memorial Fund (VVMF), a non-profit, volunteer organization devoted solely to the creation of a national memorial to the veterans of the Vietnam War.[1] The VVMF began its planning, after nearly a year of fundraising, by asking Congress for permission to erect a memorial on a two-acre section of Constitution Gardens in the northwest corner of the Mall in Washington, D.C. This site was chosen because of its proximity to the Lincoln Memorial, which to the VVMF symbolized national reconciliation after the Civil War.[2]

The United States Senate, led by Sen. Charles Mathias (R-Md), approved this site on May 22, 1980, with unanimous passage of Senate Joint Resolution 119. Then, after this auspicious beginning, came the first of many delays and political skirmishes: the House of Representatives blocked the Resolution by passing a bill, sponsored by Rep. Philip Burton (D-Cal), which would allow the Secretary of the Interior, then James Watt, to select the site.[3] The Senate and House finally reached an accord on June 24, 1980, when both houses unanimously passed Senate Joint Resolution 119 to allow construction on the Constitution Gardens site. The bill stipulated that any design selected by the VVMF was to be subject to the approval of the Secretary of the Interior, the Commission of

Fine Arts (CFA), and the National Capital Planning Commission (NCPC).[4] When President Carter signed the bill into law on July 1, 1980, few could have predicted the complicated scenario that was to follow.[5]

After further fund-raising efforts, the VVMF announced a national design competition on November 10, 1980, and two weeks later the VVMF released a fourteen-page design competition package which outlined the purpose of the Memorial and the nature of the competition.[6] The VVMF wanted the Memorial to honor the members of the United States Armed Forces who had served in Vietnam: those who were killed, those who remained missing in action, and those who returned home. The Memorial was intended to express "a nation's respect and gratitude" and to serve as a symbol of national unity. The competition was open to all Americans over the age of eighteen, as individuals or in groups, and submissions would be anonymous. Submissions could include any design elements—landscape, sculpture, or architecture, or any combination thereof. The only stipulations to submissions were as follows: the Memorial must be "reflective and contemplative in character," harmonious with its site and with the nearby Lincoln Memorial and Washington Monument, must provide for a listing of the names of all 57,661 Americans killed in Vietnam as well as an approximate 2,500 who remain unaccounted for, and must make no political statement regarding the war or how it was conducted. The eight-person jury included architects Pietro Belluschi and Harry M. Weese; landscape architects Garrett Eckbo and Hideo Sasaki; sculptors Richard Hunt, Constantino Nivola, and James Rosati; and Grady Clay, editor of Landscape Architecture. The professional advisor to the jury was architect Paul D. Spreiregen. On December 31, 1980, the VVMF released a rules-and-information package to all competitors which further stressed the apolitical nature of the Memorial, which was "to honor the service and memory of the war's dead, its missing, and its veterans—not the war itself. This memorial should be conciliatory, transcending the tragedy of war."[7]

With 1,420 entries the Vietnam Veterans Memorial Competition became the largest design competition in American or European history.[8] All of the entries were numbered, the identity of the designers sealed in envel-

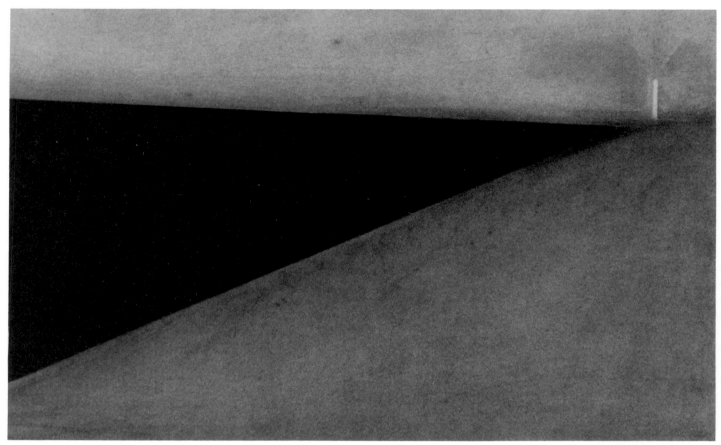

149. Detail of pastel sketch by Maya Ying Lin for Vietnam Veterans Memorial

opes taped to the back of each submission board. On May 6, 1981, the VVMF announced that the jury had unanimously selected entry No. 1026, submitted by Maya Ying Lin, a twenty-one year old senior undergraduate architecture student at Yale.

Lin's design called for a V-shaped wall on which the names of the dead and missing would be carved. Each arm of this "V" would be 200 feet long, of black granite panels that would rise from ground level to converge at a vertex where the wall would be ten feet high. Behind the wall the ground would rise with its elevation, consistently flush with its top. In front of the wall a grassy sward would slope gently upward to a screen of trees. The eastern arm of this wall would point directly to the Washington Monument, a mile away, and the western arm would point to the Lincoln Memorial, approximately 600 yards away. The names on the wall were to be ordered neither alphabetically nor by military division, as is customary with war memorials, but chronologically, in the order of each soldier's death. As the walls extended, the number of lines of names would decrease with the height of the black granite until only one line of names appeared.[9]

In its official report to the VVMF, the jury was clearly enthusiastic about its choice:

> . . . Of all the proposals submitted, this most clearly meets the spirit and formal requirements

of the program. It is contemplative and reflective. It is superbly harmonious with its site, and yet frees visitors from the noise and traffic of the surrounding city. Its open nature will encourage access, on all occasions, at all hours, without barriers. Its siting and materials are simple and forthright.

This memorial with its wall of names becomes a place of quiet reflection and a tribute to all those who served their nation in difficult times. All who come here can find it a place of healing.

This is very much a memorial of our own times, one that could not have been achieved in another time and place. The designer has created an eloquent place where the simple meeting of earth, sky, and remembered names contains messages for all who will know this place.[10]

The VVMF readily accepted the jury's recommendation. Robert Doubek, VVMF Project Director, described the initial reaction to Lin's design: "I was surprised. We were silent for a moment. But when we had understood, when the genius of this simple concept took its effect on us, we embraced and congratulated each other. We were thrilled."[11]

The designer was herself particularly aware of the simplicity of the design, and after the competition results

190

were announced, she said, "I don't think anything should be done to the design that adds or detracts from its power. I'll be stubborn about that, I guess."[12] Lin had originally conceived the design for an assigned project in a funerary architecture course.[13] Now it was destined for a world-wide audience, and her victory statement would assume special irony in view of the ensuing controversies.

Most of the immediate reaction to the design was favorable, echoing the selection jury's statement, but scattered attacks upon the proposed memorial quickly appeared.[14] On May 16, 1981, ten days after the announcement of the winning design, the *Washington Post* printed letters from two Vietnam veterans who felt that the design only honored the war's dead, while ignoring surviving veterans.[15] The following week in *The New Republic*, Charles Krauthammer claimed that the memorial would treat the Vietnam dead as mere victims without giving any context or meaning to their suffering.[16] On June 28, 1981, the architecture critic for the *Chicago Tribune*, Paul Gapp, called the wall "inane . . . something resembling an erosion control project," and he predicted that its inappropriately modernist style would alienate the American public.[17]

These criticisms seem to have had little effect on the various public hearings held by the National Parks Service and the CFA, during the summer of 1981. No testimony was presented opposing the design and, indeed, the memorial plans received the enthusiastic approval of these organizations.[18] By the end of the summer, however, the public controversy began in earnest.

On September 18, 1981, the politically conservative *National Review* published an editorial attacking the Memorial, calling it "a disgrace to the country and an insult to the courage and the memory of the men who died in Vietnam."[19] It was argued that the Memorial implied an anti-war stance because of its black color, its V-shaped plan ("the anti-war signal, the V protest made with the fingers"), and the lack of other identifying inscriptions beyond the names of the dead. The *National Review* editorial also criticized the names, for it seemed to imply individual deaths rather than deaths in a collective, unspecified cause.

These charges were answered by both Robert Doubek and the columnist James J. Kilpatrick in letters to the *National Review*.[21] Doubek wrote that the black color of the wall was as apolitical as the black color of the Iwo Jima or Seabee Memorials in Washington, and that the chronological ordering of the names served to integrate them into the entire experience of the war. He dismissed the reading of the V-shaped plan as a symbol of the anti-war movement: "More astute observers see the chevron of the PFC who bore the brunt in the fighting of the war." Kilpatrick claimed the monument "approaches a level of architectural genius," and he upbraided his conservative colleagues for the "untruth" regarding the lack of reference to Vietnam on the memorial when in fact there was such a reference in the inscription.

At a CFA meeting on October 13, 1981, originally convened to discuss granite samples for Lin's walls, the Commission was asked to reconsider its approval of the design. This appeal came from Tom Carhart, a twice-wounded Vietnam veteran and civilian lawyer for the Pentagon who had joined the VVMF as a volunteer in March, 1980, and subsequently resigned in order to enter the design competition. Carhart echoed the analysis offered by the *National Review* that Lin's design was an anti-war statement. He felt that such a political stance was inevitable, as there had been no Vietnam veterans on the competition jury. As he explained it:

> The net result is that the design the jury chose as the winner was necessarily a function of their perception of the war they lived through in

150. End of eastern arm of the Memorial

151. Visitors viewing the eastern arm

America. It may be that black walls sunk into a trench would be an appropriate statement of the political war in this country.[22]

Carhart particularly objected to the black walls, calling the memorial a "shameful, degrading ditch, a black gash of sorrow,"[23] and claiming that "black is the universal color of shame, sorrow, and degradation in all races, all societies worldwide." He then demanded a white memorial.[24] Carhart's final objection was to the chronological ordering of the names. He found it to be a "random scattering . . . such that neither brother nor father nor lover nor friend could ever be found."[25] The CFA listened to Carhart's statement but would not accept his recommendation that Lin's design be scrapped.

Carhart followed up his CFA testimony with a statement printed in the *Washington Post* on October 24.[26] While reiterating much of what he had said earlier, he lodged two new objections. First, he took up the criticism voiced by the veterans who wrote to the *Post* in May, that Lin's design did not honor the surviving veterans. Second, he claimed that even if the design was not a statement of shame or dishonor, it did denote sorrow. Sorrow, he felt, was not an appropriate comment on the war and should be replaced with a statement of pride. At this point, realizing that the CFA would retain Lin's design despite his protests, he suggested formal modifications to honor the living and to emphasize pride rather than sadness. He advocated changing the wall's color to white, "the symbol of faithful national service and honor," raising the wall above ground, and installing an American flag at the wall's vertex.

This statement in the *Post* and the publicity attendant upon Carhart's appearance at the CFA meeting served to generate interest among disaffected veterans in modifying the memorial. It was reported, furthermore, that H. Ross Perot, a wealthy Texas financier, played a large role in organizing opposition to Lin's design. Perot, who had earlier supported the VVMF with $160,000 to set up the design competititon, was not pleased with the jury's choice. In *Art in America*, Elizabeth Hess claimed that Perot tried to do away with Lin's design by creating the impression that the veterans themselves were dissatisfied with it. Hess also interviewed Jan Scruggs and Maya Lin, who both voiced suspicions that Perot had flown veterans into Washington to oppose the design. Lin also believed that Perot spread rumors around the capital that she and certain jury members were Communists. Perot denied this and maintained that he only tried to "get the Fund [VVMF] off their ego trip long enough to remember their constituency of two million vets."[27]

Whatever their source, the rumors of communist affiliation did spread until the VVMF was forced to counter them by circulating a fact sheet entitled "The Truth About the Vietnam Veterans Memorial." This fact sheet stated that

> VVMF is 100 percent pro-American. There are no communists or anti-war activists on the VVMF board of directors or staff. . . . None of the corps of volunteers who work closely with the project are communists or were anti-war activists. Most are Vietnam vets, spouses of MIA's, or Gold Star Mothers. . . . The design competition jury used their best professional judgement to recommend a design, being careful to exclude any political discussions or criteria from their decision-making. Allegations that they were attempting to make an anti-war or un-American statement are pure bunk.[28]

The fact sheet was also used to counter some of the objections raised by Carhart. While admitting that there were no Vietnam veterans on the competition jury, the VVMF explained that such veterans were integrally involved in other important stages of the selection process. Vietnam veterans set the design criteria, interviewed and selected each jury member, and approved the winning design. Also, it was noted that four of the jurors were veterans of other wars. The monument's black color was defended as being dignified and serene, as well as providing a necessary contrast to make the inscribed names legible. The names, when cut into the shiny black surface, would appear in the light grey color of the unpolished stone. White marble, it was noted, presents no such opportunity for color contrast. The chronological ordering of the names, too, was supported as displaying individual sacrifice as well as the nation's total sacrifice over time. An alphabetical sequence was deemed cold and bureaucratic and would not allow differentiation between veterans with identical names.

A design modification was also announced. To placate those who felt that the memorial would not honor the surviving veterans, an inscription, in two parts, would be added. The first part would appear on the wall just above the first line of names: "In remembrance of the men and women of the armed forces of the United States who served in the Vietnam war. The names of those who gave their lives and of those who remain missing are inscribed in the order that they were taken from us." The second part would be placed after the last line of names: "Our nation honors the courage, sacrifice, and devotion to duty and country of its Vietnam veterans. This memorial was built with private donations from the American people. Dedicated November 11, 1982."[29] The VVMF also announced that the addition of an American flag was under consideration.

Other defenders of the scheme were not lacking.

193

Maya Lin, in a statement to the *Washington Post,* explained that the surviving veterans were indeed served by her design. The actual park setting was intended as a "living gift," and the chronological ordering of the names served to involve the living in their own experience of the war.[30] The press also defended Lin's design. The *Washington Post,* the *New York Times, Time* magazine, and syndicated columnist James J. Kilpatrick all ran pieces praising the memorial, stressing its neutral, apolitical aspect.[31] A more heroic monument, as called for by Carhart, was deemed unnecessary and even fraudulent: William Grieder, in the *Post,* explained that "our shared images of the war do not include any suitably heroic images which a sculptor could convert into stone or bronze,"[32] and an editorial in the *New York Times* claimed that a heroic monument would be a "shallow monument to politics."[33] Even the *National Review* recanted its earlier anti-memorial stance, calling it a "premature evaluation."[34]

The architecture establishment also expressed satisfaction with the design. The American Institute of Architects (AIA) presented Lin with a special award, saying, "she spoke softly where others were wont to shout."[35] At the awards ceremony, Yale art historian Vincent Scully remarked that Lin was "able to find a visual equivalent to the sense of sorrow, the fundamental sorrow which is the basic fact of war."[36]

On December 4, 1981, the memorial moved one step closer to realization as the NCPC unanimously approved the original design.[37] Construction on the site could now proceed, and the VVMF planned a groundbreaking ceremony for February, 1982.

Despite the VVMF's explanations, the support of the press and architects, and the approval of the required government agencies, however, the opponents of Lin's design did not give up their fight. Four days after the NCPC decision, Carhart and other veterans called a press conference. The veterans announced that Lin's design was an insult and demanded that its color be changed to white, that the wall be raised above the ground, and that the scheme include an American flag.[38] Shortly thereafter, James Webb, Patrick Buchanan, and Phyllis Schlafly published articles in support of this group of veterans.[39] All stressed that Lin's design seemed to contain a left-wing, anti-war political message. Webb, a Vietnam veteran and novelist, and former counsel to the House Veterans Affairs Committee, also organized opposition to Lin's design on Capitol Hill.[40] Thus, in early January, 1982, a letter condemning Lin's design was circulated by Rep. Henry J. Hyde (R-Ill) and co-signed by another thirty Republican congressmen and then sent to President Reagan and Interior Secretary James Watt.[41] Part of the letter read:

> The Black Hole of Calcutta needs no re-creation on the Washington Mall. . . . This underground black memorial lists only the names of the dead. No mention or consideration is given the rest who served. . . . We feel this design makes a

political statement of shame and dishonor, rather than being an expression of our national pride and the courage and patriotism, and ability of all who served. A new jury ought to be appointed, one less intent on perpetuating national humiliation no matter how artistically expressed.

Upon receiving this letter, Watt, who had approved Lin's design some six months earlier, wrote to the VVMF, saying: "As a result of continuing modifications in the original concept, I hereby request that you advise me once the design has been finalized in order that I might proceed to a full consideration of that proposal to fulfill my statutory responsibilities."[42] But, according to Robert Doubek, when Watt met with the VVMF on January 14, 1982, the design modifications were not discussed.[43] An article in the *Washington Post* claimed that Watt personally disliked Lin's design, calling it "an act of treason."[44] Sculptor Frederick Hart believed that Watt was only responding to the opposition of his constituency, which took the form of letters written to the White House and forwarded to the Department of the Interior.[45] Grady Clay, a competition juror, thought that Watt feared a lawsuit from Carhart and that the opposition veterans intended to halt the construction of the memorial.[46]

Whatever the reasons, it became apparent that Watt had changed his mind and would withhold approval of Lin's design unless it were modified in some fashion. Anxious to speed the construction of the memorial, Sen. John Warner (R-Va), a long-time supporter of the VVMF, convened a special hearing on January 28 to allow proponents and opponents of the design to air their views. After five hours of heated emotional debate, a compromise was reached. This plan, suggested by General Mike Davison, who led the 1970 Cambodian incursion, allowed Lin's design to be constructed as planned, with the addition of two elements: an American flag and a figural sculpture of a soldier or soldiers. In early March, Watt, the CFA, and the NCPC quickly approved these additions to allow construction to begin but withheld final approval until the actual positioning of the flag and sculpture could be worked out.[47]

On March 11, Sen. Warner and the VVMF held another meeting of the dissident factions to reach an agreement on placement. After another round of testimony, the VVMF agreed to allow the flagpole to be erected forty feet behind the wall's vertex, and the sculpture to be situated 170 feet in front of the wall's vertex amongst a stand of trees. With this solution Carhart, though not completely satisfied, vowed to give up his fight and let the matter rest. Thus, with the approval of Watt on March 26, 1982, ground was broken for the memorial in Constitution Gardens, and on July 1, the VVMF commissioned sculptor Frederick Hart to design the figural sculpture.[48] Despite the apparent unanimity at this juncture, however, the battle over the added features of the flagpole and the sculpture had just begun.

The flagpole and sculpture were not the only modifications made to the original design. These two elements and the above-mentioned inscriptions were added as responses to design criticism. In the meantime other modifications to the original design were made to solve practical problems which arose in construction planning stages. Early on, the Cooper-Lecky Partnership, a respected architectural firm in Washington, had been consulted on such matters, and together the Cooper-Lecky Partnership and Maya Lin devised methods to insure that the memorial would be safe to visitors and that individual names would be properly identified and easily located.[49] For safety's sake, the slope of the ground along the wall was made more gentle. A drainage system and turf reinforcer were added, and a granite walkway parallel to the wall was planned to provide for access by the handicapped. Also, twelve feet behind the wall, an eleven-inch high warning curb was added. Lin and Cooper-Lecky also created a system to distinguish between veterans who had died and those who were missing in action. Each name would be preceded (on the west wall) or followed (on the east wall) by one of two inscribed symbols. A diamond would denote that the soldier's death was confirmed, and a cross would signify that the soldier's status at the end of the war was missing and unaccounted for. To assist visitors in finding individual names, location directories resembling phone books would be placed at both ends of the wall.[50]

For Maya Lin, the other modifications, namely the addition of the flagpole and statue, ruined the integrity of her design. In a *Washington Post* article of July 7, 1982, Lin attacked the VVMF, Hart, and the additions. The VVMF, she claimed, never informed her of the changes, which she learned of from a televised report of the compromise. She also accused the VVMF of subverting the competition process and not defending her design. Of Hart, she said: "It's unprecedented—artists don't go around scabbing on other artists' work. I can't see how anyone of integrity can go around drawing mustaches on other people's portraits." She also felt that the addition of a single flagpole to her design would make the memorial look like a golf green.[51]

Members of the original competition jury were also disappointed. Harry Weese, objecting to the political manipulations which forced the changes, said that "it's as if Michelangelo had the Secretary of the Interior climb onto the scaffold and muck around with his work."[52] Robert M. Lawrence, then President of the American Institute of Architects, opposed any modifications to the award-winning memorial, saying that any intrusions would "cut the soul out of" Lin's design.[53]

The VVMF continued to press for the realization of the Memorial. Replying to Lin's objections, Scruggs claimed that "we really fought for Maya's design, but we're completely happy with the compromise. It makes it 100 percent better, much more beautiful." Hart's response to Lin's complaints was equally direct: "It's not Maya Lin's memorial, nor Frederick Hart's memorial. It's

152. Full-size clay model for *Three Fighting Men* by Frederick Hart

a memorial to, for, and about the Vietnam veterans to be erected by the American people—in spite of what art wars occur."[54] In the press, however, only James Kilpatrick voiced satisfaction with the new additions and their placement.[55]

On September 20, 1982, Frederick Hart unveiled a maquette of his sculpture. His proposed work included figures of three young American servicemen, two white and one black, carrying weapons and dressed in Vietnam-era military attire. The completed statue would stand over eight feet high and be cast in bronze. Hart envisioned his work in relation to Lin's design as

> an interplay between image and metaphor. . . . I see the wall as a kind of ocean, a sea of sacrifice that is overwhelming and nearly incomprehensible in its sweep of names. I place these figures upon the shore of that sea, gazing upon it, standing vigil before it, reflecting the human face of it, the human heart.[56]

Hart's sculpture has itself received little critical response, either pro or con, but its very inclusion in the design scheme drew fire from the press. Paul Goldberger, architecture critic for the *New York Times*, summed up the arguments against the addition. He felt that the figural group would destroy the aesthetic integrity of Lin's design, would destroy the integrity of the competition process, and would be a political statement spoiling the intentional ambiguity of the wall.[58]

153. Visitor in combat uniform takes a rubbing of a name

A meeting of the CFA scheduled for October 13 to review the VVMF's recommendation for the placement of the flag and the sculpture caused a flurry of lobbying both for and against the additions. Maya Lin wrote to the VVMF to ask that they withdraw their recommendation, and AIA president Robert Lawrence wrote to J. Carter Brown, chairman of the CFA, claiming that any changes would corrupt the original competition.[59] Two days before the CFA hearing, Tom Carhart released the results of a poll taken of Vietnam POW's in January in which 67 percent of the respondents disliked Lin's original design.[60] Scruggs had this poll checked by experts and claimed that it was worthless. H. Ross Perot, who had paid for the poll, responded: "Losers always discredit the winners."[61]

The CFA's decision at the October 13th meeting surprised everyone. While approving Hart's maquette and the addition of the flagpole, the Commission rejected the VVMF's proposed placement of the additions. J. Carter Brown, in his decision statement, explained:

> If the sculpture is allowed to shiver naked out there in the field, to be an episodic element that is not integrated, that somehow relates to a flag-pole which is so far away and whose height and silhouette will be cut off as one approaches the existing memorial . . . they will not combine to have the critical mass and impact that those elements deserve.[62]

On its own initiative, the CFA then suggested a placement scheme that, if proposed, would be approved: the statue and flag should be grouped together at the near end of the access path from Henry Bacon Drive, creating an entranceway to the memorial site. This decision placated both Lin and Lawrence, but enraged the original proponents of the additions, who threatened to build another memorial if those additions were not placed close enough to the wall.[63]

With the issue of placement still undecided the memorial—complete as Lin designed it—was opened to the public on November 10 and formally dedicated on November 13, 1982, during the one-week National Salute to Vietnam Veterans.[64] Most major U.S. newspapers and magazines ran articles on the dedication and commentaries on the memorial's impact upon visitors.[65] The wall, and especially its litany of names, was reported to have had a deep emotional effect upon viewers, leaving many in tears and others standing and staring for long periods of time. Relatives and friends of the deceased interacted directly with individual names. Flowers, written messages, and personal mementos were taped to the wall or left by its base. Many took photographs or rubbings of the names, and almost all were moved to touch the wall, some even to kiss it. The press noted that the wall had a healing, cathartic effect, especially on visiting veterans. So pronounced is this phenomenon that psychologists who specialize in Vietnam-stress-syndrome cases regularly bring groups of patients to the memorial to help

154. Aerial view of dedication ceremonies

them come to terms with their grief, anger, and sup-pressed feelings.[66]

Praise for Lin's completed memorial in the press was almost universal. Many stressed the neutral, apolitical aspect of the wall, claiming that one could bring one's own ideas and feelings to it and come away satisfied. Some felt that the experience of the monument's vast catalytic power upon the emotions nullified all objections levied against it.[67]

The opponents to the original design nevertheless remained dissatisfied. The statue and flag were still deemed necessary, and a struggle ensued over the issue of their location. In December, 1982, Rep. Don Bailey (D-Pa) sponsored a bill that would prohibit consideration of the CFA's entrance placement suggestion, and proponents of the plan fought back. The new president of the AIA, Robert Broshnar, sent a letter to all members of Congress asking them not to further politicize the design process and to defeat Bailey's bill. In the end the House passed the bill, but it was eventually defeated in the Senate through the efforts of Sen. Mathias.[68]

In early 1983, Interior Secretary Watt re-entered the picture. On January 11, he announced plans to re-submit the placement plan which the CFA had already rejected, and he vowed to fight for its approval.[69] Three placement plans were on his desk awaiting submission to the CFA: the original plan calling for a linear alignment of the flag-pole, the wall's vertex, and the statue; the entrance grouping plan favored by the CFA; and another plan proposed by the AIA calling for placement of the flag at the entrance and the sculpture in a grove of trees separating the Vietnam Veterans and Lincoln Memorials. In this context on January 28, Watt changed his mind and decided not to submit any of the plans in order to allow time for a political consensus to emerge. He expected the matter to be resolved within twelve to fifteen months.[70]

The VVMF, weary of political meddling and anxious to complete the memorial, strongly objected to Watt's decision. Scruggs and important veterans' organizations urged Watt to submit all three plans to the CFA, saying that at this point they would agree to any of them.[71] As a result, on February 1, 1983, Watt again reversed his position and submitted the three placement alternatives to the CFA. So doing, Watt incurred the displeasure of those opposed to the entrance grouping, who felt that the CFA was sympathetic to only a small segment of the arts community and had placed trifling aesthetic concerns before the wishes of the veterans.[72]

The CFA held a hearing on the placement issue on February 8, 1983. In an emotional three-hour session, the relative virtues of the original, linear placement plan and the entrance grouping plan were hotly debated. The AIA proposal was largely ignored. Arguing for the entrance plan were the VVMF, Frederick Hart, the Veterans of Foreign Wars, AMVETs, the Vietnam Veterans of America, J. Carter Brown, and Harry G. Robinson III, Dean of the Howard University School of Architecture and Planning. They argued that if the sculpture were to be placed before the wall it would weaken the wall's impact and relegate the figural group to a spatially awkward position. A flagpole placed behind the wall "would be an intrusion into the tranquil horizontal space of the meadow and the awe-inspiring quality of the wall." If both flag and statuary were located at the entrance, however, the flag would have maximum prominence and the sculpture would benefit from the "scale giving" context of a copse of trees. Situated closer to the memorial, the sculpture would only compete with it for attention while being dwarfed by the wall.

The proponents of the original plan claimed to speak for a majority of Vietnam veterans. In support of this claim, they cited a poll taken by Milton Copulos in November 1982, which revealed that 74 percent of veterans surveyed preferred what the opposition called the more "prominent" placement of the statue and flagpole, i.e.,

with the sculpture, the vertex of the wall, and the flag in a line. The prominence of this arrangement derived from its symbolic content: the soldiers in the figural group were to gaze across the wall, a symbol of the tragedy of the war, to the flag which signified their patriotism. Such content would help memorialize living veterans, as well as the dead, and make a statement of pride to counteract the wall's emphasis on sorrow. These veterans felt that this symbolic integration was more important than the visual integration of the entrance placement plan.

After considering this testimony, the CFA voted unanimously to uphold its own suggestion: the statue and flagpole would be placed together 120 feet to the side of the standing memorial to form an entranceway to the memorial site.[73] With this decision, the veterans in favor of the original placement plan gave up their fight. At the NCPC hearing on March 3, 1983, no one testified against the entrance placement plan, though veterans were there in force to support it. On the same day, Interior Secretary Watt also gave what would be his final approval.[74] These approvals in effect ended the political controversy over the Vietnam Veterans Memorial.

Journalists had varying reactions to the final decision. Benjamin Forgey, of the *Washington Post,* applauded the CFA, citing its aesthetic arguments and the preservation of the apolitical nature of Lin's wall.[75] Jeff Kelly, writing in *Artforum,* and Elizabeth Hess, writing in *Art in America,* felt that even the entrance location of the flag and sculpture would destroy the wall's neutrality. Hess claimed that the addition of Hart's conservative statue would tend to make the otherwise apolitical wall seem to contain a left-wing statement and that the elements would be forever in opposition.[76] The statue was unveiled on Veterans' Day, November 11, 1984, and it is too early at this writing to judge the critical reaction.

What caused this controversy which divided veterans, politicians, and journalists for almost two years? To judge from published opinion, at least two different theories have emerged. One maintains that the conflict was grounded in a struggle between elitist and popular aesthetic tastes. Charles B. Leidenfrost was the first to suggest this notion, claiming that the competition jury chose a design according to its own modernist taste without anticipating its impact on a broader public. The jury failed to realize — according to this theory — that the formal qualities of Lin's design, which to them appeared understated and eloquent, would evoke an entirely different set of associations for other viewers. A public not versed in the modernist idiom saw only traditional funerary connotations in the wall's black color and recessed position.[77] Small wonder, then, that objections were so vehement. Tom Wolfe and Frederick Hart held similar opinions, but claimed that the public could not relate to the modernist memorial for less specific reasons.[78]

Benjamin Forgey developed a different explanation, political in nature, which gained currency among many writers. In the *Washington Post,* Forgey wrote that the controversy "is due to the nature of the war itself. The

155. Visitors file past the Memorial

nation is still seriously divided in its judgements of the wisdom of involvement in Vietnam and of our military conduct, once in the thick of it."[79] Such an analysis is, perhaps, extreme. It implies that Lin's design is either a pro-war or anti-war statement, with the traditional proponents of each view pitted against one another. While it is true that the antagonists in the controversy tended to fall into liberal or conservative camps, there were many important crossovers. General William Westmoreland, who led the forces in Vietnam, found the design for the wall "beautiful."[80] James J. Kilpatrick, who supported the war effort as a just cause, was one of the most avid enthusiasts of Lin's design.[81] Furthermore, an anti-war/pro-war polarity cannot be read into the conflict. Scruggs and the VVMF, despite the efforts of others, have amply proven the neutral, apolitical intentions of the jury, their own organization, and the memorial itself. The opponents of the design, who may have perceived an anti-war statement in the wall, were not trying to readjust it to make a pro-war statement. They only endeavored to inject into Lin's design an element of pride which they found lacking but necessary.

Nicholas J. Capasso

Notes

1. For a more detailed account of the formation and early history of the VVMF, see "Program Souvenir: National Salute to Vietnam Veterans" (program booklet distributed during the Salute, November 10–14), Maclean, Virginia, 1982, 5–8. Scruggs by his own account was not the first to envision a memorial (J. Scruggs, "A Vietnam Memorial," *Washington Post*, March 22, 1980, A,13). Columnist William Greider claimed to have advocated a Vietnam memorial in 1976 ("Memories That Shape Our Future," *Washington Post*, November 8, 1981, C,1); and in March 1978, the Army recommended that a plaque and display of medals be set up in the Memorial Amphitheater at the Tomb of the Unknown Soldier. This display was to be in lieu of the interment of an unknown corpse. Although a crypt at the Tomb had been prepared for a body, no unknown corpse from the Vietnam war was available intact at the time. See J. Martin, "Plaque for Vietnam," *Nation*, April 8, 1978, 389.
2. See W. von Eckardt, "The Making of a Monument," *Washington Post*, April 26, 1980, C, 7.
3. "Needless Obstacle," *New Republic*, May 31, 1980, 7.
4. C. Romano, "Moving the Memorial," *Washington Post*, June 25, 1980, B, 8. The Commission of Fine Arts was created by Congress in 1910 to give expert advice on works of art or architecture acquired or commissioned by the federal government. The National Capital Planning Commission approves structures to be built on federal land in the District of Columbia and generally follows the recommendations of the CFA. See E. Hess, "A Tale of Two Memorials," *Art in America*, 71, April 1983, 122.
5. "Carter Clears Vietnam Memorial," *Washington Post*, July 2, 1980, A, 21.
6. "Design Competition for Vietnam Memorial," *Washington Post*, November 11, 1980, B,7; and VVMF, "The Vietnam Veterans Memorial Design Competition" (rules package sent to prospective competitors), Washington, November 24, 1980.
7. VVMF, "Design Program: The Vietnam Memorial Design Competition" (information package sent to competitors), Washington, December 31, 1980, 16.
8. J. Lang, "A Memorial That Healed Our Wounds," *U.S. News and World Report*, November 21, 1983, 69.
9. The names would begin at the top of one wall, proceed to its tip, and continue from the tip of the adjoining wall toward the vertex again, thus completing a circle. See H. Allen, "Epitaph for Vietnam: Memorial Design Is Selected," *Washington Post*, May 7, 1981, F, 1.
10. "Program Souvenir: National Salute to Vietnam Veterans," 9, 34.
11. Quoted in W. von Eckardt, "Of Heart and Mind: The Serene Grace of the Vietnam Memorial," *Washington Post*, May 16, 1981, B, 4.
12. Von Eckardt, "Of Heart and Mind," B,4. For a profile of Maya Lin, see P. McCombs, "Maya Lin and the Great Call of China," *Washington Post*, January 3, 1982, F,1ff.
13. McCombs, "Maya Lin," F,3. Lin was the only member of the class to submit a design to the VVMF competition. Ironically, her instructor, who gave Lin a "B" for the project, also entered the competition but was re-

jected. Second place went to a team led by Marvin Kro-sinsky of Island Park, New York, and third place was won by a team led by Joseph F. Brown of Alexandria, Virginia.

14. Favorable reviews include von Eckhardt, "Of Heart and Mind," B,4; "Vietnam Veterans Memorial Design Competition," *Architectural Record*, 169, June 1981, 47; "Un-monumental Vietnam Memorial," *AIA Journal*, 70, June 1981, 17; and A. Freeman, "An Extraordinary Competition," *AIA Journal*, 70, August 1981, 47–53.

15. R. Lorbeer and T. Vogel, letters to the *Washington Post*, May 16, 1981, A,12.

16. C. Krauthammer, "Memorials," *New Republic*, May 23, 1981, 43.

17. P. Gapp, "Proposed Memorial to Vietnam War Inane," *Chicago Tribune*, June 28, 1981, VI, 12.

18. VVMF, "The Truth About the Vietnam Veterans Memorial," public relations press release, Washington, November 1981, 2.

19. "Stop That Monument," *National Review*, September 18, 1981, 1064.

20. *Ibid.*

21. R. Doubek and J. Kilpatrick, letters to *National Review*, October 16, 1981, 1170, 1172.

22. See T. Carhart, "Insulting Vietnam Vets," *New York Times*, October 24, 1981, 23. His entry for the competition consisted of a sculpture of an officer raising a dead soldier heavenward. It was the first work of art he had ever attempted. See W. von Eckardt, "Storm Over a Vietnam Memorial," *Time*, November 9, 1981, 103, for an enthusiastic appraisal of Lin's design by a design critic who was quick to question Carhart's evaluation of the all-civilian jury. Jan Scruggs also defended the composition of the jury in a letter to the *Washington Post*, November 24, 1981, A,16. Scruggs wondered why Carhart had waited to decry the lack of veterans on the jury, for as a participant in the competition, Carhart certainly would have known who the jury members would be.

23. Quoted in J. Eisen, "Commission Rejects Veteran's Protest, Reapproves Vietnam Memorial Design," *Washington Post*, October 14, 1981, C,3. This phrase, or parts of it, was often repeated by those who objected to Lin's design.

24. Quoted in Hess, "Tale of Two Memorials," 122.

25. Hess, "Tale of Two Memorials," 124.

26. T. Carhart, "A Better Way to Honor Viet Vets," *Washington Post*, November 15, 1981, C, 5.

27. Hess, "Tale of Two Memorials," 121–23.

28. VVMF, "The Truth About the Vietnam Veterans Memorial," 6.

29. VVMF, "The Truth About The Vietnam Veterans Memorial," 2–4. As executed, the word "remembrance" in the first part of the inscription was replaced by the word "honor."

30. McCombs, "Maya Lin," F, 10.

31. B. Forgey, "Model of Simplicity: Another Look at the Vietnam Memorial," *Washington Post*, November 14, 1981, C,1; "How to Remember Vietnam," *New York Times*, November 11, 1981, A, 30; W. von Eckardt, "Storm Over a Vietnam Memorial," 103; J. Kilpatrick, "Finally We Honor the Vietnam Dead," *Washington Post*, November 11, 1981, A, 27.

32. Greider, "Memories that Shape Our Future," C, 2.

33. *New York Times*, November 11, 1981, A, 30.

34. N. Hannah, "Open Book Memorial," *National Review*, December 11, 1981, 1476.

35. Forgey, "Model of Simplicity," C, 4.

36. Quoted in McCombs, "Maya Lin," F, 11.

37. S. Zakaroudis and L. Romano, "Personalities," *Washington Post*, December 4, 1981, D, 3.

38. "Veterans Fault Vietnam War Memorial Plans," *Washington Post*, December 8, 1981, A, 11.

39. J. Webb, "Reassessing the Vietnam Veterans Memorial," *Wall Street Journal*, December 18, 1981, 22; P. Buchanan, "Memorial Does Not Honor Vietnam Vets," *Chicago Tribune*, December 26, 1981, N,1; P. Schafly, "Viet Memorial Opens Old Wounds," *Buffalo Evening News*, January 15, 1982, 21. Buchanan, perhaps unaware of the VVMF fact sheet, charged that a juror had been a member of the American Communist Party.

40. P. McCombs, "Reconciliation: Ground Broken for Shrine to Vietnam War Veterans," *Washington Post*, March 27, 1982, A,14, identified Webb as the party responsible for organizing opposition to Lin's design in Congress. Webb's novels include *Fields of Fire* and *A Sense of Honor*, both based on the Vietnam war.

41. H. Hyde, letter to President Ronald Reagan and Interior Secretary James Watt, January 1982. Representative Lawrence DeNardis (Republican, Connecticut) urged fellow Congressmen not to sign the Hyde letter. He circulated his own letter, which read: "There is an odor of mischief in this last minute attempt to discredit the Vietnam veterans' design selection process. Congress has no business meddling in subjective judgements about the design of a memorial we are not financing. . . . The terms and conditions of the resolution permitting construction have been scrupulously met. . . ." (See "Politics Threatens to Engulf Vietnam Memorial Design," *AIA Journal*, 71, February 1982, 13). Press reports may vary with regard to the exact number of Republican signatories; a single Democrat is said to have signed the letter.

42. Quoted in "Politics Threatens to Engulf Vietnam," 13.

43. *Ibid.*

44. P. Geyelin, "The Vietnam Memorial (Cont'd)," *Washington Post*, January 11, 1983, A, 15.

45. From an interview with Frederick Hart, Hess, "Tale of Two Memorials," 124.

46. "Politics Threatens to Engulf Vietnam," 13.

47. For the Warner hearing, see B. Forgey, "Vietnam Memorial Changes Clear Last Hurdle," *Washington Post,* October 14, 1982, A, 2; "Watt Approves a Vietnam Memorial," *Newsweek,* March 22, 1982, 38; H. Sidey, "Tribute to Sacrifice," *Time,* February 22, 1982, 19.

48. For the placement compromise, see J. White, "Watt Okays a Memorial Plan," *Washington Post,* March 12, 1982, C,1; and "Compromise on Vietnam Memorial," *Washington Post,* March 25, 1982, B,3. For the groundbreaking, see McCombs, "Reconciliation," A,14. Hart, who was a member of the third prize-winning design team in the original competition, was chosen by a panel of four Vietnam veterans, two who had originally supported Lin's design (Arthur Mosely and William Jayne), and two who had opposed it (James Webb and Milton Copulos). See K. Buxton, "Personalities," *Washington Post,* July 2, 1982, D, 2.

49. Officially, Maya Lin is the designer of the memorial and the Cooper-Lecky Partnership is the architect of record, a normal procedure when the designer has no license or is not licensed by the state (in this case, District) where construction takes place.

50. During the planning stages the wall was lengthened by fifty feet to provide sufficient room for all the names. 57,939 names appeared on the memorial at its dedication. If a missing serviceman becomes accounted for as dead, the diamond symbol will be superimposed over the cross. If he returns alive, a circle will be inscribed around the cross.

51. R. Horowitz, "Maya Lin's Angry Objections," *Washington Post,* July 7, 1982, B, 1, 6.

52. Quoted in I. Wilkerson, "Art War Erupts over Vietnam Veterans' Memorial," *Washington Post,* July 8, 1982, D, 3.

53. B. Forgey, "Hart's Vietnam Statue Unveiled," *Washington Post,* September 21, 1982, B, 4.

54. Scruggs and Hart are quoted in Wilkerson, "Art War Erupts," D, 3.

55. J. Kilpatrick, "The Names," *Washington Post,* September 21, 1982, A, 19.

56. Quoted in Forgey, "Hart's Vietnam Statue Unveiled," B, 1–4.

57. Among the few statements on the subject of the sculpture, see Forgey, "Hart's Vietnam Statue Unveiled," B,4, for praise of Hart's statues: "In gesture and facial expression, especially, it is an impressive ensemble: The soldiers are portrayed at a telling moment, all the more tense because of its expectant ambiguity," J. Carter Brown, chairman of the CFA and director of the National Gallery of Art in Washington, suggested that "the three soldiers act as a kind of Greek chorus, facing the monument, commenting on its meaning. We were lucky with the statue; it could have been kitschy, but it isn't" (quoted in "Vietnam Memorial War," *Art News,* 82, January 1983, 12). Others were less enthu-

siastic: Hess, "Tale of Two Memorials," 125, called Hart's design merely "competent."

58. P. Goldberger, "Vietnam Memorial: Questions of Architecture," *New York Times,* October 7, 1982, C,25.

59. Goldberger, "Vietnam Memorial," C, 25.

60. "Most Ex-POW's Polled Dislike Vietnam War Memorial Design," *Washington Post,* October 12, 1982, C,2. The poll also yielded the following data: of the 265 respondents (587 polls were sent out), thirty-three percent liked Lin's design, seventy percent wanted a white memorial, ninety-six percent wanted a flag, eighty-seven percent wanted the memorial above ground, fifty-six percent felt that the original design would appeal specifically to those who had not served in Vietnam, and eighteen pecent felt that the original design would appeal to those who did serve.

61. Hess, "Tale of Two Memorials," 123.

62. J. Carter Brown, "The Vietnam Memorial Decision: 'Part of the Healing'," *Washington Post,* October 16, 1982, A, 15.

63. For the CFA proposal, see Forgey, "Vietnam Memorial Changes," A,1. Lin said of the proposal: "I don't know where they (the additions) will end up, but care will have to be taken so you don't have three isolated elements floating in space" (Forgey, "Vietnam Memorial Changes," A,2). Robert Lawrence pledged the AIA's full support for the CFA's recommendation, saying: "By recommending a complete separation of the conflicting design elements, the Commission has preserved the integrity of Maya Lin's award-winning design and served the best interests of the public" ("Art Commission Compromises on Compromise Design for Vietnam Memorial," *Architectural Record,* 170, November 1982, 51). Regarding the opponents' threat to build another memorial, see C. Murphy, "Reconciliation in Granite," *Washington Post,* November 7, 1982, A, 9.

64. For other events scheduled during the National Salute to Vietnam Veterans, see "Program Souvenir: National Salute to Vietnam Veterans," 17–19.

65. E.g., "The Vietnam Memorial," *Washington Post,* November 13, 1982, A,18; B. Forgey, "A Mood Is Built—Stillness and Force in the Vietnam Memorial," *Washington Post,* November 13, 1982, C,1; R. Cohen, "Roll Call," *Washington Post,* November 14, 1982, B,1; W. Broyles, "Remembering a War We Want to Forget," *Newsweek,* November 22, 1982, 82–83; K. Anderson, "A Homecoming at Last," *Time,* November 22, 1982, 44–46; "What's in a Name," *New Republic,* December 6, 1982, 6ff; M. Scrogin, "Symbol of the Valley of Shadow," *Christian Century,* January 5–12, 1983, 7–8; H. Maurer; "The Invisible Veterans," *New York Review of Books,* February 3, 1983, 38–39; "Notes and Comments," *New Yorker,* June 20, 1983, 25–26; D. Hoekema, "A Wall for Remembering," *Commonweal,* July 15, 1983, 397–98; P. Gailey, "Vietnam Memorial; Touching, Tears, Roses,

Rain," *New York Times,* August 30, 1983, B,6.

66. For the wall and psychological therapy, see Lang, 70; and P. McCombs, "Flag, Statue Approved for 'Front Door' of Lin's Vietnam Design," *Washington Post,* February 9, 1983, F, 1.

67. I have found only two negative reports published: C. Krauthammer, "Washington Diarist," *New Republic,* November 29, 1982, 42, who called the memorial a tomb, and a "monument to death"; and W. Hubbard, "A Meaning for Monuments," *Public Interest,* Winter 1984, 17–30. Hubbard believes that the memorial is inadequate because it acts only as a catalyst for personal emotions rather than as a stimulus for public thought about the historical event it represents.

68. For the Bailey bill controversy, see McCombs, "Flag, Statue Approved," F,6; "Vietnam Veterans Memorial: Once More into the Breach," *Architectural Record,* 171, March 1983, 61.

69. Geyelin, "The Vietnam Memorial (Cont'd.)," A, 15.

70. P. McCombs, "Watt Stalls Addition to Vietnam Memorial," *Washington Post,* January 29, 1983, C, 1.

71. McCombs, "Watt Stalls Addition," C, 1.

72. P. McCombs, "Watt's Memorial Turnabout," *Washington Post,* February 2, 1983, D, 3.

73. For the CFA hearing and testimonies, see McCombs, "Flag, Statue Approved," F,6; B. Forgey, "A Solution with Pride, Harmony and Vision," *Washington Post,* February 9, 1983, F,4; "Statue and Flag Voted for Vietnam Memorial," *New York Times,* February 19, 1983, A,25. The VVMF had Copulos's poll evaluated by polling consultants who found it to be seriously flawed.

74. B. Forgey, "Vietnam Memorial Approved," *Washington Post,* March 4, 1983, D, 1.

75. Forgey, "A Solution with Pride" F, 4.

76. J. Kelly, "Maya Ying Lin, Vietnam Veterans Memorial, the Mall," *Artforum,* 21, April 1983, 76–77; and Hess, "Tale of Two Memorials," 126.

77. C. Leidenfrost, "Memorial to Whom?," *Washington Post,* July 21, 1982, B, 7.

78. T. Wolfe, "Art Disputes War: The Battle of the Vietnam Memorial: How the Mullahs of Modernism Caused a Stir," *Washington Post,* October 13, 1982, B,1ff. Wolfe's article is an extension of his anti-modernist views as voiced in his popular books *The Painted Word,* New York, 1975; and *From Bauhaus to Our House,* New York, 1981. Frederick Hart expressed his opinions in an interview conducted by Hess, "Tale of Two Memorials," 124; and in F. Hart, letter to *Art in America,* 71, November 1983, 5–6.

79. Forgey, "Model of Simplicity," C,1. Hess, "Tale of Two Memorials," 125–126, writes at length of this political division.

80. In a letter to Tom Carhart, General Westmoreland wrote that the simplicity of Lin's design "strikes me as beautiful." See McCombs, "Reconciliation," A, 14.

81. See notes 21, 31, 55.

PHOTOGRAPHIC CREDITS

Peter Aaron ©Esto: 19, 24, 133, 135, 136, 138-140
Ted Bickford: 134a-d, 137
The Darkroom, Inc., AT&T Photo/Graphic Center: 25
Courtesy of Eisenman/Robertson Architects: 96, 112-114
Kathleen Enz Finken: 1, 95
Courtesy of Frank O. Gehry and Associates: 80-82
Courtesy of House & Garden © 1978 Conde Nast
        Publications, Inc.: 97, 115
Wolfgang Hoyt ©Esto: 31, 33, 34, 36
Alan Karchmer ©Architectural View: 23, 124-128, 130,
        132
Christopher Lark ©Lark, Ltd.: 150, 151
Tod A. Marder: 72, 77
Norman McGrath: 29, 30
Courtesy of the Office of General Services, Governor
        Nelson A. Rockefeller Empire State Plaza: 70, 71
Courtesy of I.M. Pei and Associates: 9
Charles Pereira, U.S. Park Police: 154
Courtesy of Perez Associates: 3
Courtesy of John Portman and Associates: 15, 141-147
Victor Pustai: 5, 26-28, 32, 53, 63, 67, 87, 88, 91, 98-
        111
Julius Shulman: 11, 12, 86, 89, 90, 92-94
Courtesy of SITE, Inc.: 14, 18, 116-123
Ezra Stoller ©Esto: 7, 8, 10, 17, 20, 21, 37-52, 54-62,
        64-66, 68, 69
Tim Street-Porter: 13, 73-76, 78, 79, 83-85
Tom Van Eynd: 4, 149

LENDERS TO THE EXHIBITION

AT&T
John Burgee Architects with Philip Johnson, New York
Cooper-Lecky Partnership, Architects, Washington, D.C.
Eisenman/Robertson Architects, New York
Ron Filson, New Orleans
Richard and Suzanne Frank, New York
Frank O. Gehry, Santa Monica, California
Archives of the J. Paul Getty Trust, Malibu, California
Michael Graves Architect, Princeton, New Jersey
K. and M. Hoffman, Venice, California
Langdon•Wilson•Mumper Architects, Los Angeles,
        California
Maya Ying Lin, New Haven, Connecticut
National Gallery of Art, Smithsonian Institution,
        Washington, D.C.
Office of General Services, Governor Nelson A.
        Rockefeller Empire State Plaza, Albany, New York
Museum of Oregon Historical Society, Portland, Oregon
Perez Associates, Architects, New Orleans, Louisiana
John Portman and Associates, Atlanta, Georgia
Renaissance Center Venture, Detroit, Michigan
SITE, Inc., New York
Vietnam Veterans Memorial Fund, Inc., Washington, D.C.